NEW APPROACHES TO
LANGUAGE MECHANISMS

NORTH-HOLLAND
LINGUISTIC SERIES
Edited by S.C. DIK *and* J.G. KOOIJ

30

NEW APPROACHES TO LANGUAGE MECHANISMS

A Collection of Psycholinguistic Studies

Editors:

R.J. Wales
University of St. Andrews
Scotland

Edward Walker
Massachusetts Institute of Technology
U.S.A.

1976

NORTH-HOLLAND PUBLISHING COMPANY
AMSTERDAM · NEW YORK · OXFORD

North-Holland ISBN for the series: 0 7204 6180 4
North-Holland ISBN for this volume: 0 7204 0523 8

Published by:

North-Holland Publishing Company – Amsterdam/New York/Oxford

Distributors for the U.S.A. and Canada:

Elsevier/North-Holland Inc.
52 Vanderbilt Avenue
New York, N.Y. 10017

Library of Congress Cataloging in Publication Data

Main entry under title:

New approaches to language mechanisms.

    (North-Holland linguistic series ; 30)
    Includes indexes.
    1. Psycholinguistics--Addresses, essays, lectures. I. Wales, Roger J. II. Walker, Edward, 1942-
P37.N4   401'.9   76-22710
ISBN 0-7204-0523-8

Printed in The Netherlands

PREFACE

One classical view of science holds that the outcome of experiments and the theory which motivated them are related. If the results of the experiments and the theory are consistent, then the theory is supported. If the results and the theory are inconsistent, then the theory is incorrect or the experiments are irrelevant. Surely even those readers who entertain some other opinion admit to a fundamental constraining relationship between theory and data. Unfortunately, most research in the psychology of language fails to impinge on theory: either the theoretical issues involved are so well-founded that the outcome of the experiment is immaterial, or else the methodology of the research is so abominable that the results can't be trusted.

Doing psycholinguistic research is hard. All but the gross features of linguistic theories are vague and in dispute; and in psychology, there is an unfortunate tendency to substitute disputes about how to get and evaluate results for disputes about what the results imply. In consequence, the research that is considered sound (if it relates to the psychology of language at all) merely demonstrates that the obvious aspects of linguistic theories have behavioral manifestations, and the research about theoretically more risky issues tends to be unbelievably crude.

The articles collected here depart from both tendencies and demonstrate that the hope for interesting and believable research in the psychology of language is not inherently paradoxical. Taken separately, the articles discuss and comment critically on important issues in language acquisition, speech perception, reading, sentence production, and sentence processing. For a change, the facts cannot be dismissed; nor is their interpretation foregone.

Taken together, the articles apply the commitment to do theoretically interesting, believable research to most of the current subject matter of research in the psychology of language. That commitment rests on the belief that, although consistency with each is necessary, neither a linguistic nor a psychological theory of language is a sufficient theory of psycholinguistics. The mechanism of learning and using language provides the subject matter of the field, and the articles here are an overview of that mechanism in action.

This volume grew from the spade-work we did in St. Andrews during the spring of 1975. The authors represent some fruits of our association at MIT, Edinburgh, and St. Andrews. An aspect of the new approach represented here which gives us particular pleasure is to have successfully persuaded some researchers in

the field to publish their ideas. In this respect we are sad to
observe that some of our friends remain old-fashioned.

We wish to thank the Leverhulme Trust for making our col
laboration possible by granting an Overseas Fellowship to Edward
Walker. We owe special thanks to Monica Pettijohn, who produced
the final typescript.

St. Andrews and Natick   Edward Walker
April, 1976

                                                Roger Wales

TABLE OF CONTENTS

USING LANGUAGE IF YOU DON'T HAVE MUCH

Robert Grieve

and

Robert Hoogenraad
Psychological Laboratory
University of St. Andrews

I Introduction

A regularly reported, and apparently reliable, phenomenon exhibited by the early utterances of young children concerns their so-called overextension. This phenomenon, found in data from many of the diarists, has recently been summarized by Clark (1973a), who proposes a "criterial features" hypothesis to account for it.

In a series of overextensions, the child employs a word across a range of applications wider than that of an adult; e.g., dog may be found to range over dogs, cats, cows, horses, sheep, etc.. Clark suggests that overextensions are motivated by "criterial features" of the objects or events involved, features such as size, shape, texture, sound, movement, etc., which are predominantly derived from perceptual input to the child through visual, tactile, olfactory and auditory sources. Thus, although the range of early utterances may be wider than that of the adult language, the child's behavior may be more systematic than it initally appears, especially if we suppose that more than one feature is involved in a series of overextensions, say two features operating in combination or alternating in dominance in a way reminiscent of the "chain complexes" described by Vygotsky (1962).

While the accuracy of this view will be challenged, there is no denying its appeal, for the elegance with which Clark seems to account for data can be readily illustrated. For example, she suggests that a series of overextensions relating to shape is illustrated by Pavlovitch's data on a child's application of wau-wau, first to a picture of a hunting dog, then to a small black dog, then to all dogs, then to a cat, then to a woollen toy dog (Pavlovitch, 1920--see Clark, 1973a). Or, a series of overextensions relating to size are illustrated by Moore's data on a child's application of fly, first to a fly, then to specks of dirt, then to dust, then to all small insects, then to his own toes, then to crumbs of bread, then to a toad (Moore, 1896--see

Clark, 1973a); or by data from Romanes where a child first applies quack to a duck on water, then to all birds and insects, then to all coins after seeing an eagle on the face of a coin, then to flies (Romanes, 1888--see Clark, 1973a).

But while Clark's proposal often seems to have some chance of success (her paper provides numerous examples of extensions related to features of size, shape, sound and movement), there are already hints in Clark's examples, themselves, that all may not be well. In the data from Romanes cited above, for example, the similarity in size between ducks, coins and flies is not clear. And in the example from Moore, while flies, specks of dirt, all small insects and crumbs of bread do exhibit some similarity in size, the addition of the child's toes, and especially of a toad, to the set of overextensions begins to strain the size hypothesis. Presumably at this point appeal is made to the notion that more than one feature is operating--e.g., from small things like flies, specks of dust, insects and crumbs, the child gets to his toes because they are small in relation to the rest of his body, and he gets from his toes to a toad because of similarity in the sound of the words? However, although some plausible story might be constructed for the sort of data summarized by Clark, our suspicions that all may not be well are brutally confirmed by other data in the literature, not discussed in Clark's paper, such as that reported by Piaget on a series of overextensions made by one of his daughters between the ages of about 1 year 2 months and 1 year 4 months. Jacqueline first used bow-bow to indicate dogs; then the landlord's dog seen from her balcony, and few hours later a geometrical pattern on a rug; then a horse seen from her balcony; then a pram, with the baby clearly visible, seen from her balcony; then hens; then dogs, horses, prams and cyclists; then everything seen from her balcony including animals, cars, the landlord, and people in general; then trucks pulled by porters at the railway; then again for the pattern on the rug; and finally the term "seemed to be definitely reserved for dogs" (Piaget, 1951, Chapter VIII, Observation 101a).

The notion of overextension is undoubtedly of interest and deserves examination, and there is no doubt that the child will employ a term across a wide range of different situations. But, it seems to us, what is in doubt is that the enterprise in which the child is generally engaged is that of overextension on the basis of criterial features, and that what the child is doing across these different situations is in some way homogeneous; --e.g., with respect to some such activity as naming.

In this discussion we give grounds for our dubiety about the child's early utterances being heavily involved with naming and overextension on the basis of criterial features. We will argue that with his early utterances, the child is attempting to employ limited linguistic resources to achieve a variety of purposes, and that this variety of purposes becomes apparent not by trying to identify criterial features of objects and events to

which early utterances refer, but rather by trying to identify
the intentions which underlie the child's early utterances.
Attempting to build up a picture of the child's system via inferences as to his intentions has certain methodological consequences. In considering these, we propose a set of methodological procedures for study of child language whose essential aims
are to make as explicit as possible the grounds for inference as
to the child's intentions, and to test the validity of such inferences via informal experimentation. We argue our case with
respect to observations from a recent study of early semantic
development in which we have been engaged.[1]

II Observations

The examples of early utterances given here are based on 46 hours
of observation of six young children, ranging in age from 1 year
2 months to 2 years 10 months, obtained in 81 audio and video
recorded play sessions conducted in the children's own homes.
In these sessions, which usually lasted about 30 minutes, one of
us would play with the child at a low desk which was part of a
playbench apparatus that incorporated our audio and video recording equipment (for a detailed description, see Grieve and
Hoogenraad, 1976). From large envelopes or boxes we would produce materials (such as models of people, animals, furniture,
vehicles, and so on, as well as wooden blocks, crayons, paper,
books, etc.) and ask the child to name objects or to indicate
objects named by us. We also engaged in a great deal of more or
less free play. Three of our six children were studied only
briefly, and most of our observations come from three children
studied at regular intervals (at least once every fortnight)
over a period of nine months: Roderick, Alison and Jane, aged
respectively 1:8:21, 2:1:2 and 2:2:6 (years:months:days) at the
start of the study.
    Before we question the ubiquity of naming in the child's
early utterances, we can first note that naming certainly occurs,
as in the spontaneous naming of (1)[2], or in the naming on request

----

[1] 'Studies of semantic development in young children', SSRC
(London) Grant HR 2516 to R. Grieve and R.N. Campbell, assisted
by R.M. Hoogenraad and R.M. Bowe. The assistance of the SSRC in
this research is gratefully acknowledged.

[2] In our observations we give the child's name and age, the session number, and the time (in minutes and seconds) from the beginning of the session at which the episode occurred. The observer is identified as O. The phonetic transcription is explained
in the appendix.

in (2):

(1) <u>Spontaneous naming</u>

Alison, 2:4:8. Session 11.

8:30. A has been given two chairs, which she is placing on the
desk. She has named these frequently on request. O: <u>You know</u>
<u>what they are. Don't you.</u> A, picking up the baby's high chair
from the desk: /dɑs bebiz tjıêr/ (that's baby's chair), studying
it. <u>Yes, that's right. That's baby's chair.</u>

(2) <u>Naming on request</u>

Roderick, 1:9:18. Session 5.

2:25. R is holding the motorbike and rider. O couples a steam
engine and two open railway wagons: <u>Do you know this? Do you</u>
<u>know this one?</u>, slightly lifting the whole assembled train. R
looks up from playing with the motorbike: /tjê·ın/ (train).
<u>That's right. Can you put the motorbike in the tráin? Put the</u>
<u>motorbike in the tràin.</u> R scans the train from the engine back-
wards, and puts the motorbike in the front wagon. <u>Good.</u>

Another aspect of the naming game in which the child exhi-
bits his knowledge of a word produced by the adult by identifying
an appropirate referent, is seen in (3), where Roderick responds
appropriately to the words 'gloves' and 'boots':

(3) <u>Responding to a name</u>

Roderick, 1·9:19. Session 6.

24:00. R studies the man on the motorbike. Finally, reaching
for the moulded-on helmet: /ʌn haēt op/ (a hat off). <u>I don't</u>
<u>think the hat will come off.</u> R continues to try. <u>It's on there,</u>
<u>isn't it? Uhuh. What about his gloves; will his gloves come</u>
<u>off?.</u> R tries the man's gloves. <u>No they don't, do they? No,</u>
<u>they're stuck on there.</u> R continues to study the man. <u>What</u>
<u>about his boots? Will his boots come off?.</u> At this, R turns
and looks down at his shoe, extending his foot; then he considers, looks at the desk, then the man. <u>See if his boots come</u>
<u>off.</u> Finally, R touches the boots, tugging at them. <u>No, they</u>
<u>don't come off either. They're all stuck on, aren't they?.</u>

However, it is inadequate to suppose that we can establish
the child's system merely by attending to his spontaneous namings, his namings on request, and his responses to names, for
the results of such procedures cannot always be taken at face
value. This is because the child may make mistakes, and these
mistakes may arise for a variety of reasons. For example, he
may make a slip in the pronunciation of a word, as in (4):

(4) <u>Slip in pronunciation of word</u>

Roderick, 1:9:4. Session 3.

1:15. R is playing with the tip-truck. <u>Shall we put</u> ....?
<u>What are these?</u>, proferring a toy brick. R studies it for a
moment, then looking down at the truck again: /dìk/. <u>Uh?</u>....
<u>yes</u> (not immediately interpreting this), as R corrects himself:
/bh̲ı̲k/. <u>Ah</u>.

Alternatively, the child may make a slip in identifying an
object, as in (5), or he may make a slip in the term he employs,
as in (6), where the error is eventually turned to good effect
by making a joke out of it:

(5) <u>Slip in identifying object</u>

Jane, 2:5:19. Session 13.

2:25. <u>Now</u>. <u>Oh, here</u>. <u>This's ... a ... uh</u>. <u>I think you like</u>
<u>this one, don't you</u> (looking into envelope), bringing out the
elephant. O shakes free a kangaroo which is stuck between the
elephant's legs. <u>Oops; oops</u>. The kangaroo falls back into the
envelope. J takes the proferred elephant without looking at it,
her eyes being fixed on the kangaroo which still partly pro-
trudes from the envelope: /wà.../,/ıs daet sʌ mʌ̃ngi/ (What ...
is that a monkey). <u>That's not a monkey, is it</u>. <u>What is it?</u>.
J has retrieved the kangaroo: /ıs ʌ kàeŋgʌrù/ (is a kangaroo).
<u>Yes</u>.

(6) <u>Slip in choice of word</u>

Roderick, 2:0:25. Session 17.

In the previous session, a fortnight earlier, R had asked for
/rɔbi kiz/ (Robbie keys). O had emptied out his pockets for R,
giving him amongst other things keys and a small penknife with
which he played for some time.
13:15. R: /kn ʌ hàevıs rɔbıs kĭz/ (can I haves Robbie's keys).
<u>My keys?</u>. R: /ʌhʌ/. <u>Do you want to play with my keys?</u>.
R: /ʌh̃ʌ̃/. <u>OK, I'll give you my keys to play with</u>, reaching into
his pocket. R: /wı j gıv ʌ fɔ̀rk/ (will you give a fork). <u>What?</u>.
R: /gıv dʌ na̲jv/ (give the knife). <u>The knife?</u>. R: /dʌ nàjf̲/.
<u>Oh, you want the knife, too</u>, continuing to search in his pocket,
<u>Oh</u>. <u>Did you call it a fork first of all</u>. <u>I think that's what</u>
<u>you said</u>. O exchanges some remarks with R's mother as he gives
R the bunch of keys. R, looking up into O's face as he accepts
the keys: /wʌndıt fɔ̀rk/ (want it fork). O holds out the knife:
<u>It's not a fork</u>. R, reaching for it: /wʌz àet/ (what's that).
<u>What's this?</u>, holding up the knife. R, triumphantly: /ıs ʌ vùn/
(is a spoon). O and R's mother laugh. R: /ıs ʌt nàjf/ (is it
knife), chuckling.

Thus, in naming, naming on request, and responding to names, the young child may meet with success as in (1) - (3), or he may make slight mistakes which are little more than temporary deviations from what he knows the case to be, as in (4) - (6). However, genuine mistakes in naming do occur, although again for a variety of reasons. For example, the child may fail to provide a name for an object with which he is clearly familiar, either because he does not have or cannot recall the word, as in (7); or the child may be uncertain of what the pronunciation of a word should be, as in (8); or the child may be uncertain of the meaning of a familiar word, as in (9):

(7) Does not have or cannot recall a name

Jane, 2:4:21. Session 9.

17:05. J reaches for the mop held by O. Do you know that one?. J: /hʌ̄/. Do you?. J: /hʌ̀/. You don't, do you?. J: /jàeh/. What is it then?. J runs it once along the desk, considers, then: /ûlʌh haev lajk dǎet/ (Oolah have like that). Does she?. J: /jaeh/. Oh. J: /grènpa/ (grandpa). A what?, misunderstanding completely, but J ignores this. (Jane's grandfather has a mop on his sailing boat, for mopping up water.) 28:50. J finds the mop and uses it to mop the desk top, looking at O for approval. That's right.

Jane, 2:5:6. Session 12.

14:40. J takes the mop from O: /wɔs dāet/ (what's that). You kn ... you remember that one, don't you?. J, excited: /āhs swipɩŋ daun ... ʌ wȝtʌr/ (I sweeping down ... a water). Yes, that's right. J mops the desk, sweeping then dabbing: /ǎt sʌ wȝtʌr/ (that's a water).

(8) Uncertain of pronunciation of word

Roderick, 1:9:19. Session 6.

14:35. R has found a petrol pump for the first time. Do you know what that is?. R: /t sʌ vhîʔthar/ (it's a petrol), picking it up. It's a what?. R touches it uncertainly and whispers uncertainly: /vʌr dʌ vhîthar/ (for the petrol). O does not understand. I'll show you. It's for putting petrol in the car. Ok. So let's put some pet ... petrol in the truck, pretending to do this with the hose. Put petrol in the truck. O makes a noise imitating the flow of petrol.

15:10. R, truck in one hand, picks up the petrol pump by its hose: /put pèthɩ dǎer/ (put petrol there), applying the hose to various parts of the truck. Ooh, are you putting petrol underneath there too?. R: /vur pɛtȝjs/ (for petrol).

17:40. R picks up the petrol pump, and looking at it: /piter/.
Peter, is that what you call it, a meter?. R's mother whispers
'Petrol'. Petrol! Ah! I see, yes. Ah well. R: /pɛtɔl/.
Petrol, yes.
R makes various attempts at the word during the next few min-
utes. E.g., /pitar/ at 18:00, /pitat/ at 18:30, /pɪki/ at
22:15, and /gitar/ at 23:10.

(It should be noted that the child's utterances are not always
as clearly articulated as the phonetic transcription may suggest: phonetic transcriptions are themselves based on interpretation.)

(9) Uncertain of meaning of word

Jane, 2:2:19. Session 3.

1:25. J has taken out a mechanical mouse. What's that then.
J: /wʌs dɪs/ (what's this). Remember what it is?. J: /fwɔg/

Jane, 2:2:6. Session 4.

0:55. Showing an emu: And do you know what this one is?.
J looks at it: /ʔdɑ̀h/ (yes). Do you know what that one is?.
J looks at it: /his ʌ fwʌ̂g/ (he's a frog).

2:05. For a pelican on the desk: And what's that one?. J
whispers: /fwɔg/.

4:10. Putting on the desk a green rubber frog (a good likeness):
Now; hey! Look! Do you know this animal?. J studies it:
/ɑ̀t s .../ (that is ...). She picks it up. Do you know what
that one is?. J considers: /ɑt sʌ ..../ (that's a ...), studies it: /gɪ̂siz/ (geeses). It's a what?. J; /ʌ gɪ̂s/ (a geese).

6:20. J has been questioning what the frog is. Will I tell you
what it is. J: /tɛh dɪs/ (tell this). It's a frog. J, looking
at the frog: /jàez/ (yes). It's a frog. Can you remember that
one now?. J: /jɛh, ɛ fwɔ̄g/ (yes, a frog). Have a good look at
it; have a good look at the frog, giving it to her. J: /ʌ fwɔg/.
Fwog!.

     Thus, while slips in aspects of naming as in (4) - (6) may
be no more than deviations from the child's own system, (with
the methodological implication to exercise caution in taking the
child's behavior at face value; errors in performance not necessarily entailing inadequacies in competence), the examples of
error in (7) - (9) seem rather different in nature. Rather than
appearing to be deviations from an already defined system, they
indicate that the child is operating in terms of a system which
is not yet well defined. Since the child is learning, this is
of course to be expected.
     Another consequence of the child's inexperience and lack of

practice may be seen in (10) where the child's pronunciation of
a word is erratic:

(10)   Erratic pronunciation

Roderick, 1:10:30. Session 10.

21:10. R pushes a railway wagon towards the gate of the field:
/tjēr kʌm àht/ /ɪt kʌm aht thɛ̀r/ (trailer come out, it come out
there - /tjɛr/ usually = 'chair', but here it is an approximation to 'trailer').

Roderick, 1:11:6. Session 11.

2:05. What's this one here then? What's that one?, showing R
the railway wagon. R, taking it: /tjɛ̀·ʌr/ (trailer). Uhuh.
It's what?, rather sharply: What is it; what did you say it
was?.

6:00. R, sitting on the desk, is playing with the excavator:
/ʌ têlar/ (a trailer), and turns around to get the railway wagon,
which is behind him.

     In (4) - (10) we have illustrated some of the ways in which
the child's utterances and other behavior may fail to directly
reflect his intentions as a result of various sorts of slips,
errors or inaccuracies. In the remainder of our examples such
departures from intention occur quite frequently.
     However, if the problem of early utterances consisted of
distinguishing cases of successful naming (despite minor slips)
from cases of genuine error, and then mapping out the resolution
of the latter into the former during the course of development;
investigation would be comparatively straightforward. We do not
accept this, for we doubt whether the child's early utterances
are concerned exclusively, or even frequently, with naming or
responding to names. Our misgivings can be introduced with observation (11), an early precursor to the sort of responding to
a name illustrated in (3) above:

(11)   Name as an aspect of a game

Jacob, 1:6:3. Session 1.

23:10. (O knows J very well. Although J's utterances are very
indistinctly articulated, though with a pronounced intonation,
O knows that he responds to the word 'shoe'.) Picking up a
man: Jacob! Where's ... where's ... where's his shoes?. J
switches his attention to O, then to the man, and reaches for
it. Where's his shoes? Where's his shoes?, withholding it.
J: /àh/, pulling it out of O's hand. Where's his shoes?. J,
looking at the man: /wû, dae̅/ (?). Hmm?. J: /da̅/(?), looking
elsewhere. O takes the man: Jacob! Jacob! Jacob! Where's his
shoes?, holding out the man. J leans across the desk. Shoes?
Shoes! Huh?. J sits back, looks down at his right foot, moving

it: /ɪ hě/(?), holding out his right foot at 0. <u>Ah, shoes!</u>
<u>That's right.</u> <u>Clever boy!</u>, lifting J's foot and tapping the sole
of his shoe. <u>There</u>. J again lifts his foot for inspection:
/lu dà/(?). <u>Yes</u>. J touches his shoe. <u>Hmm. That's the shoes</u>.
<u>Yes. And where's the man's shoes, where's his shoes</u>, holding
up the man again. J looks at the man, and reaches for him, but
<u>Oops</u> as 0 drops it by mistake. J laughs as he reaches for the
man, but 0 picks it up. <u>Where's his shoes? Where's his shoes?</u>
<u>Show me his shoes</u>. <u>Where's his ....</u>, withholding it from J who
is trying to take it. J, looking at 0: /dụwu:w:/(?). <u>Shoes?</u>.
J looks at his extended foot again and laughs. <u>Bah!</u>, as 0 pokes
J's nose with the man.

Thus rather than 'shoe' being used for any shoe, the word
functions as an aspect of a much enjoyed game, and for the child
'shoe' only has meaning within that game's confines where it
serves to direct attention to one of the game's components, in
this case touching a shoe. The function of the word then is not
to name but rather to direct attention in a certain way. Later,
when a word is used as a name, its use may still serve the function of capturing and directing an adult's attention in various
ways. This can be seen in (12):

(12) <u>Name used to draw attention</u>

Jane, 2:2:13. Session 2.

26:10. J is putting toys away inside the desk. Looking over
the lifted lid she sees a cow, out of her reach at the far end
of the lid: /gɪz ʌ kạu ʌp/ (give's a cow up). <u>Hm?</u>. J, continuing to put books into the desk: /wɪl ju du ʌ kau ʌp, plịz/
(will you do a cow up, please). <u>Hm?</u>. J, reaching, wiggling
her fingers impatiently: /kàu/ (cow). <u>Oh, OK. There you are,</u>
<u>there's the cow</u>, getting it for her.

Besides being used to draw the attention of others, the
child may employ words in setting up his own attention, as in
(13). This is reminiscent of the "directive function" aspect of
language discussed by Luria (1959), but note here that the directive function is self-initiated, at age 1 year 9 months. Note
also that the first indication of the plan comes when the child
says 'a horsie', uttered when he notices <u>the man</u>:

(13) <u>Word used to direct child's own action</u>

Roderick, 1:9:18. Session 5.

22:25. R has put a doll (man with white hair) into the rear
wagon of the train. <u>Hmhm. Now, into the ... into the train,</u>
pointing to a donkey, a sheep and a penguin, <u>Put them into the</u>
<u>train</u>. R picks up the donkey, places it into the rear wagon
which knocks the man out. Noticing <u>the man</u>, he sits back and

says: /ʌ hɔrsi/ (a horsie), scanning the train. <u>Where's the</u>
<u>horsie</u>. R picks up the model horse from the front wagon. <u>Yes</u>.
R, man in one hand, is putting the horse on the desk with the
other animals. O picks up the donkey, and showing it: <u>Is this</u>
<u>a horsie too? Roderick. Is that a horsie too? Hm?</u>. R ignores
this, places the man on the horse. This knocks the horse off
the desk: /ʌ̄p/ (up). O assists: <u>There y'are</u>. R: /maen ʌ
hɔrsi/ (man a horsie), turning the horse so as to place the man
on it.

In these observations, the child employs words, either to
draw the attention of others or to set up his own attention, in
relation to objects which are present. However, the child may
also employ a word to try and draw attention to something which
is absent, as Roderick does in (14) for an event in the past:

(14) <u>Word used to draw attention to a past event</u>

Roderick, 1:9:11. Session 4.

12:00 R is given a duck and four ducklings, all mounted on the
same green plastic base. <u>And ... and what's this one then?</u>.
R, taking it: /bôt/ (boat—his usual response to this stimulus).
<u>Do ... do you think it's a boat? What's a boat say then</u> (R has
just supplied the appropriate noise for a dog and for a duck).
R looks down, considering, then sings /hū:/ on a high note.
<u>Hm! Toot toot</u>; at the same time R turns to his mother: /pʌ̂mi/
(mummy), and turning to the window, /tēk gɔn ʌwêɪ/, and turning
to O who looks questioningly at him, /têktʊ/. <u>The what's gone</u>
<u>away?</u>. R: /têktʊ gɔn ʌwêɪ/.

Roderick's mother explains that R is saying 'tractor gone
away'—there had been a tractor outside the window that morning.
Given the child's limited resources, we can appreciate the difficulty he must have in trying to make reference to things which
are absent and to events in the past, especially in relation to
adults who have not shared the child's experiences. When the
child is older and has greater resources at his disposal, he can
draw and refocus attention much more successfully, sometimes in
a sophisticated way, as we can see from Jane in (15):

(15) <u>Drawing and refocusing of attention</u>

Jane, 2:2:26. Session 4.

21:10. J is placing the penguin upright in the toy field:
/ɪts bʊrd/ (it's bird). <u>Aha</u>. J: /ɪs ʌ pɛnwʌn/ (is a penguin).
<u>That's it; yes. Hm</u>. J, reaching for another animal: /aj lajk
pêŋgwʌns/ (I like penguins). <u>Yes, so do I. I think they're</u>
<u>really nice</u>.

Jane, 2:4:8. Session 8.

7:15. Looking through a book of animals, including a picture of penguins, J: /pêŋwʌns/ (penguins) Penguins, yes. J: /aj lajk pêŋgwʌns/ (I like penguins). You like penguins, do you?. J: /dɛh, ə̀/

Jane, 2:5:19. Session 13.

17:40. O gives J the penguin. J: /wʌ̄t ʌ pêŋgwɪn/ (What a penguin!) looking at it delightedly. Yes, you like those, don't you. Hm. Is a peng ... . J, who has placed the penguin on the desk, points to it, and looking at O for his reactions: /aj ìt daet pêŋgwɪn/ (I eat that penguin). O, surprised: Eat it?. J: /jaes/. O looks at her in mock horror: Oh!. J, pointing at the wall behind her (where the kitchen is): /aj ɪ̄t sʌm ɔv daet .../, ɪn dɑt tɪn/ (I eat some of that ..., in that tin). Looking pleased, she looks expectantly at O. Oh! Those!. ('Penguin' is the trade name for chocolate biscuits which children regard as a treat—the biscuits are individually foil-wrapped, with the picture of a penguin on the wrapper.) Are they like those, pointing to the model penguin. J: /hm̄/ (thumb in mouth). Yes?. J: /jɪh/. You like those. J: /hm/. Hm. Is that why you like penguins?. J: /hm̂/. Is that why you like penguins. Hm? There you are, giving her the model penguin. But you wouldn't eat him, would you?, pointing to the model penguin. J: /nò/. But you'd eat those other penguins. J: /hm/. Yeah?. J: /hm/. Hm. I see!.

Jane, 2:5:20. Session 14.

4:10. J has called a crocodile a 'penguin', then, with greater certainty, called a seal and a penguin 'penguin'. O puts a second penguin on the desk: Oh, and here's another one. There you are. J: /hir sʌ nʌ̀dʌr pɛŋ:gwɪn/ (here's another penguin). Hmhm. J: /ō̄h/, /ɑts fɔ dâun7/ (oh, that's fall down), the penguin falling as she places it in the field with the other animals. Oh, did it fall down. J: /jʌ̀h/. Dear me. J, picking it up: /hi gɔt ʌ bìg jɛlow nò̄z/ (he got a big yellow nose). He does, doesn't he. A big yellow nose. Yes. J, looking at it again: /hi gɔt ʌ bɪg jɛlow noz/. Yes. They've got lovely noses, haven't they. I think penguins are very nice. J, placing the model penguin in the field again: /aj ìt pɛngwʌns/ (I eat penguins). You eat penguins?. J, looking at him: /ʌh/. But I wouldn't eat those poor little things. J: /nò e w̄udn/ (no I wouldn't—last part indistinct). No. J, half turning towards the wall behind her where the kitchen is, and flapping her hand: /ī̄t ɪn dʌ tīns/ (eat, in the tins). Oh, eat in the tins! Oh, you don't eat those ones. You eat the other sort of penguins. J: /jàe:s/. And are they the same?. J: /jaes/. Are they. Do the ones in the tins go in the water too (J had earlier remarked

that she had seen a penguin in the water on TV). J: /nò e
dʌ̃snt/ (no, they doesn't). They don't. J: /no̱/. Ah, I see. Ah.
J: /ōnli pɛ̀ntetos go ɪn ʌ... ɪn dʌ wɔtʌr/ (only pentatoes go in
a... in the water). Only what?. J: /onli pòtetos go ɪn dʌ
wɔtʌrs/ (only potatoes go in the waters). Only potatoes! Oh,
I see, when you cook them. J: /jɛ̀s/. Yes. Or when you wash
them. J: /jɛ̄h/.

In this example, it is not clear what Jane is referring to
on the many occasions when she says 'I like penguins', as for
example in Sessions 4 and 8. She may be referring to the model
penguin and the picture of the penguins respectively, or she may
be trying to inform the adult that she likes the chocolate biscuits of that name. In Session 13 she not so much draws as
rivets the adult's attention by pointing to the model penguin
and saying 'I eat that penguin'. And then she makes clear that
she is in fact talking of penguins 'in that tin'. Note also her
slip at the end of Session 14, which blends 'penguins' and 'potatoes' into 'pentatoes'.   .
Up until now, our observations have concerned the child's
early use of words to name, identify, refer or draw attention to
objects or events in the past, present or future. However the
child may employ a variety of names for the same object as in
(16):

(16) Variety of names for the same object

Roderick, 1:10:2. Session 7.

5:50. R, placing a cow in the wagon coupled to the steam engine:
/ɔn ʌ têɪn/ (on a train).

18:00. O is tapping R on the nose with a pig: What's that?.
R, warding it off, trying to take it: /ah vūt t tîn/ (I put it
in). But ... yes, OK, put it in. What're you going to put it
in?. R puts it in the wagon, which moves, revealing that it
is not coupled to the engine. In the train? OK. R looks at
the engine, and withdraws the pig: /nʌ ɪn ʌ tî·ʌn/ (not in a
train). R then tries to put the pig into the cabin of the engine. Oh, you're going to put it inside the train. R /ʌh hʌ/.

Roderick, 1:10:30. Session 10.

3:15. O couples the railway wagon to an excavator, and asks what
the wagon is. R: /kɛrʌvaen/ (caravan).

11:50. R has placed the excavator and the steam engine, both
with an open railway wagon hooked to them, side by side on the
desk. O has suggested that R should put petrol in the tractor:
there is a short interlude as they discuss the petrol pump, then
R: /vɪkɸ..., pētɔl go ɪn ʌ thʌ̃k/ (vika ... petrol go in a truck),
as he pretends to fill the chassis of the wagon hooked to the

excavator with the petrol pump hose. <u>Yes, good, uhm.</u>

21:10. R pushes the railway wagon towards the gate of the field:
/tjɛr kʌm âht/ /ɪt kʌm aht thêr/ (trailer come out, it come out
there. /tjɛr/ usually = chair, but here it is used as an approximation to 'trailer'--cf. (10) above).

Here Roderick refers to the railway wagon with four different words: 'train', 'caravan', 'truck' and 'trailer'. It is not
clear why he does this--possibly he is uncertain about the appropriate name, or it could be that he knows this quite well, the
main criterion which determines the word used in (16) being concerned with the function that the wagon is to serve.

Naming an object not with its customary name but in terms
of the function it is currently serving is not unusual. For
example, in observation (4) above Roderick named a brick appropriately at 1:15; yet a little later he employs the word 'chair'
to indicate the function that the brick is serving at that point
in the game, as in (17). Note that the latter part of (17) shows
that calling the brick 'chair' does not arise from any failure
to know what a chair is:

(17) <u>Word used to indicate function of object</u>

Roderick, 1:9:4. Session 3.

2:40. R places a man in sitting posture on a toy brick: /ah sɪt
tâun/ (he sit down). <u>Sit down, that's right</u>, giving assistance.
R finally leans the man against the brick. <u>Against there</u>, adjusting the doll's position. R looks on, put out because he
wants to do it. <u>Now can you bring out a chair? There's a chair
in there too</u>, referring to the box of toys on the desk. Still
adjusting the doll: <u>Can you bring out the chair for me? Rod?</u>.
Pointing to the box: <u>Can you give me the chair</u>, sitting back.
R takes the man, and, turning the brick over: /ʌh tĕh/ (<u>this</u>
chair).

3:45. R takes a chair out of the box, looks at it, and: /tĕh/
(chair). <u>Hmm.</u> R reaches into the box again: /gut/ (good),
brings out an armchair: /tĕh/ (chair), and studies it. <u>Yes.</u>
<u>They're nice ones aren't they.</u> R, not attending to this:
/dɔbʌdub/ (R sometimes produces such wordlike noises for no
special reason. Cf: Keenan and Klein's (1974) report on twins
who constructed elaborate and lengthy games on the bases of such
word distortions.)

This game is remembered two weeks later:

Roderick, 1:9:18. Session 5.

10:45. R finds the brick in the toybox. Bringing it to the
desk: /ʌ mĕn/ (a man). <u>Oh yes. Yes.</u> R scans the desk as he
puts the brick on it: /ʌ mĕn ɪn ʌ jɛr/ (a man in a chair),

Yes. Hmm. R, searching: /màen gɔn ʌwe/ (man gone away). Oh,
has the man gone away?. O produces the man, verbalising all the
while. R, taking the man: /sɪ daun mah sɪ̂t/ (sit down his seat--
/ah/ and /mah/ have been translated as 'he' and 'his', as
Roderick uses these for first, second, and third pronouns and
possessive pronouns).

A similar phenomenon arises in (18) where Alison names the
kangaroo's joey as a baby; yet denies it is a baby when she is
looking for a baby to put in the highchair:

(18) Word used in relation to current function

Alison, 2:4:9. Session 12.

On the previous day, shown a female kangaroo with a joey in its
pouch, A identified the joey as /ʌ bebi/ (a baby).

6:35. A is given the baby's high chair. She studies it carefully, then putting it on the desk: /wɛs ʌ bĕbi/ (where's a
baby). The baby. It's in here I think, picking up an envelope,
Here y'are. A: /nô, ɪts ɪn iʌ̂r/ (no, its in here), pointing to
another envelope. No, and O picks up the joey: I thought that
was a baby, showing it to her, Didn't you say that was a baby?.
A: /nô/, and she turns to point to another envelope; No. Is that
the one you want, holding out the human baby. A taking it,
/jaeh/. Yes. She places it in the high chair.

It is also the case that when the child appears to be
naming, he may in fact be engaged in some quite different purpose. In the next two observations, (19) and (20), the most
obvious interpretation--that the child is overextending his use
of a name from one object to another that is similar--may not be
correct. Instead, the child may be employing a word to obtain
information:

(19) Use of a word to elicit information

Roderick, 1:19:19. Session 6.

34:15. R shuts and latches the gate of the model field, then
picks up a highland cow in the field, and butts at the gate with
it: /bɛ̄k/ (back--this is a game which O had played earlier).
R stands back, the cow in one hand. Oh, yes, can't he get out?
R walks round the desk, studying and touching the field, until
he is holding the section of fence opposite the gate: /shʌ̄t dʌ
gɛ̀t/ (shut the gate), /fan ʌ gɛt/ (find a gate), looking closely
at the section of fence and tugging at it. Standing up: /ʃʌbn
bɛk dʌ gɛ̀t/ (shut back the gate). There's ... that's ... there's
only one gate here. That's not a gate, indicating the section of
fence R tugged at; That's the gate over here, touching the gate.

Another example, perhaps even clearer, is this:

(20) Use of a word as a question

Roderick, 1:10:3. Session 8.

(At this stage in our studies, the playbench apparatus had three microphones, which protruded slightly from the front of the bench; above this the camera lens, surrounded by shiny metal, protruded from the camera cover.)

0:10. R looks at the centre microphone, then touches it: /ha lâjt, dɔbar/ (a light, Robert). O misinterprets this as: 'I like (it), Robert'.
2:25. R points suddenly at the centre microphone: /ʌ lâjt/ (a light).

Roderick, 1:10:30. Session 10.

17:10. R gestures at the camera lens: /s ʌ lâjt/ (it's a light). This allows us to make sense of something Roderick said nearly two months previously:

Roderick, 1:9:4. Session 3.

24:00. R, standing on the playbench desk, pointing at the camera lens: /ɪs sɪs ʌ fɛ̌t/ (is this a light).

Here O did not know what Roderick meant by /fɛt/, and so did not react. Then in Session 8, the child's utterance was misinter-preted, and only later in Session 10 does it click that what he is doing is asking if the camera lens, among other things, is a light. Apart from the questioning function illustrated by this observation, we can also note a phenomenon to which we will re-turn: namely, the adult's misunderstanding of what the child is trying to do, which may persist over several sessions. Inter-estingly, when we eventually spot these, tracing them back may show that despite persistent misunderstanding, the child has been attempting to communicate by producing a series of phono-logical variants of misunderstood words--for an example, see Grieve, 1976.

Earlier we noted that the child may use more than one word for the same object. While this might arise for a variety of reasons--uncertainty, for example, or where the words stand in certain semantic relation to one another such as synonymy, hyponomy, etc.--when the child uses two words for the same object, he may not be naming the object in two different ways because he thinks it has these two names, but for some other purpose, as in (21):

(21) Word used to comment on likeness

Roderick, 1:8:28. Session 2.

13:10. Proferring a chimpanzee which has moveable arms: <u>There</u>
<u>you are</u>. <u>Here</u>. <u>What's this</u>. R takes it and studies it with
interest. <u>Do you like that one?</u> <u>Do you know what that is?</u>
R continuing to study it: /ʌn tìtada/ (a ?), and running to his
mother with it: /tɪs ..., ʌ mâen/ (tis ..., a man).

Roderick, 1:9:4. Session 3.

29:55. O puts the chimp on the desk. R spots it, points towards it, and (excitedly): /mʌ́ki:/ (monkey). <u>Yes, that's a</u>
<u>nice one, isn't it</u>, handing it to R, who, taking it: /s ʌ mʌ́keɪ/
(it's a monkey). <u>Yes, yes</u>. <u>It's got long arms, hasn't he</u>,
while R studies it. R hands it back, and:/sʌ mâen/ (it's a man).
<u>Hm</u>. R: /n ʌ lâpɑt/ (another example of verbal play?).

32:30. O holds out a gorilla (standing, with arms raised):
<u>What's that?</u>. R: /mʌ́keɪ/ (monkey). <u>Yes, that's right</u>, placing
<u>it</u> on the desk. R, a moment later: /maen/ (man).

35:00. R spots the chimp: /mȝki/ (monkey), picking it up.
<u>Yes</u>. R studies it, then throws it back on the desk.

     Thus instances where the child is apparently naming may be
serving quite different purposes, such as questioning, comment-
ing, drawing or planning attention, etc.. Perhaps the clearest
example of this comes from when the child is ostensibly naming
objects, but does so in an outrageous fashion. For example, in
(22) Jane becomes bored with a naming game, and she attempts to
divert attention towards a more interesting topic:

(22) <u>Outrageous naming</u>

Jane, 2:4:8. Session 8.

14:30. J has been playing a game with O, naming a series of
different animals, but she now seems a bit bored. Ignoring
further questioning by O she turns to the usual observer (O2)
who sits off to one side, and shows him some animals, including
a polar bear. O2 takes them and holds out the polar bear:
<u>What's that one there, Jane</u>. <u>You ... you know what this one is,</u>
<u>don't you?</u>. J: /jaeh/. <u>What's that</u>; O2: <u>You have a good</u>
<u>look at it and tell us</u>, placing it on the desk. J, head cocked
to one side, looks at it: /dɑs ʌn têprɪkɔrdʌr/ (that's a tape-
recorder). O2: <u>A what!</u>. J, reaching for it without looking:
/têprʌkɔrdʌr/, looking at O2 for the effect of her utterance.
(The playbench apparatus used to record each session is brought
to the child's home, and the various sections assembled beforehand, an activity of great interest with which the children
invariably help. On this particular occasion our tape-deck was
not working, and the tape-recorder replacement was spotted by
Jane, who was greatly interested in this departure from routine.)

17:10. J is bored with naming the animals which are being put
away in an envelope held by O, who asks what they are as J drops
them in. J reaches for the polar bear on the desk: <u>What's that?</u>
As she picks it up, J: /d<u>ae</u>s pôl^baer/ (that's polar bear), and
she drops it in the envelope. <u>Uh-huh. And the next one?</u>. J
reaches for the baby elephant, looks at it, then: /ɪs pôl^baer/,
and drops it in the envelope. <u>And the next one?</u>. J picks up a
giraffe and as she drops it in the envelope: <u>What's that?</u>.
J: /ʔaes ^ djirâf/ (that's a giraffe).

There is no doubt that J can correctly name sheep and ele-
phants if she wants to: in fact, she did so correctly earlier
in this session. We might also note that Alison and Roderick
name outrageously when the mood takes them, but Jane is particularly accomplished at it.

III <u>Methodology in the study of child language</u>

These observations are not intended to indicate all of the purposes to which the young child puts his early utterances.
Rather, they are intended to indicate that the young child does
employ his limited linguistic resources for a variety of purposes besides naming. Our observations attempt only to illustrate, not exhaust, that variety of purposes. To some extent,
this has been noted before; for example, by Leopold (1948), who
records that his daughters Hildegard and Karla "both made ex-
cessive use of the word <u>pretty</u>, not because a strong power of
abstraction allowed them to subsume a great number of expressions under one abstract concept, but because they lacked
specific terms for many things and had to be satisfied with a
vague emotional reaction." Thus, when the child is using
language at a stage where he does not have much, his language
must none the less serve a host of different functions. If we
are to do more in the study of child language than merely take
what the child says at face value and assume that he is engaged
in little other than naming, then clearly we must attempt to
establish what that variety of functions might be. To do this
we suggest that what is required are inferences as to the intentions which underlie the child's early utterances, for such
inferences might establish a more adequate picture of the child's
linguistic-cognitive system.

Such a proposal carries implications for methodology which
need to be considered. If the study of child language is to be
placed on a sound empirical basis, it might be supposed that the
only really objective data available are what the child says
and the immediate context of his utterance; e.g., his accompanying behavior, such as pointing, orientation and direction
of gaze, manipulation and so on; what his interlocutors say and
do; and the objects so acted upon. While there is no doubt that

these are the most objective data available, we should bear in
mind that many aspects of behavior are far from unambiguous:
for instance consider (23) and (24), which indicate that pointing does not unequivocally determine what is being referred to:

(23) Misinterpreted reference

Jane, 2:6:3. Session 15.

6:00. J, touching the head of the tortoise: /irz hɪz hâed/
(here's his head). O agrees, then points to its shell and asks
what it is called. J: /è kɔld sârkʌlz/ (they called circles),
referring to the pattern of concentric hexagons on the shell.
O repeats the question, pointing to the whole shell, delineating
it with his finger. J, putting it aside: /daets ..., ah dõn no
wɔt ɪt ɪs/ (that's ... I don't know what it is).

(24) Interpretations pass each other by

Alison, 2:3:25. Session 9.

21:15. What's this one here?, holding up the parrot on a perch.
A's gaze has fallen on her pedal car, behind O. She points
(sloppily) over O's shoulder: /stɛ màj/ ('s that mine). Hm?
Oh, where's yours?, imagining that A is talking of the panda
which they have just discussed, and which O placed on the bench
near his shoulder—it is also approximately along the line of
A's pointing finger. A, insistent: /tɛ màj/ (that's mine).
Oh, it's up there is it?, imagining she is pointing to the table
behind him where A's toys are kept, and that she is referring
to her own toy panda. A: /hm̂/, /sì, ɪts mâjn/ (see, it's mine).
Is it. Uhuh. What about this one? What's that thing, holding
up the parrot again. A, again looking briefly at her car:
/mʌh kàr/ (my car). This one?. A: /kàr/. That's not a car.
A: /ʌ kàr/. No. A: /kàr/. She points: /sì/ (see). Where?

Also, while the implication of observations (4) - (10)
above—that performance does not necessarily directly reflect
competence and that the child's competence is incomplete and
changing—is generally accepted, the extent of the problem is
perhaps not so widely recognized. It seems to us that what is
required is a good knowledge of the child's ability, gleaned
from longer term observation and interaction with the child,
against which to judge his behavior on particular occasions.
Also, access to audio and video records of episodes allows us
to reconsider initial interpretations and judge the fine details and precise timing of the various events. Without this
reconsideration, there is a considerable possibility that insignificant errors, such as those illustrated in (4) - (10), will
be taken as intended behavior instead of deviations from intended behavior, and we speculate that some of the reported

quirks of child language may be based on such misinterpretations.
We should point out that we have illustrated this point with
examples of fairly gross deviation from intention, where the correct interpretation is reasonably certain. In many cases, deviation from intention may be far more subtle, where interpretation of what was in fact intended becomes correspondingly less
certain.

     In proposing that the data required in studying child
language is data from which we can infer the child's intentions,
we must also note that it is not enough to infer what the child
intended the form of an utterance or other behavior to be. We
must also infer what the child intended to accomplish by means
of its utterances and accompanying behavior. How we can arrive
at such inferences, and the nature of the data needed to accomplish this, can be considered in relation to four separable
sources of data. What is at issue is, first, identifying the
sources of pertinent data; and second, suggesting how the data
can best be described so that it is made maximally transparent
how inferences were arrived at.

(a) <u>What the child says and does</u> This aspect of the data has
already been covered in some detail: the pertinent point is
that what is ultimately required from the data is what the child
intended to do and say. This raises the question as to what
form the description should take, for even a young child's intentional behavior is sufficiently rich to require a rich language for its description. Ordinary English--or some other
natural language--has the required resources but tends to be
imprecise in important respects. Take intentionality as an
example: 'R drops the cow'--here there is no indication whether
the action was intentional or accidental. Or, to take another
example, consider real versus imaginary actions: 'R walks the
cow on the desk.' The problem is to define a descriptive language that is sufficiently rich, yet sufficiently terse, to
make the task of description feasible. An augmented natural
language may suffice, provided such augmentation can capture
certain essentials, such as: intentionality, the sequencing of
actions, the nature of their duration, the success of the outcome, as well as specifying the relation between actions: e.g.,
is this action self-initiated, a response to a request, a consequence of the preceding action, or whatever?

     As regards the child's utterances, a fairly broad phonetic
transcription will usually prove adequate, although the child's
protolanguage vocalizations (Halliday, 1975) need a rather different system of transcription--Halliday suggests a postural
and prosodic notation which specifies the postures of the articulatory organs. The greatest danger is not that the transcription of utterances will be insufficiently precise, but that
the transcriber will allow his knowledge of the language which

the child is learning, and his 'quest after the child's meaning',
to transform what he hears. There is a similar problem in describing the child's actions. Visual and auditory recordings
which allow the same episode to be seen and heard repeatedly
provide an opportunity for constant review and reassessment of
what is taking place.

(b) <u>The child's attitude towards what he says and does</u> Clearly
we always use more than what the child says and does in judging
what his intentions are. This additional information comes from
what might be termed the child's affective state. Some aspects
of this form a background to the child's activities over a more
or less extended period of time: e.g., the child may habitually
use a characteristic intonation, his articulation may be habitually lax, his actions habitually staccato, his interest and
focus of attention habitually diffuse or concentrated over a
certain definable range of activities. Other aspects are of
shorter duration: e.g., the child has a cold which affects his
articulation, his level of interest, the decisiveness of his
actions, etc.. Others modulate particular utterances and
actions: e.g., his reply is offhand, he points hesitatingly,
he drops the cow to provoke, etc.. And finally, there are those
clues carried for instance by facial expressions and by tonus:
e.g., he is embarrassed, tense, delighted, etc.. There is no
doubt that we use some of this information some of the time: it
is important that we should use it consistently and as explicitly
as possible.

(c) <u>What the child sees and hears</u> This aspect of observation
of the child probably bears the greatest burden of what is normally meant by 'context of utterance'. It seems straightforward
enough in principle: we record what is said to the child, what
is visible to the child, what he can feel and so on. But that
would be to miss the first essential: what the child does is
informed not by what is visible to him but by what he sees, not
by what was said to him but by what he hears, and so on. While
in practice we cannot be sure of what the child attends to, what
we record of the 'context of utterance' must include our best
assessment of what was attended to, for if we do not, much of
our description will not be merely superfluous but actually
misleading. Consider this in relation to (25):

(25) <u>What is said and what is understood</u>

Graham, 2:4:5. Session 3.

39:00. There are horses and cows in the field. O places a box
on its side on the desk, opening facing forward: <u>This is a ...</u>
<u>that's a stable; that's where the horses live. OK? Now you</u>
<u>open the gate and put the horses in their stable. OK?</u>. G places

a horse on top of the box: /ʔʌ hârziz ʌ te bʌl/ (the horses a table).

It is quite clear that Graham has not attended to, or not understood, the explanation 'that's where the horses live'. Or, in (23), although O may have intended to point to the shell, what Jane saw was O pointing to the pattern on the shell. (25) raises another related point: what is seen (or heard) is not independent of what is understood. We may be sure that the aspects of O's request that Graham attended to were the portions he understood, and that the pertinent piece was: 'put the horses in their stable'. But since Graham does not know the word 'stable', what he understood was 'table', either because that was what he heard, or because he heard 'stable' and inferred--wrongly in this case--that O meant or intended 'table'. What of 'in'? Three possibilities are: he heard 'on'; or he heard 'in' but inferred that 'on' was intended; or 'in' and 'on' are undifferentiated for him, variants of the same word. A fourth possibility seems more reasonable, however: in (23) Jane answers the question 'what are these called' though the question asked was 'what is this called'. She almost certainly differentiates between these two forms, but we must suppose that the child, faced with various sources of information, many of which are ambiguous or imperfectly understood, reaches the best possible interpretation rather than the only possible interpretation. In doing this he is willing to forego or ignore information from speech, since as a learner he cannot place great confidence in the accuracy of his understanding of speech. Watch this in operation in (26), where a situation very like that in (25) leads to a similar result that, nonetheless, differs in a subtle way, for Jane decides that perhaps 'in the table' is the right expression after all:

(26) An erroneous inference leads to an erroneous change of
      mind

Jane, 2:2:19. Session 3.

17:10. O has placed two boxes on their side on the desk, opening facing forward. He reaches inside to clear out some tiddlywinks, and J bends down to peer inside to see what he is doing: Now. Let's make ... let's make believe that these are stables. Can you put the ... the cow in the stable?. J first clears out the rest of the tiddlywinks, helped by O. Then: OK. Now. Can you put the ... cow in the stable?. J, reaching for the baby giraffe: /ʌn dᴛs/ (on/in this). Where's the cow; put the cow in the stable. J changes her mind and picks up the duck and ducklings: /njɛ/, and placing it on top of the box questioningly: /ɪn dɛ/ (in there?). Uhuh (offhand). J puts the baby giraffe on top: /ɪn dɛ̄/ (in there), and then questioningly: /ʌn dɛ/ (on/in there?). Uhuh. And what are you doing now

(offhand). J, inclining her head to look at the giraffe, and
adjusting its position on the box: /pu̱ʔ ɪn dʌ tê̠ʔʌl/ (put in the
table).

    Note that (25) and (26) contradict the predictions of
Clark (1973b) where she argues that the young child will respond
to questions involving 'in', 'on' and 'under' on the basis of
the perceptual features of the stimuli, using ordered rules
which predict that the child will place the one object inside
the other if that is possible, on it if not, and under it only
if the first two possibilities are not realizable. But we see
that the basis for the child's response is the meaning it imposes on the stimulus, in this case on the basis of misunderstanding the language, not on the form or criterial features of
the stimulus, though clearly the form of the stimulus restricts
the possible interpretations. Thus, again, we come to the conclusion, as we did earlier, that it is not the criterial features of the stimulus that determine how it will be referred to,
but rather the meaning imposed by the child.
    It will be apparent that throughout this paper we have not
attempted to maintain a clear distinction between observation
and inference. This is not unintentional, for we reject the
notion that observation is theory-neutral. Our main plea is
for an attitude: the attitude that looks for rational explanations of the child's behavior on the basis of an understanding
of the child's limited experience, the consequence of this on
what he sees and hears, and the limited means which the child
must, perforce, use to accomplish a rich variety of ends.
    Such an attitude has consequences beyond those we have
mentioned. Consider (27):

(27) <u>Using a word in a deviant way</u>

Jane, 2:3:4. Session 6.

11:55. <u>Yes, I'll show you something you know</u>, and holding up
the helicopter: <u>You know that one, don't you</u>. J, touching the
rotor: /jɛ̀h/. <u>What is that</u>. J, taking it: /lɛ́plen/ (aeroplane). <u>Uhuh. Yes. Where does it go?</u>. J: /dɛ̀r/ (there),
placing it on the desk. <u>And ... what about this one, what's
that one</u>, giving her an aeroplane. J, taking it: /ɔ̂fʌs/ (office). <u>Uhuh,</u> as J puts it on the desk too.

    There is no reason to believe that the child is not naming
and intending to do so in a straightforward way. But if we en-
quire into the experience that gave rise to Jane believing that
'office' refers to aeroplanes, we see that she came to this belief quite rationally. Jane's father works at a local airbase,
and every day he goes 'to the office', so she has been familiar
with the word 'office' for some time without any clear idea of

its meaning. When she finally went to the airbase, 'to Daddy's office', the family went up in an aeroplane, and she came to the rational conclusion that this was the 'office'. Adults get the wrong end of the stick in exactly the same way, as in Jespersen (1922): "I may mention here that analogous mistakes may occur when missionaries or others write down words from foreign languages with which they are not familiar. In the oldest list of Greenlandic words (1587) there is thus a word panyginah given with the signification 'needle'; as a matter of fact it means 'my daughter's': the Englishman pointed at the needle, but the Eskimo thought he wanted to know who it belonged to." Jespersen suggests that many etymological changes arise from this sort of misunderstanding.

In interpreting an example like (27) we used a source of data not so far discussed:

(d) The background to the child's utterances   In many of our examples we could not have arrived at an adequate interpretation if we had not had access to a great deal of background information on the child. One source is our continuing observations of the child, for many of the child's utterances become clear only when we observe them against subsequent events, as in (28):

(28) Clarifying the meaning of a word

Roderick, 1:8:28. Session 2.

10:00. What's that?, giving R a cow. R, accepting it: /maēs/ (?). What's that?. R, inspecting it, touching its horns: /pi māj ti maes/ (?), /ʃɪp/ (sheep). He then 'walks' it on the desk, intoning: /dɔkix dɔkiˀ/ (doggie, doggie).

10:10. What about ..., producing an elephant: What's that one. R, looking at it: /hɔrz/ (horse). Yes? 're you sure it is? OK, as R reaches for the envelope. What about ... what about this one? What's that, producing a horse. R, reaching for it: /dɔkî/ (doggie).

10:20. R runs to his mother with a duck, a horse and a cow: /hɔrz/ (horse), as he gives her one of these. Mother: "Thank you". R, giving her another: /dɔgî/ (doggie).

10:40. What's this one here?, drawing R's attention to the elephant. R takes it by the trunk. Do you know that one. R, as he turns to take it to his mother: /dɔkī/ (doggie).

12:00. R pulls a pelican out of the envelope. Looking at it: /āh dɔki/ (a doggie). What ...? Yes.

23:00. O has lined up the elephant, the pelican, the horse, the dog and the duck. Can you find me the ... the horse. Where's the horsie. R immediately picks up the horse: /ōh hî ıt ıs/

(Oh here it is). Yes! That's a lovely one, isn't it. Look at
his white nose. R gets up, reaching for the duck. Now what
about the ... dog. Where's the dog, restraining R. R picks up
the duck and handing it to O: /t ʌ dʌkɪ̄/ (it a duckie). What
is it? R's mother: "Duckie". Uhuh. R picking up the pelican
with his left hand: /hi̱r ha/ (here y'are(?)). He drops it, and
his eyes follow it as it falls: /dūk/ (duck). Then, dropping
the horse which he has held throughout in his right hand, he
picks up the dog: /he̱ dɔ̂g/ (here dog). Ahah. Yes.

28:15. Here, why don't you put the ... why don't you put the
duck in the truck, pushing the tiptruck towards R. Can you put
the duck in the truck?. R, turning around: /gɔn ʌwêɪ/ (gone
away). Gone away? Oh, where's it gone to? I think it's ...
up there, pointing back to the desk as he walks away, I think
it's just down here, on the desk. You have a look for the duck;
it's down there. R returns to the desk, scanning it, all serious. You put it in the truck, OK. R reaches for the elephant
across the desk, then his eyes fall on the duck, dog and pelican. Picking up the dog: /dʌ̄k/ (dog(?)). Put in in the truck
then. R: /dʌ̂k/ (dog(?)).

Roderick, 1:9:19. Session 6.

34:35. There are horses, cows and calves in the field. R,
returning to the desk: /dʌ dɔ̂g .. hi ɔh/ (the dogg..ie off),
and he takes all the animals out of the field, throwing them
aside: /dɔgi ɔ̂v/ (doggie off).

The observation in Session 6 shows that 'doggie' is roughly
equivalent to 'animal', and this in turn suggests that in
Session 2 Roderick employed two words, 'dog' with a (more or
less) conventional meaning, and 'doggie' with the approximate
meaning 'animal'. We do not, of course, have sufficient background information to determine how he arrived at these meanings.
     In interpreting the child's utterances we also make constant
use of our developing knowledge of his phonology and syntax, and
although these have not been considered systematically here,
being beyond the scope of our present study, a fuller treatment
is clearly desirable. Another source of information is the
child's mother or other caretakers. We have had some recourse
to this already but it is a source that should be treated with
considerable caution, for the observations and interactions on
which their information is based is not generally open to
scrutiny. Furthermore, mothers are no freer from presupposition
than investigators: mothers may claim their children can count
if they can recite numbers or that they know colors if they produce color terms, but further investigation may reveal that
the words are virtually all that the child knows. However this
is not to deny that accurate auxiliary information may be

invaluable. Consider (29):

(29) <u>Overextension</u>
Roderick, 1:8:28. Session 2.

4:30. O has opened a box of crayons. R, to his mother: /lùk/,
/his ʌ kì, mʌ̀mi/ (look! here's a key, mummy).

8:30. R is touching, in a desultory fashion, a drawing pin
which is pushed into the desk. The pin has in its head a tri-
angular hole: /kî ho/. <u>It's a key hole, is it; is that what
you said</u>.

9:00. There is a scraping noise from the rear of the bench, as
R pulls the key for the door in the back of the bench out of the
lock, and pushes it into a hole in the door. R: /ki gɔ̂n:/,
/hi hʌ gî ki, mʌ̀mi/ (key gone, here a ? key, mummy).

9:45. R having been given a crayon, walks around the desk and
puts the crayon into the crayon box. Then, to his mother:
/kì bɔk hì, mʌ̀mi/ (key box here, mummy).

Here we would appear to have a classical case of overextension based on the criterial feature of shape. But consider the
auxiliary evidence available to us. Roderick is fascinated by
keys and key holes. He has not seen crayons before this session
and does not at this stage know what they are for, what their
function is. He also likes to poke things into holes. So we
might suppose that for <u>him</u> 'key' does not yet carry any implication of 'locking, or securing from entry', but rather means
'something that can be poked into an appropriate hole'. Faced
with a new object, the crayon, he infers on the basis of shape
that crayons are 'things for pushing into holes', and hence
'keys', where the extension is not on shape, but on the basis
of identity of (here, wrongly) inferred function. When he does
learn the customary function of crayons he calls them 'pussy
cat', because that is what they are first used to draw.
    Having considered sources of observational data, we can
also note the importance of attempting to delineate the child's
knowledge by means of experiment. Although formal experiments
may suffer various drawbacks, such as the difficulty in being
sure of the child's co-operation, our incomplete knowledge of
the child's abilities and experience, his propensity for inci-
dental and one-trial learning, etc., informal experiments may
be more satisfactory, where the experimenter chooses an appropriate moment, and is ready to modify the procedure where
necessary, including giving hints and help to the child. The
experiment can then be interpreted as it was done, rather than
as it was intended, and never purely in terms of its outcome,
but always in terms of how that outcome came about. Such

informal experimentation not only provides a means of checking
what the child can accomplish, but can also allow us to check
our suppositions in an explicit way.

IV Summary

The arguments presented in this paper are these. When the child
begins to produce language, he has at his disposal limited
linguistic resources. But, while the resource may be limited,
the variety of ends which it must serve is not. Besides using
words as names, the young child tries to use his early utterances for such varied purposes as drawing attention to matters
both present and past, setting up his own attention for future
action, eliciting information, making comments, indicating current functions of objects, etc.. Any attempt to capture the
ways in which the young child uses his early language requires
inferences to be made about the intentions underlying utterances.
The grounds of such inferences--what the child sees and hears,
what he says and does, the characteristics of his production,
and the background information of his previous experience--need
to be established as explicitly as possible in longitudinal
study, with inferences being checked in informal experimentation.

Appendix: Phonetic Transcription

The child's utterances are given in a broad phonetic transcription, using more or less standard IPA symbols. Apart from
consonant symbols whose phonetic value is well known, we use in
this paper:
/ʃ/ ship, /ŋ/ sing, /x/ loch (Scottish pronunciation), /ʔ/ do'y
(as when doggy is said with the g unpronounced), /r/ is not a
rolled r but the sound usually represented by /ɹ/ in IPA, /j/
yes , /w/ was; /i/ beat, /ɪ/ bit, /e/ bait, /ɛ/ bet, /ae/ bat.
/a/ part, /ɑ/ French pâte. /o/ boat, /ɔ/ pot, /u/ boot, /ʌ/ but,
/ʊ/ bird, /φ/ French feu; /:/ indicates that the preceding vowel
or consonant is prolonged, /·/ indicates a syllable boundary
where this is not otherwise clear.

We have marked stress placement and intonation by giving
an indication of the intonation on the vowel of the stressed
syllable:

a̲ mid or low level   à falling   â rising falling

ā high level   á rising   ǎ falling rising

The transcriptions of the child's utterances are not fully
satisfactory, especially as regards intonation, but a fuller
treatment was beyond the scope of our study. We give a trans-
literation or translation of the child's utterances where
necessary, but a fuller treatment of the developing syntax assumed in the translations was beyond the scope of our study.

Most examples give the adult's utterances, in ordinary
script, regardless of whether or not the child attended to them.
We have also attempted to describe as much of the relevant context as seems pertinent, including comments on the child's
affective features, information on what the child is doing when
utterances are produced (e.g., direction of gaze, what is being
held, touched, etc.), as well as any available information on
the child's previous experience.

References

Clark, E.V. (1973a) What's in a word? On the child's acqui-
    sition of semantics in his first language. In T.E. Moore
    (Ed.), Cognitive Development and the Acquisition of
    Language, 65-110. New York: Academic Press.
Clark, E.V. (1973b) Non-linguistic strategies and the acquisi-
    tion of word meanings. Cognition, 2, 161-182.
Grieve, R. (1976) Problems in the study of early semantic de-
    velopment. To appear in G. Drachman (Ed.), Salzburger
    Beiträge zur Linguistik, II (Salzberg Papers in Linguis-
    tics, II). Tübingen: Gunter Narr (in press).
Grieve, R. and Hoogenraad, R. (1976) A playbench apparatus for
    studies of cognitive and linguistic development. Journal
    of Experimental Child Psychology (in press).
Halliday, M.A.K. (1975) Learning How to Mean - Explorations in
    the Development of Language. London: Edward Arnold.
Jespersen, O. (1922) Language - Its Nature, Development and
    Origin. London: Allen and Unwin.
Keenan, E.O. and Klein, E. (1974) Coherency in children's dis-
    course. Paper presented at the Summer Meeting of the
    Linguistic Society of America, Amherst, Mass., July.
Leopold, W.F. (1948) Semantic learning in infant language.
    Word, 4, 173-180.
Luria, A.R. (1959) The Role of Speech in the Regulation of Nor-
    mal and Abnormal Behaviour. London: Pergamon Press.
Piaget, J. (1951) Play, Dreams and Imitations in Childhood.
    London: Routeledge and Keegan Paul.
Vygotsky, L.S. (1962) Thought and Language. Cambridge, Mass.:
    MIT Press.

MORE OR LESS THE SAME: A MARKEDLY DIFFERENT VIEW OF CHILDREN'S
COMPARATIVE JUDGEMENTS IN THREE CULTURES

R.J. Wales
Psychological Laboratory, University of St. Andrews

M.A.G. Garman
Department of Linguistic Science, University of Reading

P.D. Griffiths
Department of Language, University of York

This paper is in the classical mould, in that it has three
parts. There is I a Prologue, which sketches the immediately
relevant studies of children's relational terms. The second
part presents II The Studies, some new data from children
of three very different languages and cultures. These studies
on the understanding of the meanings 'more' and 'less', and
'same' and 'different' by these children, indicate serious differences with past results. Specifically we argue that young
children can distinguish between the terms, and that this has
been missed in the past (a) because of the particular tasks
used and (b) because the analyses of the children's responses
have been in adult terms rather than their own. The third
part, III Schematic Models, explores the constraints that need
to be placed on any theorizing which assumes that the observed
children's regularities do not constitute a simple (if partial
or progressive) reflection of the adults' regularities.

I Prologue

Not so long ago that it deserves to be forgotten, Dewey (1897)
castigated certain students of children's language because

The data reported here was gathered in the course of research
supported by a grant from the Social Science Research Council
(HR/1109/1). We are grateful to Dr. Beatrice Clayre who
analysed the Bornean data, to Bulan Racha who collected it, and
to R. Kotandaraman who collected the Indian data. Our work
was sponsored by the Centre for Advanced Study in Linguistics
at Annamalai University, Tamilnadu; and by the Sarawak Museum,
Kuching. Linguistic and logistic help was also given in Sarawak by members of the Borneo Evangelical Mission. We also wish
to thank Alison Macrae for her comments.

they simply applied adult categories to it, instead of being
concerned about what those categories might signify for the
child. Naturally all sage persons nod their heads in agreement
when confronted with this constraint, but few there be who follow it! On reflection this is hardly surprising since it is
exceedingly difficult to see how some degree of coercion by
adult categories can be avoided in pursuing the child's language system. This paper can be taken as a worked-out example
of an attempt in this direction, with an indication of some of
the rewards that may be waiting.

While others had been there beforehand, this paper takes
off from a series of studies on preschool children's understanding of relational terms by Donaldson & Balfour (1968),
Donaldson & Wales (1970), and Wales & Campbell (1970). These
were studies of a set of antonym pairs from the semantic field
of dimensional adjectives. Characteristically the children's
performance with one term of the pair was better (i.e. more
like the assumed adult response) than with the other term.
The term that seemed to be acquired first was always what some
linguists would call the 'unmarked' term - i.e. the one that is,
in some sense, more neutral in the set of linguistic contexts
in which it might appropriately be used. (The opposite term is
spoken of as 'marked' in its opposition to the more general
and basic 'unmarked' term.) With reference to the semantic
field of dimensional adjectives, we found acquisition differences not only between terms of a pair, but also between pairs,
approximately in accordance with the dimensionality of the
referents concerned.

A somewhat more striking finding, for which there was not
clear evidence on the dimensional terms, had to do with the
children's responses to questions about which was 'more' or
'less', and 'same' or 'different'. In the former case it seemed
as if the children, in judging between apples on apple trees,
interpreted 'more' as adults would and 'less' as if it meant
the same as 'more'. This result has been systematically replicated by Palermo (1973). With the second pair of terms it was
a more complicated state of affairs, but at least on the first
response in a matching task, questions requesting an item 'the
same in some way as this one' produced typical items that were
similar in color or shape (or both) to the standard; and the
question asking for 'different' resulted in responses similar
to those for 'same'. Campbell, Donaldson & Young (1975) report
much the same results and interpretations. Thus it looks as if
both 'more' and 'less' mean 'more', and that 'same' and 'different' both mean 'same'.

Notice two important points before we proceed further.
First the children's responses and their interpretations are
classified directly in adult terms. Second, H. Clark (1970)
and E. Clark (e.g., 1973) have supposed that the apparent

initial assimilation of the marked term to the meaning of the
unmarked can be applied as part of a general model of semantic
development, when there is no hard evidence for this anywhere
else than with the 'more/less, same/different' pairs. There
is a hint of such wicked generalization even in Wales & Campbell
(1970), but at least they characterize that part of their discussion with the qualification that it is 'highly speculative'.
However, in this regard it is important to remember that we are
all in the business of making sense of the data, and not merely
collecting it. From this point of view a simple and powerful
generalization is useful, even if at points inconsistent with
crucial aspects of the data. Presumably what we want to do is
not only criticize, but also present better principles of gen-
eralization--better, to include a truer representation of the
data, and better, to provide deeper and more significant generalizations. To start to do this then we must quickly indicate the current options.

Donaldson & Wales (1970) suggest a complexity ordering to
account for the acquisition of relational terms, and argue in
general for relatedness between cognitive and linguistic onto-
genesis. H. Clark (1970, 1973), using markedness as an organizing principle, argues that 'the perceptual features in the
child's early cognitive development (his P-space) are reflected
directly in the semantics of his language (his L-space)" (1973).
Further, "that he acquires English temporal expression in turn
by extending the spatial terms in a metaphor about time" (1973).
H. Clark's thesis is largely theoretical. E. Clark, building on
her own work on the acquisition of temporal expressions (1970),
which reflects many of the generalizations already sketched for
spatial terms, elaborates (1973) a complementary hypothesis to
H. Clark's--the semantic feature hypothesis. This hypothesis
posits that children learn to apply words to perceptual categories one semantic feature at a time. Thus, the child is
assumed to start off "identifying the meaning of a word with
only one or two features". Further, "the principal difference
between child and adult categories at this stage will be that
the child's are generally larger since he will use only one or
two features criterially, instead of a whole combination of
features". (1973) This aspect of her thesis particularly is
applied to overgeneralizations of children's early speech and
to studies of relational terms already mentioned, where the
principle of markedness is used in characterizing the acquisition of the contrasting polarity as the last feature in the
child's lexicon of those terms--and hence the apparent assimilation of marked to unmarked.

Wales & Campbell (1970) and Campbell & Wales (1970) have
taken the view that the more specialized dimensional terms are
acquired by differentiation within a quasi-superordinate field
of 'big-small'. This view is somewhat at variance with Clark's

in that it 'predicts' that errors (in terms of the adult model)
concerning unmarked terms (such as 'tall, fat, long, wide' etc.)
would gravitate to the unmarked 'big'; whereas those involving
the marked terms ('short, thin, narrow' etc.) would gravitate
to 'small'. That is, the polarity would antecede the acquisition of the specialized dimensions since what is being differ-
entiated is a semantic field. This 'prediction' is in fact
reflected in Clark's own results (1972), (but for her own view
see 1973).

One more theoretical option is canvassed by Sinclair-de-
Zwart (1967, 1970) who (roughly) takes the position that any
account of children's appropriate (i.e. logical, consistent
and adult-like) use of relational terms cannot be seriously
entertained until the child is seen to have the necessary underlying logical equipment, by virtue of its transition in
Piagetian terms to the relatively ordered existence of concrete
operational thinking.

In all these cases, though in different and, therefore,
interesting ways, there is a general acceptance of the position
that there is a systematic assymmetry in the child's acquisition and use of relational terms. In each instance this interpretation is maintained with reference to adult norms. In
the strongest (that is, the most restricted) cases, the assymmetry is seen initially as absolute, with the marked term
assimilated to the unmarked as if they were synonymous. These
views, in the most restricted cases in particular, are supposed
to refer to principles of acquisition of all spatial and temporal terms (not an insignificant part of language, even without the proposals of 'localist' theories to extend them widely
within the language system; e.g., Anderson 1971). Although
there seem to us some serious problems with them, the more
restricted views have achieved a wide currency. For both these
reasons the topic justifies a second look.

II   The Studies

The studies were motivated by two particular considerations.
First, a feature model of relational terms may be an unnatural
way of expressing such information. The features might be said
to belong more to the objects related than to the relation itself i.e. 'moreness', 'bigness', 'sameness', 'length' etc. do
not exist, at least for the child, independently of the set of
objects of which such relations may be predicated. To assert
that 'long' has more features in its representation than 'big'
is merely to say that the set of objects which may be described
as 'long' is smaller than the set described as 'big'. In other
words, the features of a relational term constitute selectional
restrictions on the items which can be related by it. It

might follow directly from this that there could be evidence of
task variables influencing the child's comprehension of the
term in question. Secondly, it also seemed to us (in the words
of a famous pejorative expression) theoretically incoherent to
suppose that the complete assimilation of one word to another
already understood in an adult fashion could ever occur, at
least without much stronger evidence. If task variables enter
in, the proposed assimilation presumably cannot be construed in
strictly linguistic terms. The interpretative problem would
then be at least as difficult to cope with as the traditional
hornets' nest of prescribing conditions on synonymy. Further,
it might be the case that there are regularities in the children's use of the terms which mark a distinction which is not
shown by classifying the responses simply in adult terms. If
this should be the case, we certainly will have been theoretically stung, and some strong medicine will be required to set
us going again! Since the matching task has so much potentially
rich data, a series of virtual replication studies was performed
on same/different to check this latter possibility. The more/
less task was left open for variation of task and questioning.
Nonetheless, both studies help to answer both points.

Background on subject groups

There were three main groups, except where otherwise stated.
Each group consisted of twenty children, ten three year olds,
and ten four year olds. The 'English' group were from Edinburgh, Scotland; the 'Indian' group were Tamil speakers from
Chidambaram, Tamilnadu--i.e. speakers of a Dravidian language
(not one of the Indo-European language family); the 'Bornean'
group, from Long Sebangang, Sarawak, spoke Lun Bawang, a tribal
Malayo-Polynesian language. The data in all cases was collected
by trained native speakers.

IIA MORE AND LESS (with a little same/different)

Preliminary pilot tests with pictures of trees with variable
amounts of fruit (which has more/less?) and with a jug and cup
of water (make it so there's more/less to drink) suggested the
same pattern of results as reported in the past. One trouble
with these sorts of task is that there is a real life association between fruit and the trees they grow on--be they apples
or mangoes--and, similarly, one between water to drink and the
cups used to drink it. This latter relation is shown well by
S. Carey's (unpublished) work asking children confronted with
a jug and a cup with water in them to 'make it TIV to drink'.
The children typically pour water into the cup. We do, not,

however, draw the inference from this that the terms 'more' and
'less' are wholly redundant in the instructions to the children,
since supplying TIV for 'more' or 'less' in the following series
of studies does not give the same results--too many blank stares
were encountered for the experimenter (in this case in English)
to continue!

To simplify the situation and not have strong natural relations between the items being compared, we devised a series
of tasks involving marbles (or large beads) on saucers. Thus,
we might present in one series five marbles in one saucer, five
in another, and five loosely grouped on the table between the
saucers. We represent this state of affairs as

$$(5)_A, \ 5, \ (5)_B$$

There were three series of tasks with various sub-sets of instructions or questions. The order of items was systematically
varied between and within series.

Note as we proceed that (a) the Tamil and Bornean children
make the requested discriminations better than the English, but
(b) in all groups, especially the English, there is a good deal
of variation in performance between one task and another, although the structural requirements may be identical in linguistic terms if all that is at stake is the interpretation of the
relational term. The order of presentation of the series here
is arbitrary. + = affirmative responses, - = negative ones.
'Add' = addition, 'Sub' = subtraction, * = touching or rearrangement. NR = no response. C = correct (adult) response,
$\overline{C}$ = incorrect. Unless otherwise stated missing responses (from
sum of 20) are 'no response'.

MORE - indicates an instruction 'make it so there are
more beads/marbles here'--pointing to sauces.

LESS - indicates same instruction substituting the term
'less'.

MORE? - indicates a question 'are there more beads?' or
(where relevant), 'which has more beads?'

LESS? - indicates one of these questions substituting
'less' for 'more'.

N.B. - the data from both age groups has been pooled
wherever this is warranted.

Series I (5), 5

Language	Tamil			English				Lun Bawang		
Group	Add	Sub	*	Add	Sub	*	NR	Add	Sub	*
MORE	16	2	2	14	2	2	2	15	5	0
LESS	3	15	2	7	7	1	5	7	13	0

	+	−	c	c̄	+	−	c	c̄	+	−	c	c̄
MORE?	19	1	17	3		0	14	3	20	0	15	5
LESS?	20	0	15	5	15	0	7	8	20	0	14	6

As already emphasized, there is some variation between groups, but even in the case of the English group the data could hardly be said to unequivocally support the assimilation of 'less' to 'more'; two children go the other way!

Series II 1. $(5)_A$, 5, $(5)_B$

	Tamil			English			Lun Bawang		
	Add	Sub	*	Add	Sub	*	Add	Sub	*
MORE	14	4	2	13	3	4	17	3	0
LESS	3	15	2	9	6	5	4	13	0

(3 responses here of Sub and Add)

	+	−	c	c̄	+	−	c	c̄	+	−	c	c̄
MORE?	17	3	15	5	17	1	14	4	20	0	17	3
LESS?	20	0	15	5	15	3	6	12	20	0	14	6

2. $(3)_A$, 5, $(7)_B$ or $(7)_A$, 5, $(3)_B$ as appropriate

	Add	Sub	*	Add	Sub	*	Add	Sub	*
MORE	16	2	2	16	2	2	18	2	0
LESS	2	16	2	6	8	6	5	15	0

	+	-	C	$\overline{C}$	+	-	C	$\overline{C}$	+	-	C	$\overline{C}$
MORE?	18	2	16	4	17	1	16	2	20	0	18	2
LESS?	20	0	16	4	14	2	5	11	20	0	17	3

Notice that in instructions to 'make it less' never as many as
half the children add beads. Yet there are approximately
twice as many incorrect answers to 'is one less - which one?'
If we note the incidence of the rearrangement responses, it
looks as if at least some of the children take a rather different view of what is being asked than perhaps we first thought.
Of course, it might be possible to construct an interpretation
which ignored the possibility of any regularities across languages, but that would be to throw out the applicability of
universals! We must not be too hasty in assuming there are no
generalizations for such data.

Series III 1. $(5)_A$ $(5)_B$

In this case SAME? = 'Is there the same number of beads?'

DIFFERENT? = 'Is there a different number of beads?'

	Tamil		English		Lun Bawang	
	+	-	+	-	+	-
SAME?	17	3	13	6	19	1
DIFFERENT?	15	5	7	12	17	3

	+	-	A	B		+	-	A	B		+	-	A	B
MORE?	20	0	8	11		10	9	4	6		14	6	6	8
LESS?	17	3	10	7		9	10	5	4		15	5	7	8

The AB here shows which choice was made if they replied 'yes'.

2. $(3)_A$ $(7)_B$

	+	-		+	-		+	-
SAME?	18	2		12	8		8	12
DIFFERENT?	16	3		14	6		17	3

	+	-	A	B		+	-	A	B		+	-	A	B
MORE?	19	1	1	18		17	3	1	16		19	1	1	16
LESS?	19	1	17	2		18	2	8	10		20	0	15	3

First note that in the first task there is a close approximation to the "'different' equals 'same'" pattern, although interestingly, not for the English group. But one might just as well argue the inverse in the second task! Furthermore, while the Tamil and Bornean groups have done particularly well up to now in distinguishing 'less' from 'more', on task 1 they are thoroughly inconsistent with an adult model; whereas, the English group does much better than before.

As part of another study using different groups of children of the same age, the following situation and questions were put to the children: there are three piles of sand (one large, one medium and one small) and three similar piles of small blocks. The child is handed a small doll and asked to 'place it next to a pile which has more' (or 'less', or 'does not have more'.) Pooling the results of the 32 English children and those of the 20 Tamil children across types of pile we get the following picture:

	English			Tamil		
	Large	Medium	Small	Large	Medium	Small
MORE	25	7	0	19	1	0
LESS	1	16	15	0	6	16
NOT MORE	0	11	21	0	10	10

No significant variations occurred when either the sand and
blocks were presented separately, or when the children were
simply asked 'which pile has more' etc. The important generalization here is that in this task, where there is some degree
of option, neither the English nor the Tamilians have any difficulty in distinguishing 'more' from its opposite--although there
is some indication from the difference in the distributions of
the two groups on the negative terms (which remains constant
across tasks) that even here subtle variations in response
strategy are being picked up. Incidentally, 20 of the English
group were checked against the earlier series and found to have
similar scores there; e.g., on Series III2 $(3)_A$ $(7)_B$

	A	B
MORE?	5	15
LESS?	12	8

Hence, the difference in performance has to do with task, not
subject, variation.

   If, as we believe, the English children can make a distinction of sorts but pursue their own strategies as a result of
uncertainty as to how to apply their model (like the other
groups, only more so (sic)), then asking the question again and
again as to 'more' and 'less' ought to result in important
changes in response. We started with the beads: $(7)_A$, $(3)_B$
situation, repeated it for $(3)_A$, $(7)_B$, and repeated these for
$(6)_A$, $(4)_B$ and $(4)_A$, $(6)_B$. Thus there were four trials of
'which has more? (or less)' questions counter-balanced. Here
we perceived one interesting age difference, with 10 three year
olds, and 10 four year olds.

		Trial 1 $(7)_A$ $(3)_B$		Trial 4 $(4)_A$, $(6)_B$	
		C	$\bar{C}$	C	$\bar{C}$
MORE?	3 years	9	1	10	0
	4 years	10	0	10	0
LESS?	3 years	5	5	1	9
	4 years	4	6	8	2

Clearly there is an interaction of representation of meaning and response strategy, as a function of repetition. Either way, the result can be interpreted as the children having a representation of the distinction. In the younger children, uncertainty results in a shift to greater (erroneous) certainty as to the form of the relation, and apparent 'assimilation' behavior. in the older children, repetition forces the distinction into the open.

In summary; as predicted, task variation makes a difference not only relatively, but also to the kind of interpretative claim that can be made of the distinction between 'more' and 'less'. There is some evidence that the children operate with the distinction; but if so, their use of it is inconsistent with respect to the adult model. However, no child in any group consistently made a response of assimilating 'less' to 'more'.

IIB SAME AND DIFFERENT

To declare A as 'the same as' B immediately suggests the question 'same what?' Allowing similarity to be predicated presupposes the identification of the relevant parameters, which in turn implies the corresponding and complementary discrimination. Difference is predicated on similar presuppositions and discriminations but on inverse judgements. Identity in all respects, including being the identical object, is something of a special case in the use of 'same', as shown by such hedges as 'self-same' or 'one and the same'. Thus, to look for the range of use of 'same', which the child might use initially to articulate his own sense, it is perhaps more useful to look at the possible senses which might be restricted in some way. Let us look at the matter this way: first, there is present sameness, attaching to a present context, bounded perhaps by constraints such as memory span; second, there is remote sameness, a meaning attaching to the establishment of a convertible memory

context; third, there is recurrent sameness, the meaning
attaching to the re-established object as recurring, or the
meaning attaching to the confirmation of remote sameness by its
repeated fulfillment. These three notions may (as suggested
by Baldwin, 1906) be the senses of 'same', or they may be clues
as to the strategies used to get to that sense. What is of particular interest to us here is that the third notion of recurrence points particularly to the importance of the conditions
determining agreement between two contexts which enable us to
start to answer the 'same what?' question.

When scanning spontaneous speech records of preschool
children it is clear that 'same' is not used frequently, and
'different' is even more infrequent. However, in many of the
contexts where similarity and difference is being referred to,
the children use 'like' (in forms such as 'is like') and
'another' respectively. That 'like', used as 'same', involves
the notion of recurrence or duplication of relevant parameters
is fairly self-evident. That 'same' and 'another' may be defined in terms of each other can be shown as follows: 'A is
the same F as B' can be restated as 'A is an F and B is an F
and A is not another F than B'; and 'A is another F than B' can
be restated as 'A is an F and B is an F and A is not the same
F as B' (see Geach, 1966). Thus, we can see why it might be
that 'another' is picked up and used as the opposition to 'same'
or 'like'. Again it carries the force of recurrence or duplication. If we look at past results it seems at first rather
strange that any difficulty with 'different' should be encountered. We have already seen that with many dimensional adjectives like 'big' and 'more', the children rarely run into
trouble. Obviously, the children can operate with at least
some differences of extent and with recurrence. That this is
the natural way for them to start is borne out by the observation on older children. When they were asked to say how two
objects 'were different', they almost invariably started by
referring to size, then color or shape, then function--in that
order. The particular advantage of using variations of color
and shape in experiments is that we can look further at the
child's preparedness to shift category in making its judgement.
Although we shall use this form of variation we must note now
that making sense of the child's responses is peculiarly tricky
since it is technically perfectly possible that one and the
same object may be appropriately judged to be both the 'same'
as and 'different' from a given standard of comparison--the
same in either color or shape (or both), and different in being
another instance of either or both of these. Only when the
child responds to a 'different' instruction with an object that
differs in both shape and color can we be sure it is following
an adult interpretation--but there is no <u>linguistic</u> requirement for it to do so. If and when we obtain the kind of result

which apparently shows assimilation of 'different/same' to 'same' we are honor bound to look for regularities which may betray strategies of interpretation which betoken some systematic understanding. As is presumably apparent by now, we were forced to try to do just that. The situation is simple. Nine objects are placed in random array in front of the child, and the experimenter establishes with the child the colors and shapes of the objects. He/she then produces and points to a primary standard which is identical in both color and shape to (at least) one of the objects on the table and starts by saying 'Give me one that's the same as / different from / not the same as this'. The experimenter proceeds by saying 'give me another one that's the same (etc.) as this' until the child either does not respond, or the set of objects on the table is exhausted. The point of introducing 'not the same' in some cases was because the term in Tamil for 'different' is, as far as we could determine, late in acquisition (and felt to be part of the non-native vocabulary by adult speakers).

In Series A the objects were: 3 green squares, 3 red circles, 3 black triangles; i.e., color and shape overlapped.

In Series B1, the three non-overlapping colors and shapes were green, red and black; books (covered paperbacks), pens, matchboxes (covered). Thus, there were three different colored pens etc. (We call these shapes 'representations'.)

Series B2 were also non-overlapping colors and shapes, green, red and black squares, circles and triangles. (For convenience we call these shapes 'formal').

Series B3 used similar shapes as B2, but the colors were yellow, red and black. The colors were uniform since in all cases the shapes were covered by parts of the same plastic coated sheets.

The order of series A, B1 and B2 and their respective questions were counterbalanced across subjects. B3 was performed on another occasion. The subject groups were the same as for the main more/less study; that is, 20 children each, split between 3 and 4 year olds, speaking Tamil, English or Lun Bawang.

Series A. In this case, where color and shape are conjoined, it is easy to see if the child follows the adult model and chooses for 'different' a set of objects that differ--since to differ in one respect is to differ in the other. Looking just at the first three responses in this sense of 'correct' we obtain:

	Tamil		English		Lun Bawang	
	C	$\bar{C}$	C	$\bar{C}$	C	$\bar{C}$
SAME	17	3	19	1	18	2
DIFFERENT	–	–	4	16	15	5
NOT SAME	13	7	14	6	–	–

It does look as if there is some evidence that the children can
handle the sense of 'different'; even if, as is especially clear
in the English speaking group, this requires the aid of explicit
negation to force recognition of what the adult may be asking.

Series B. The non-overlapping nature of the materials in these
series allows of more options in interpretation; thus, the child
is arguably in a better position to show us how it is construing
the instructions. The latter were B1 'same' or 'not same', B2
'same' or 'not same', B3 'same' or 'different'. It is again
clear that if the results are categorized in the manner of
Donaldson and Wales (1970), then a similar pattern emerges:
responses to 'same' show an adult-like match of color or shape
to the standard, at least for the first few choices; those to
'different' show a sequence which is not distinct from this.
However, with the notion of recurrence particularly in mind, we
looked for possible and plausible sources of 'error' in applying an otherwise suitable and regular interpretation. The
obvious (to us) place to look was a possible switch of attention
from the standard to some preceding response object. (i.e. one
given as a response by the child. We developed 'rules' allowing
for this possibility, and allowing us to still categorize any
response:

1. Select response object (RO) that is the same color as
    Primary Standard (PS).

2. Select RO that is the same shape as PS.

3. Select RO that is the same color as preceding RO.

4. Select RO that is the same shape as preceding RO.

3^1. Select RO that is the same color as last shape standard.

4^1. Select RO that is the same shape as last color standard.

*   No response: 'there aren't any' etc. What we call the

'stop function'.

In generating a list of possible 'appropriate' response sequences, apart from No. 1, the constraint was that each
sequence of three to be judged regular share an attribute with
either the primary standard or the first member of an immediately preceeding sequence. Clearly, where the first RO was the
same shape and color as PS, we could appeal to both Rules 1 and
2. In such cases, we looked at the subsequent ROs and invoked
Rule 1 if a color sequence emerged after the first RO, and Rule
2 if a shape sequence followed. If a response was not classi-
fiable in these terms, it was judged random. Obviously, an
enormous number of random (in this sense) response sequences
is possible.

B1 <u>SAME</u> Appropriate responses are:

Type

I   1/2 * (absolute similarity requirements; then refusal)

II   1 3 3 * (Color similarity; then refusal)

III   2 4 4 * (Shape similarity; then refusal)

IV   1 3 3 2 3 3 2 3 3

V   2 4 4 1 4 4 1 4 4

VI   1 3 3 4 3 3 4 3 3

VII   2 4 4 3 4 4 3 4 4

VIII   1 3 3 4'3 3 4'3 3

IX   2 4 4 3'4 4 3'4 4

X   1 3 3 4'4 * ---- /2 4 4 3'3 * --

Looking just at the first six choices we have:

B1 SAME	Tamil		English		Lun Bawang	
	C	$\overline{C}$	C	$\overline{C}$	C	$\overline{C}$
	17	3	17	3	15	5

However, there are great differences in response type: (type
in brackets)

Tamil   4(VII), 13(IX)

English   8(I), 2(II), 4(III), 1(VII), 2(IX)

Lun Bawang   1(III), 2(VI), 3(VII), 3(VIII), 6(IX)

B1 NOT SAME

Appropriate response sequences are types I-X as for SAME instructions, plus any sequence involving starting with D--a choice
that differs in both color and shape from Primary Standard.

Tamil		English		Lun Bawang	
C	C̄	C	C̄	C	C̄
14	6	12	8	12	8

Types

Tamil   4(VII), 8(IX), 2(D)

English   1(I), 2(II), 4(III), 1(VII), 4(IX)

Lun Bawang   2(V), 3(VII), 2(IV), 5(D)

If we expand the set of appropriate response sequences to include anything that does not involve a sequence break with
reference to either Primary Standard or preceeding response
object(s), we get:

Tamil		English		Lun Bawang	
C	C̄	C	C̄	C	C̄
15	5	19	1	18	2

The most striking datum of all however, is that in comparing the
response sequences of each child for 'same' and for 'not same',
only one Tamil and one English (no Lun Bawang) child used the
identical sequence for both. Virtually all the children, therefore, are marking, in their own way, a distinction which would
be missed if their responses were categorized merely according

to 'normal' adult criteria. Naively, it might be argued that it would be remarkable if the children did produce 'identical' response sequences to both instructions. But then, naively, we would also not expect assimilation behavior! Of course, we could forget about assimilation and markedness and wonder further why the children produce non-adult-like, but regular sequences when the options available to them are very much wider. The crucial point here is that each subject's variation is systematic.

<u>B2</u> This is formally analogous to B1 except that geometrical shapes are used. First we take the appropriate responses as for B1 and look just at the first six responses:

<u>B2   SAME</u>

	Tamil		English		Lun Bawang	
	C	$\bar{C}$	C	$\bar{C}$	C	$\bar{C}$
	4	16	11	9	13	7

However, if we extend the list of appropriate sequences to include: (6) 1 3 3 4 3 4' ....., (6") 1 3 4 3 3 4 ..... which involve continuous linking of response objects (i.e., we now exclude as inappropriate only those sequences which involve a break in the similarity with reference to both Primary Standard and preceeding object at once), then we get:

	Tamil		English		Lun Bawang	
	C	$\bar{C}$	C	$\bar{C}$	C	$\bar{C}$
	14	6	14	6	16	4

<u>B2   NOT SAME</u>   Appropriate response sequences as for B1

	Tamil		English		Lun Bawang	
	C	$\bar{C}$	C	$\bar{C}$	C	$\bar{C}$
	6	14	7	13	9	11

D responses: Tamil (2) English (4) Lun Bawang (6). (It is worth noting here that these figures do not include those that produced initial D responses but continued with irregular sequences).

By the expanded set of appropriate response sequences we have:

Tamil		English		Lun Bawang	
C	$\bar{C}$	C	$\bar{C}$	C	$\bar{C}$
13	7	12	8	15	5

This time there is no child in any group which produces in its responses two identical sequences.

<u>B3</u> The same kind of material as for B2 but different instructions.

SAME

	Tamil		English		Lun Bawang	
	C	$\bar{C}$	C	$\bar{C}$	C	$\bar{C}$
	8	12	12	8	12	8
expanded set	13	7	15	5	17	3

DIFFERENT

	Tamil		English		Lun Bawang	
	C	$\bar{C}$	C	$\bar{C}$	C	$\bar{C}$
	5	15	10	10	9	11
expanded set	12	8	14	6	15	5

D responses at beginning of regular sequences were:
Tamil (2) English (3) Lun Bawang (7). Again note here that there were (especially in the Lun Bawang case) many more single D responses--in Lun Bawang 14!

The notion of a 'regular sequence' does not whitewash the child's performance! That is, the notion of continuous linking of ROs (the expanded set of rules) in no sense constitutes an opening of the floodgates in accepting response sequences as 'appropriate'; even in these terms, 'inappropriate' ones are numerous.

Again there were no children that produced identical sequences to both sets of instructions.

Let us summarize the overall results here:
(1) There is now clear evidence that children, <u>in their own terms</u>, express a distinction between 'same' and either 'different' or 'not same'.

(2)   The difference in lexicalization of the opposition to
'same' seems to make a striking difference in Series A, but not
Series B, suggesting room for further study.
(3)   In Series B the children's performance on 'same' with
'representational' shapes (Bl) seems better, i.e. more internally consistent, than with 'formal' shapes (B2 and B3).
(4)   In Series Bl--i.e., 'representational' shapes--the children in all groups concentrate on shape in their sequences--
varying between 75 and 83 per cent of their responses. This
is true for both 'same' and 'not same'. In Series B2 and B3,
where the shapes may be said to be less functionally meaningful
for the children, they concentrate their attention on color
matches--varying between 64 and 77 per cent.
(5)   There are striking cultural variations in the sequencing
strategies used. The most immediately obvious is that the
English children quite often stop to decline a response well
before the set of objects is exhausted, whereas the Tamil group
never do. The Lun Bawang group is somewhere in between. Nevertheless, with a rich enough data source, it is possible to show
in each group how the sequencing operations used by the child
reveals the regular use of the lexical distinctions studied.
Should anyone be stimulated by the earlier discussion to wonder
how the distinction between 'like' and 'another' might be responded to, the answer is that, in an equivalent English group,
the same pattern of results as those reported here was obtained;
the only interesting difference being that the 'stop function'
was applied rather less frequently.

III   Schematic Models

It is now clear that the 'markedness' model will not do as a
model of acquisition. It is hardly surprising that this should
be the case since if it had worked, it would have been the first
time a specifically linguistic model had been directly and
reliably translatable into a psychological model. The more
searching question is how to proceed from here. Notice that,
to arrive 'here', a radical departure from the convention relating children's behavior to adult categories has been made.
An attempt has been made to pursue the children's regularities
in their own terms. The possibility of doing this is both exciting and disturbing: it is exciting that some plausible
sense can be made of children's developing regularities; disturbing, since if no constraints are placed on models pursuing
this goal, only the universe of undecidable and disconnected
hypotheses lies ahead. What then might be the general conditions on this kind of approach to 'grammars of action'? Part
of the problem lies in the kind of organism the child is at a
given time. The other part has to do with specifying conditions

on the segmentation of the context of language use. The former
invites a descent into the abyss of mechanistic reductionism;
the latter, a flight to the infinite possibilities of cloud-
cuckoo land. To keep our model feet on the ground we suggest
that both aspects need to be both accepted and constrained.
The statement of the conditions should allow of three inter-
dependent levels of description.
(1) A physiological description from which the anchor points of
the possible set of behaviors may be derived.
(2) A psychological mechanism for articulating the behavioral
repertoire and taking it through time.
(3) A social description from which idiosyncratic and ecological
variations may be derived.
     Constraint (1) is needed (a) to restrict hypothesis testing,
and (b) to constrain the possible set of segmentations. (2) is
needed to specify the kind of mechanism which would enable the
organism to learn within the constraints imposed by (1) and at
least in this way take the organism through time. Such a
mechanism would direct segmentation e.g. in subclasses, and
thereby set up a contextual 'frame of reference' within which
the organism could perform. The structural conditions of such
performance would then effectively specify its 'grammar of
action'.
     (3) presupposes that there are variations of performance
conditioned by social and environmental constraints which build
on, rather than against, the regularities specified by (1) and
(2). It follows that, if the organism operates in a way that
is at variance with the principles derived from (1) and (2), the
behavior derived in (3) will be unlearned.
     Now to illustrate these generalities in operation; first,
take color naming. It has been, until recently, a structural-
ist commonplace that color names are arbitrarily assigned to
variations in brightness, wavelength and saturation. However,
in 1969 Berlin & Kay indicated that with 'basic color terms'
(roughly; single morphemes, solely used for color naming) there
was great commonality as regards the identification of 'best
instances'. They also proposed a partial ordering in the cultural development of the assignment of spectral colors; and
further hypothesized that that partial order might predict
ontogenetic development. Some evidence (with problems) for the
latter proposal has been forthcoming; for example, Heider (1971)
and Rosch (1973). For the moment we ignore problems raised as
to the veracity of this account. Looking to implement the
structure of our model, we have (1) two physiological anchor
points are necessary as a minimum, namely brightness discrimination and neural specialization for red. (The reader will
recognize that for brevity and clarity some precision is being
lost!) The work of de Valois and Jacobs (1968) might be said
to allow us to go thus far but raises the problem of why red

before green. For (2) we need a learning strategy which operates by maximizing the relevant contrast (this looks super-
ficially like markedness). Applying this to brightness will
predict 'black' and 'white'. Applying it to 'red' leads to
'green', then back to 'yellow', then to 'blue'. If 'brown' is
now to be added, brightness must be manipulated. Since red is
fixed, yellow would shift up to allow brown in. We have some
developmental evidence for this state of affairs in all three
of our language groups. If brightness interacts with hue earlier in the developmental sequence, this might help to indicate
why some results, e.g., Rosch (1971) suggest an earlier acquisition of yellow.) Then in contrast to brown we have purple
at, approximately, that level of brightness. Note that this
disallows the Berlin & Kay subsequence of red to yellow to
green, etc.; however, all their data (bar one unpublished
study) for this ordering is derived from a particular subset of
Malayo-Polynesian languages, in which the word for yellow derives from that for tumeric (i.e., it is not a basic color
term) - see Bartlett (1929).

The relevance of (3) is seen in a number of factors: (a)
the variance in <u>range</u> of application of color terms both within
and between language groups; (b) the influence of secondary
color terms; for example, Lun Bawang adults, who only have one
basic term for green/blue, 'mebata', randomly identified the
focal instances of this color term in the blue and green ranges
(contrary to Berlin & Kay's prediction)--which are overtly dis-
tinguishable in Lun Bawang on the model of 'sky blue' and 'grass
green' ('sky-mebata' and 'grass-mebata'); (c) social/ritual
overlays in usage as described for example by Conklin (1955).
None of these need by contrary to the principles of development
of (1) and (2)--although they might be found to mislead the
child for a time, and predict 'erratic' responses.

Coming now to consider relational terms and comparative
judgements, the crucial problem appears to be how to relate
visuo-spatial representations to linguistic representations.
This is not only a problem of deriving the appropriate mapping
from one to the other <u>and</u> vice versa. It is also a problem to
construct the appropriate contexts for each, in order for the
mapping to operate appropriately. This problem has been considered in its biological and cultural perspective in Marshall
& Wales (1974). For the present, therefore, we merely point out
that the problem of mapping representations of this sort seems
to have biological analogue in the differences in specialization
of function between the two cerebral hemispheres. Typically
these are stated in terms like left hemisphere--'language';
right hemisphere--'visuo-spatial'. That these ascriptions do
not fit all the facts, yet carry more than a half-truth, is wit-
nessed to by more than a century of debate. Suppose we try to
simplify the matter in terms of our model framework: (1) the

developing linguistic representation is largely stored in a
memory mechanism similar to a tape recorder--Fong (1969) argues
for the possibility of construing RNA coding as a ferro-electric
recording mechanism. The visuo-spatial representation is stored,
by analogy, in a video-like mechanism. Another, and perhaps
more plausible speculation on these lines, would be to see the
left hemisphere as a filing system, operating with primitive
categories and rules, relating them on 'brute' input. The right
hemisphere would then be taken as our tape for handling items
already analyzed. One useful result of trying to force the discussion into considering alternative underlying mechanisms in
this way is that different empirical consequences follow from
one view, as opposed to the other. Whatever the appropriate
view is, we may further suggest that these stores may come to be
functionally separated (to avoid interference?) during the
course of development and the laying down of different representations. On the basis of such differences in biological store,
we then again posit (2), a contrastive learning model. However,
in this case particularly there is the possibility, from con-
textural variation, of attention being difficult to relate
accurately and simultaneously to two different representations.
This is not a handicap, however, if (1) provides different constraining gradients; such as, intensity, etc. Then a model such
as that proposed by Bateson for the simultaneous development of
preferences for familiarity and novelty might be operative.
Given a gradient of intensity or extent, we then ought to be
able to stipulate the structural conditions on what Bateson
(1973) calls a 'slightly novel stimulus', which comes to be preferred, along with the familiar.

     Hence we come (by a jump or three) to the acquisition of
'specialized adjectives', say, from the familiar 'big-small'
superordinate (i.e. undifferentiated) category. The applicability of this kind of model is particularly useful since one
fact it predicts is that on the acquisition of the 'slightly
novel' stimulus, it becomes preferred to the learned 'preferred'
one. This is directly in accord with the phenomenon of children
acquiring language in a 'correct' to 'incorrect' to 'correct'
sequence, with 'novel' terms being used in the intermediate
slot (see Wales & Campbell, 1970, for discussion). Clearly,
for this model to be in business, the minimal set of perceptual constraints provided by the organism needs to be specified.
Some of these may be inferred from the way in which categories
are segmented into subclasses (as suggested by Garner (1966)).
The degree to which these are invariant will point to the necessary biological invariants. The degree to which the structural redundancies are manipulable will point to the structural
constraints on the learning model. For example, the asymmetries
characteristically found in development may all be simply predictable from differences in the salience of different

discriminable gradients. It is striking that nearly all the
asymmetries found thus far involve spatio-temporal oppositions;
e.g., directional opposites are also asymmetric (Wales, 1974),
although this cannot be attributed simply to differences in the
specification of source and goal (Garman, Griffiths & Wales,
1970). When the opposition does not involve this, e.g., in
converse terms like 'buy and sell' and 'brother and sister',
the developmental asymmetry disappears (MacCrae, 1976). The
only clear case where an asymmetry might be present which is
not obviously spatio-temporal is in that of evaluative terms
like 'good' and 'bad'. This could be a special case for (3),
but it is much more probable that it is based on the same principle of (1) and (2) above, deriving from the relation of
mother and child sharing contrastively certain action patterns.
This seems necessary anyway, as the basis for early acquisition
of utterances.

The interaction of (1) and (2) with (3) would now be seen
in the social contexts of cognitive and linguistic performance
which condition related behavioral variants--e.g., the 'like'
and 'another' instances given earlier. That this is a necessary
level of description is based on the assumption that, from the
start, the language acquisition problem (and the child's attempts to solve it) are all cast in a communicative context.
While we have argued for the necessity of trying to account for
the child's language in its own terms, we do not wish to say
that that language is wholly private. What we are proposing at
this level is the kind of account which sees language acquisition as a child/adult learning system, the two being coupled and
constraining each other. This communicative constraint is going
to apply to both why and how we look at contexts (Campbell &
Wales, 1970); to what the prevocal child/mother do to each other
(Bruner, 1975; Huttenlocher, 1974; and Trevarthan, Hubley and
Sheeran, 1975); to what the mother says to the child (Snow,
1972); and to understanding what the child can usefully say
for itself (Grieve & Hoogenraad, this volume).

The main point here is that if we collate what is known of
perceptual and linguistic development, much of it should be ex-
pressable in this framework. If this is so, it seems likely
that the main mechanisms for acquisition are found to be remarkably simple and general. In borrowing necessary constraints
from different levels, each level is prevented from following
the unreal path of reductionism without recoverability, or in-
finitely many unspecified options. What is more, the child may
be able to learn a language.

References

Anderson, J. (1971) The Grammar of Case: Towards a Localistic
    theory. London: Cambridge Univ. Press.
Baldwin, J.M. (1908) Thought and Things: or Genetic Logic.
    New York: Sonnerschein.
Bartlett, H.H. (1929) Colour nomenclature in Batak and Malay.
    Papers of Michigan Academy of Sciences, Arts and Letters
    10:1-52.
Bateson, P.P.G. (1973) Preferences for familiarity and novelty:
    a model for the simultaneous development of both.
    J. Theor. Biol. 41, 249-259.
Berlin, B. and Kay, P. (1969) Basic Color Terms: Their Univer-
    sality and Evolution. Berkeley: Univ. of Calif. Press.
Bruner, J.S. (1975) From communication to language – a
    psychological perspective. Cognition, 3, 255-287.
Campbell, R.N., Donaldson, M.C. and Young, B. (in press)
    British J. Psych.
Campbell, R.N. & Wales, R.J. (1970) The study of language ac-
    quisition. In J. Lyons (Ed) New Horizons in Linguistics.
    Penguin: Harmondsworth.
Clark, E.V. (1970) How children describe events in time. In
    G. Flores d'Arcais and Levelt (Eds) Advances in Psycho-
    linguistics. North-Holland: Amsterdam.
Clark, E.V. (1972) On the acquisition of antonyms in two
    semantic fields. J. of Verbal Learning and Verbal Behavi-
    or, 11, 750-758.
Clark, E.V. (1973) What's in a word? On the child's acquisi-
    tion of semantics in his first language. In T. Moore (Ed).
Clark, H.H. (1970) The primitive nature of children's rela-
    tional concepts. In J.R. Hayes (Ed).
Clark, H.H. (1973) Space, time, semantics, and the child.
    In T. Moore (Ed).
Conklin (1955) Hanunoo colour categories. Southwestern J. of
    Anthropology 11, 339-344.
de Valois, R. and Jacobs, G. (1968) Primate color vision.
    Science 533-540.
Dewey, J. (1894) The psychology of infant language. Psych.
    Rev., 1, 63-66.
Donaldson, M.C. and Balfour, G. (1968) Less in more: A study
    of language comprehension in children. Brit. J. Psych.
    59, 461-472.
Donaldson, M.C. and Wales, R.J. (1970) On the acquisition of
    some relational terms. In J.R. Hayes (Ed).
Fong, P. (1969) Brain memory and ferroelectric recording
    mechanism of R.N.A. Physiol. Chem. and Physics 1, 24-41.
Garman, M.A., Griffiths, P.D., and Wales, R.J. (1970) Murut
    (Lun Bawang) preposition and noun-particles in children's
    speech. Sarawak Museum J. 20, 1-24.

Garner, W.R. (1966) To perceive is to know. Amer. Psychologist, 21, 11-19.

Geach, P. (1966) Reference and Generality. Ithaca, New York: Cornell University Press.

Hayes, J.R. (Ed.) (1970) Cognition and the Development of Language. New York: Wiley.

Heider, E. (1971) "Focal" color areas and the development of color names. Developmental Psychology, 4, 447-455.

Huttenlocker, J. (1974) The origins of language comprehension. In R. Solso (Ed.) Theories in Cognitive Psychology. New York: Houghton-Mifflin.

Macrae, A. (1976) On the acquisition of converse terms. Thesis submitted for the degree Ph.D., University of Edinburgh.

Marshall, J.C. and Wales, R.J. (1974) Pragmatics as biology or culture. In C. Cherry (Ed.) Pragmatic Aspects of Human Communication. Dordrecht-Holland: Reidel.

Moore, T. (Ed.) (1973) Cognitive Development and the Acquisition of Language. New York: Academic Press.

Palermo, D. (1973) More about less: a study of language comprehension. Journal of Verbal Learning and Verbal Behavior, 12, 211-221.

Rosch, E. (1973) On the internal structure of perceptual and semantic categories. In T. Moore (Ed.).

Sinclair-de-Zwart, H. (1967) Acquisition du Langage et Développement de la Pensée, Sous-systemes Linguistiques et Opérations Concrètes. Paris: Dunod.

Snow, C. (1972) Mother's speech to children learning language. Child Development, 43, 549-565.

Trevarthan, C., Hubley, P., and Sheeran, L. (1975) Les activites innes de nourrison. La Récherche, 6, 447-458.

Wales, R.J. (1974) The child's sentences make sense of the world. In F. Bresson (Ed.) Problèmes Actuels en Psycholinguistique, Colloques Internationaux. Paris: C.N.R.S.

Wales, R.J. and Campbell, R.N. (1970) On the development of comparison and the comparison of development. In G. Flores d'Arcais and W. Levelt (Eds.) Advances in Psycholinguistics. Amsterdam: North-Holland.

ADAPTING THE PROPERTY DETECTORS FOR SPEECH PERCEPTION

Anthony E. Ades

University of Sussex
Centre for Research on Perception and Cognition
Laboratory of Experimental Psychology

INTRODUCTION

Adaptation experiments are probably the most rapidly expanding part of current speech perception research. They began with a paper by Eimas and Corbit (1973); and since the writing of Cooper's (1975a) review, the number of research reports has increased greatly. As a research method, adaptation is familiar to many other branches of perceptual psychology. An example from vision is the motion after-effect, in which prolonged viewing of a river flowing from left to right causes the stationary bank to appear to move from right to left. The importance of the method is that it provides a basis for the discussion of property detectors. For instance, there could be a pair of detectors, each responding to motion across the retina in one direction. Exposure to motion will activate the appropriate detector, and over-exposure will selectively fatigue it. Assuming that the final percept is a function of the output of both detectors, the result of fatiguing one is that stationary objects appear to move in the opposite direction.
Frequently cited as examples of property detectors are single cells in the visual systems of animals that respond to lines, edges, or corners at given orientations moving in given directions (e.g., Hubel and Wiesel, 1965) and cells in the cat auditory cortex responding to frequency change (Whitfield and Evans, 1965).
Several authors (Abbs and Sussman, 1971; Stevens, 1973) have suggested that property detectors could play an important role in speech perception, mediating at some point in the process that transforms the acoustic waveform into a string of phonemes, syllables, or words. The general problem of speech perception is that there appears to be no simple relationship between the acoustic and phonetic levels; it is therefore difficult to know a priori what types of property might be usefully detected, and when in the process they are detected.
Much of the controversy surrounding speech perception is concerned with the acoustic/phonetic relationship, the constancy, or lack of it, in the acoustic cues to each phoneme. Some have taken the position that there is considerable invariance in the acoustic cues to each phoneme; that is, a given phoneme has the same acoustic properties in every context in which it appears

(Cole and Scott, 1974a). If this view is correct,[1] we might
expect adaptation to reveal detectors for these fixed acoustic
cues. The outputs of such detectors could be mapped very directly into a phonetic description of the utterance.

The phoneme, linguistically, can be decomposed into a small
set of binary distinctive features (Jakobsen, Fant and Halle,
1952; Chomsky and Halle, 1968); these too, must be considered
properties, albeit linguistic ones, for which there might be
detectors. Earlier adaptation experiments (Eimas and Corbit,
1973; Eimas, Cooper and Corbit, 1973; Cooper, 1974a) were, in
fact, interpreted as evidence for linguistic feature detectors.
The force of this view is largely in the term "linguistic".
Eimas and his colleagues were perhaps influenced by the view
opposite to that of Cole and Scott (1974a), that there are in
general no fixed acoustic properties for phonemes, nor therefore,
for distinctive features (Liberman, Cooper, Shankweiler and
Studdert-Kennedy, 1967). This could be interpreted as meaning
that only the linguistic properties of the signal are sufficiently stable to be likely candidates for property detectors.

These two views of speech do not necessarily generate different hypotheses about detectors, because detectors for linguistic features would be substantially the same as detectors for
any acoustically invariant cues that could be directly mapped
into them. The difference, and it is not a difference to which
we expect adaptation experiments to be sensitive, is that in
one case the detectors could operate immediately, in the putatively invariant cues in the signal, while in the other case
their operation must follow considerable recoding of the signal,
operating closer to the phonetic finished product.

A third, quite different type of detector would be one that
picked up specific acoustic cues, but whose output could not be
mapped directly into linguistic description. This proposal,
although distinct from the linguistic feature detectors of Eimas
and Corbit (1973), again reflects the lack of acoustically invariant cues to phonemes or linguistic features. Of particular
interest here is Fant's (1962, 1968) description of the acoustic
features of speech. Put simply, speech is seen as consisting of
a number of temporal segments, not necessarily synchronous with
the sequence of phonemes. Each segment can contain a number of
acoustic cues relating to the type of sound (e.g. voiced excitation of the larynx, noise, silence), to the manner of its
production (e.g. vowel-like, nasal, fricative, transitional) and
to the place of articulation (e.g. labial, dental, velar). Typical of the acoustic cues within segments would be the frequencies of individual formants and simple functions of several

---

[1] Some of Cole and Scott's evidence for invariant acoustic cues
to phonemes (Cole and Scott, 1974b) has recently been challenged
by Darwin (1976).

formants, which provide the basic information about place of articulation. There might, therefore, be detectors for cues at this level: but the mapping from their outputs into a phonetic representation must be quite complex (Fant, 1970).

A scheme that is perhaps in a similar spirit can be found in a theoretical paper by Abbs and Sussman (1971), where detectors for acoustic speech events were first explicitly proposed. These authors mention, for example, detectors for frequency-change from one specific frequency to another in a given time. Again, the outputs of such detectors will be far from a phonetic description. Furthermore, detectors either for the components of Fant's segments or of the type proposed by Abbs and Sussman are qualitatively different from the linguistic feature detectors of Eimas and Corbit (1973) in that they would not necessarily give binary outputs. Returning to visual perception for analogies, such detectors would be closer to the channels tuned to specific ranges of spatial frequency, which are, incidentally, also capable of adaptation (Blakemore and Campbell, 1969), than to the pair of detectors responding to left-to-right and right-to-left movement suggested for the motion after-effect (Barlow, Hill and Levick, 1964).

Although phonemes cannot be defined in terms of single fixed acoustic cues like those for which Abbs and Sussman propose detectors, they can in some cases be defined as fixed combinations of several cues. In response to this, Stevens (1973) has put forward more sophisticated detectors, which are sensitive to global properties of the spectrum, to combinations of cues rather than to individual components. Designed to reflect the presence of invariant, though complex, acoustic cues to phonemes, detectors of this sort could, for the most part, be mapped directly into a linguistic distinctive feature table.

Evidently, many types of detector can be imagined, and most investigators have in fact felt that more than one level of detector might be amenable to the adaptation technique (Cooper, 1975; Tartter and Eimas, 1975; Bailey, 1975a; Darwin, 1976). In the pursuit of parsimony, we shall attempt, rather strenuously, to argue for a single type of detector. Detectors relating to the linguistic features on which adaptation experiments have been performed will be discussed in turn, and the degree and significance of the variability of the acoustic substrate of the feature, in natural and synthetic speech, will be assessed in each case. For, as we have seen, beliefs about the invariance problem tend to condition very different a priori conceptions of possible detectors. The basic issue will be whether the detectors are sensitive to individual acoustic cues or to combinations of them. This is rather different from most discussions of adaptation (cf. Cooper, 1975a; Studdert-Kennedy, 1975), in which auditory and phonetic detectors are contrasted. A treatment of the relationship between feature extraction and segmentation is then given, the link between detectors and speech production is reviewed and finally we try to account for a puzzling class of recent experiments, which show that the operation of the detectors depends on seemingly irrelevant variables. To begin with, however, we develop a basic model of the voicing distinction, which will serve as a basis for discussion of adaptation experiments and will place these experiments in the broader field of speech perception.

VOICING

The six English stop consonants can be classified by voice (voiced, b,d,g; voiceless, p,t,k) and by place of articulation (labial, b,p; dental, d,t; velar, g,k).

In initial position, the acoustic difference between a voiced and voiceless stop lies in the onset time of voicing, the periodic waveform caused by vibration of the larynx, relative to the burst of noise caused by the rapid flow of air at the place

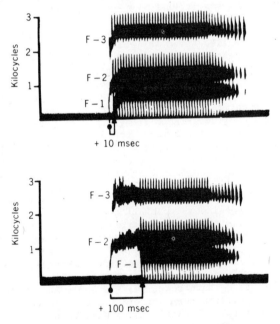

Fig. 1. Spectrograms of synthetic speech: [ba] (above) and [pa], showing the time between the burst and the onset of voicing or Voice Onset Time in each. (From Eimas and Corbit, 1973)

of articulation when the vocal tract is opened. Spectrograms of synthetic syllables heard as [ba] and [pa] are shown in Fig. 1. In the [ba] voicing begins only 10 msec after the burst, while in the voiceless stop [pa], voicing lags by 100 msec. The period between the burst and the onset of voicing is occupied by aspiration, a non-periodic turbulent flow of air through the open glottis, which excites mainly those formants higher than the first. These values of voice onset time (VOT) are fairly typical of the natural speech of languages where this distinction is made (Lisker and Abramson, 1964), and they occur in dental and velar, as well as, labial stops.

With the help of a computer it is possible to synthesize a series of stimuli ranging from voiced to voiceless in equal steps of VOT. In practically all the experiments discussed here, stimuli from such series are presented in a random order to subjects whose task it is to identify them as "B" or "P", "D" or "T", depending on the series; i.e., as voiced or voiceless. Stimuli with a short VOT are classified as voiced; those with long VOT, as voiceless. The Phoneme Boundary is defined as the point on the stimulus continuum that would be labelled "B" and "P" to an equal degree. The voiced/voiceless boundary generally lies at VOT values between 20 and 40 msec..

In an experiment which established adaptation as a research method in speech perception, Eimas and Corbit (1973) selectively fatigued either the voiced or voiceless end of a [ba-pa] continuum. The procedure was as follows. First, the baseline phoneme boundary was measured in the manner described above. Then one of the stimuli from the extreme end of the series, for example the extreme [ba], was repeated 75 times in the course of one minute, after which a single stimulus from the test series was presented for identification. The cycle of adaptation and testing was repeated until each test stimulus had been identified ten times. The result of this adaptation is to shift the identification curve toward the voiced end of the continuum (see Fig. 2); sounds that were formerly reported as [ba] are now heard as [pa]. Of particular importance is the finding that repetition of [da] has the same effect as [ba]; namely, that it also shifts the phoneme boundary toward "voiced". Repetition of the extreme voiceless stops [pa] and [ta] shifted the boundary in the opposite direction, toward "voiceless". Analogous effects were observed on another voiced-voiceless series ranging from [da] to [ta].

Because both voiced stops, [ba] and [da], had the same adapting effect irrespective of the place of articulation of the test series, and both voiceless stops [pa] and [ta], had the opposite effect, Eimas and Corbit concluded that they had fatigued property detectors for the linguistic features voiced and voiceless, respectively. Repetition of a voiced sound, they proposed, weakened the output of the detector for voiced

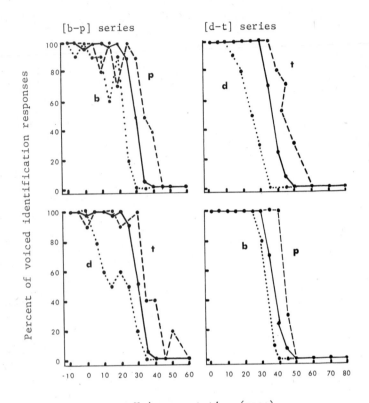

Fig. 2. Identification functions on voiced/voiceless series,
[ba-pa] and [da-ta], before (solid lines) and after adaptation
with [ba], [pa], [da], and [ta]. (From Eimas and Corbit, 1973).

relative to the detector for voiceless. Each detector responds
to a range of stimuli, and these ranges overlap somewhat. A
boundary stimulus will stimulate both detectors equally; but
after the voiced detector is fatigued, the same stimulus will
activate the voiceless detector relatively more strongly. The
equilibrium point, the phoneme boundary, is therefore shifted
toward the voiced range.
    [b] and [d] have several attributes in common besides the
linguistic feature voiced. Detectors for any of these attributes would be able to explain why they have the same adapting effect. The question that is therefore addressed in many
of the subsequent adaptation studies is: "exactly what is being
adapted?". To provide a framework in which to discuss the

alternative views of adaptation and to place them in a larger
context, I shall attempt to motivate, on independent grounds,
a class of models of the voice distinction proposed by Summerfield (1974).

1. A General Framework for Voicing

Voiced-voiceless continua have several interesting perceptual properties, one of which is that they are perceived cate-
gorically. Listening to the stimuli in order, they do not
appear to become gradually more voiceless as VOT is increased;
instead, there is an abrupt perceptual break between voiced and
voiceless categories. In "same-different" and in other discrimination tasks with these stimuli, subjects can distinguish
between two test items only if they are taken from different
sides of the phoneme boundary (Liberman, Harris, Kinney and
Lane, 1961; Strange and Halwes, 1971). In its ideal form, categorical perception is characterized by poor discrimination of
stimuli that are within the same phonetic category and by a discrimination of stimuli that are within the same phonetic category and by a discrimination peak at the phoneme boundary.
Categorical perception has been linked with a special mode of
perception that is unique to speech (Studdert-Kennedy, Liberman,
Harris and Cooper, 1970); however, in the case of voicing, it
now seems likely that the discrimination peak is generated by
perceptual mechanisms sensitive to certain acoustic properties
of the stimulus series, not to a process of categorization into
phonemes.

Inspection of the spectrograms in Fig. 1 reveals two cues
which could be carrying the voicing distinction and which could
be responsible for its perceptual properties. Firstly, there
is the variable time separation between the burst at the beginning of the sound and the voicing. A continuum analogous to
voicing may thus be constructed with a hiss of variable duration,
which represents the aspiration between burst and voicing, followed by a buzz representing voicing. Stimuli from such a continuum are not identifiable as speech; yet they are maximally
discriminable when the hiss lasts for about 20 msec (Miller,
Pastore, Weir, Kelly, and Dooling, 1974), a value that agrees
well with the position of the phoneme boundary. We can regard
the perception of the separation cue as a judgement of temporal
order of hiss and buzz. According to Hirsch (1959) and Stevens
and Klatt (1974), sounds must be more than about 20 msec apart
before judgement of relative order can be made. A subject could
therefore, in principle, discriminate a [pa] with a VOT of 50
msec from another with VOT 65 msec by using the output of a
mechanism that measures relative temporal order. On the other
hand, a [ba] with VOT 0 msec and a [ba] with VOT 15 msec could
not be distinguished in this way, as in both sounds the relative

onset time of the burst and voicing is below the simultaneity
threshold (Stevens and Klatt, 1974). The behavior of the separation cue in non-speech contexts, then, not only predicts the
location of discrimination peaks in synthetic speech continua,
but also suggests an asymmetry between voiceless stops in
consonant-vowel (CV) syllables, for which temporal order of
burst and voicing can be judged, and voiced stops for which it
cannot.

The second cue (See Fig. 1) is the presence or absence of
voiced transitions in the First Formant (F1). In a fully voiced
stop (i.e. VOT 0 msec) the F1 transition may last about 45 msec,
depending on the place of articulation. But as VOT is increased
and the onset of voicing cut back, the duration of voiced F1
transitions is correspondingly shortened; until at long VOT's,
it is entirely absent. Like the separation cue, the F1 transition may also be able to generate discrimination peaks. Nebelek
and Hirsh (1969) found that discrimination of the duration of a
frequency glide preceding a steady state sine wave was best at
durations in the range 20-30 msec. Where the total extent of
the transition period is 45 msec, this corresponds to a VOT
value of 15-25 msec, again in reasonable agreement with the perceptual boundary in speech in spite of the non-phonetic nature
of the stimuli. In addition, note the potential for an asymmetrical mechanism, this time in the other direction: a mechanism which measures the duration of transitions would be quite
valuable in the voiced range, but when voicing onset is cut back
as far as 45 msec or longer, there is no frequency transition
left to detect.

Experiments where both the separation cue and the F1 transition cue are varied independently demonstrate that both cues
are, in fact, used (Stevens and Klatt, 1974; Summerfield and
Haggard, 1974; Summerfield, 1974; Lisker, 1975). Viewing the
mechanism for the voicing distinction as composed of these two
sub-parts immediately explains a fact that would otherwise be
puzzling. The VOT value of the phoneme boundary varies as a
function of place of articulation, being shortest in labial
series and longest in velar series (Lisker and Abramson, 1970;
Summerfield, 1975a). For reasons related to the inertial properties of the vocal tract, the overall duration of the transitions also increases from labial to dental to velar. In both
the above studies, stimuli were used that reflected this; so
that, while a VOT of 20 msec will leave only a short F1 transition in the labial series, longer voiced transitions will still
remain in the velar series. The longer remaining F1 transitions
in the velars lead to a greater tendency to perceive a voiced
stop, and the separation will have to be correspondingly longer
before voiceless judgements are given.

Our view that the voice distinction is to be explained in
terms of very basic mechanisms that can be engaged by non-speech

sounds is strongly supported by the curious finding that the
increase in VOT value of the phoneme boundary from labial to
dental to velar also occurs in the Chincilla (Kuhl and Miller,
1975). To the extent that this is a correct account of phoneme
boundary phenomena, the same mechanisms may be expected to underlie adaptation in both animals.

The research reviewed so far gives the impression of two
"hard-wired" property detectors, one for the F1 transitions
present in voiced initial stops and the other for the separation
cue which predominates in the voiceless range. Furthermore, we
appear to be pre-wired from birth: one month old infants show
a discrimination peak at the same point on the voice continuum
as adults (Eimas, Siqueland, Jusczyk and Vigorito, 1970). However, property filters of such an inflexible nature would on
their own be of only limited utility if natural speech does not
contain fixed, invariant cues. Furthermore, they cannot explain some recent results described below that call for a more
"active" perceptual mechanism.

Are the acoustic cues to voicing in natural speech sufficiently invariant to permit reliable recognition by fixed property
detectors? The data gathered by Klatt (1973) suggest that for
CV syllables, the distributions of VOT in voiced and voiceless
stops are quite distinct: a relatively high degree of invariance exists. Roughly the same value of VOT will also serve to
distinguish voiced and voiceless stops followed by a sonorant
(e.g. [br] versus [pr]). However, voiceless stops preceded by
[s] (e.g. [sp] or [spr], have a very short VOT, scarcely longer
than that in voiced stops ([b] or [br]). While this last result does not present insuperable problems for passive theories
in general, it at least indicates that some processing must intervene between the extraction of acoustic cues and the final
voicing decision.[2]

Another source of variability in the acoustic substrate of
voicing originates in the rate of speech. Measurements of
the voice onset time of voiceless stops taken from real speech,
vary over a range of about 20 msec, depending on how fast the
speaker is talking (Summerfield, 1975b). If the perceptual
system could compensate for this we would expect that, at apparently fast rates of speech, the voice onset time does not

---

[2]An alternative is to suppose that the speech perception system
decodes all short VOT sounds, both [b] and [sp], as phonetically
voiced, and that a phonological rule then interprets them as
voiced and voiceless respectively. This simplifies the speech
perception system, because all short VOT sounds can be voiced
and all long ones voiceless, but at the expense of the phonological rules.

have to be so long in order to satisfy the conditions for a
voiceless judgement. Such compensation does in fact occur: a
given synthetic syllable with intermediate VOT may be heard as
[pa] when preceded by a rapidly uttered precursor phrase, and
as [ba] after a slow one (Summerfield, 1974, 1975a). Furthermore, the magnitude of the perceptual compensation is of the
same order as the distorting effect that changes in rate have
on the VOT cues.

To recapitulate, there is on the one hand evidence from
studies of the psycho-acoustic bases of the separation and transition cues, and from voice perception in infants and chinchil-
las, for property detectors that are hard-wired, in the sense
that they would always give the same output to the same stimulus.
On the other hand it is clear, particularly from the effects of
apparent rate of speech, that the perception of voicing is
partly controlled by factors other than the stimulus itself. A
class of models capable of integrating these two aspects of
speech perception have been discussed by Summerfield (1974) and
by Summerfield and Haggard (1974) (see Fig. 3). Essentially,

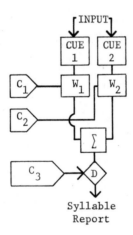

Fig. 3. Information flow model of voicing perception, from
Summerfield (1974).

the outputs of two detectors, which we shall assume extract from
a "neural spectrogram" the F1 transition and the separation cue,
respectively, are weighted (see below) and then interact in
some unspecified way to produce the final voicing decision.[3]

---

[3]The nature of the interaction between cues when they combine is

We shall make the further assumption that the F1 transition detector gives a stronger response for longer F1 transitions, and that the separation detector gives a higher output for larger separations. In view of the asymmetries already noted, we could suppose, additionally, that separations less than 20 msec are indistinguishable to the separation detector, 20 msec being the threshold of temporal order judgements (Hirsh, 1959; Stevens and Klatt, 1974). The simplifying assumption means that separation will act as a cue for voicelessness but that the lack of it will not be a cue to voiced. Also, the fact that two different voiceless stops with VOT greater than about 50 msec do not differ in F1 transition duration (because neither have any) will be interpreted in the same way: lack of F1 is not a cue to voicelessness.

The outputs of the detectors are weighted (w_1, w_2) for the following reason. Experiments on two voiced/voiceless continua, [ga-ka] and [gi-ki], in which the two cues have been varied independently, reveal that the F1 cue has greater influence on judgements of voicing in the [a] series, while separation is more important in the [i] series (Summerfield and Haggard, 1974). The model can explain this because for the vowel [i] the steady state of the first formant is so low that rising transitions in [gi] are so shallow as to be negligible. The F1 transition detector will therefore scarcely distinguish [gi] from [ki], its output being of similar magnitude in both cases. But, aside from the strength of the cues inherent in the stimulus itself, it seems that the relative importance of the outputs of the detectors can be readjusted in light of the demands a given ensemble of stimuli place on the subjects' decision mechanism. In a condition where subjects are confronted with both [gi-ki] stimuli and [ga-ka] stimuli (rather than one or the other), the [ga-ka] boundary is shifted toward voiced. Summerfield and Haggard argue that the presence of the [i] series causes subjects to weight the separation cue more highly, so that less separation is required in the [a] stimuli to bring it into equilibrium with the F1 cue.

In addition to weighting, a recalibration is called for to explain the effects of apparent rate of speech, as manipulated by syllabic rate in a synthetic precursor phrase (Summerfield,

---

obscure. If it is multiplicative rather than additive then the discrimination peaks at the phoneme boundary (categorical perception) (Liberman et al., 1960) can be explained. Another possibility which would have the same effect is to have the output of each detector inhibit the other before the information is combined (Abbs and Sussman, 1971).

1974, 1975a). The question arises as to whether this effect
occurs at the composite level (C in Fig. 3), or on the outputs
of the cue detectors (c_1, c_2). Because the effect of rate is
much greater in the [i] context, where the separation cue predominates, Summerfield (1974) concluded that the recalibration
responsible for rate normalization occurs only on the output of
the separation detector.

There are, then three conceptually distinct types of influence on the phoneme boundary. 1. The outputs of the property
detectors can be reweighted. 2. Outputs of detectors can be
recalibrated. 3. Finally, as we saw from the experiment of
Eimas and Corbit (1973), the phoneme boundary can be shifted by
adaptation, which, as a working hypothesis, might occur at the
two cue detectors, weakening their response to all stimuli that
activate them. Because they contain long Fl transitions, voiced
stop CV's will fatigue the Fl detector, while the long separation in voiceless stop CV's fatigues the separation detector.
For purposes of discussion, we shall assume that both detectors
give a graded response; e.g., the more Fl transition in the
stimulus, the stronger the output of the Fl detector; and the
stronger the degree of adaptation that that stimulus would incur.

2. Adaptation of Voicing Cues

Eimas and Corbit (1973) attributed adaptation to a pair of
linguistic feature detectors for voiced and voiceless. As noted
before, some of the force of this view is contained in the word
"linguistic". Within a speech-mode theory (see, e.g., Studdert-
Kennedy et al., 1970), a linguistic detector can only be engaged
by a phonetically identifiable (speech) sound. Non-speech sounds
are made by synthesizing the extreme syllables from the test
series in a highly reduced form (See Table 1), preserving some
of the acoustic cues but making them sound like "chirps" or
"bleats" rather than human speech. To the extent that such
sounds are not speech-like (not identifiable as phonemes, or as
"voiced-like", "voiceless-like", etc.), adaptation with them is
taken to indicate that the fatigued detectors are not linguistic
in nature. Another reason for studying the adapting effects of
various reduced versions of the voiced and voiceless syllables
is that, ideally, they show exactly what parts of the full syllable are able to activate the detectors responsible for fatigue.
The results of such non-speech experiments are summarized in
Table 1 (Eimas, Cooper, and Corbit, 1973; Tartter and Eimas,
1975; Ades, unpublished data). The boundary shift due to each
non-speech adaptor (e.g. the p-bleat) is expressed as a percentage of the effect of the full syllable of the same class (e.g.,
the p-syllable). All the adaptors shift the phoneme boundary
in the same direction as the syllable from which they are derived (e.g. toward voiceless for p-derived non-speech adaptors).

Adaptor	CV Syllable		Chirp		Bleat		F1
	/b/	/p/	/b/	/p/	/b/	/p/	/b/
Spectrogram							
Percent Adapting Effect	"100"	"100"	13 a 28 b 40 c	3 a 21 c	48 b	83 b	79 c

Table 1. Size of adapting effects of non-speech adaptors on voiced/voiceless continua (a, [da-ta]; b and c, [bae-pae]) expressed as a percentage of the size of the boundary shifts resulting from adaptation with the syllable from which they were derived. Circles represent aspiration, and solid lines voicing.

a) Eimas, Cooper and Corbit (1973).
b) Tartter and Eimas (1975).
c) Ades (unpublished data).

Of particular interest is the fact that the stimuli with
the greatest adapting effects are the p-bleat (the entire p-
syllable minus Fl), and the isolated Fl of the b-syllable.
These stimuli rather closely satisfy the respective requirements
of the separation detector, in that a period of aspiration is
followed by voicing excitation, and of the Fl transition detector. It should be noted that both the p-bleat and the b-Fl
resemble stimuli in which heightened discrimination has been
found at a point corresponding to the phoneme boundary as
measured in speech continua (Miller et al., 1974; Nabelek and
Hirsh, 1969). Whether or not these sounds are phonetically
identifiable as being p-like and b-like is not really clear:
not all investigators would, therefore, accept that their strong
adapting effect shows that the adapted detectors can be activated by non-phonetic sounds.

Interpretation of the adapting effects of the other non-
speech sounds like the b-bleat and the b-chirp is complicated
by the fact that a given boundary shift may be significant in
one study, while a larger effect of another stimulus might be
insignificant in another. But it is not obvious why non-speech
adaptors, if they have a significant effect, never have an
effect as strong as the syllable from which they have been derived. This problem is dealt with more fully in a later section.

The Fig. 3 model does not suggest any particular mechanism
for a level of adaptation higher than the two cue extractors.
But it does distinguish between those processes that precede the
integration of information from the two extractors, and those
that come after. All the evidence presented so far can be explained quite adequately by having adaption occur only at the
level of the Fl and separation detectors: but, relaxing the
requirement which a speech-mode theorist might make, that the
integrative level only be activated by speech stimuli, we could
equally well suppose that the effects are at the integrative
level. One way, ideally, of showing that at least some of the
effect is beyond the point where the two cues are united, is to
adapt one cue and look for boundary shifts in stimuli that differ only in the other cue. This experiment has not been done,
but a similar one by Cooper provides a basis for discussion.

Cooper (1974b) used a standard [ba-pa] test series in which
both cues are simultaneously varied; as the separation is increased, the duration of the Fl transitions is reduced. In this
series, the overall transition duration was 20 msec. There were
two adapting [da] stimuli, both with the same separation between
initial burst and onset of voicing (25 msec), but differing in
the length of voiced transitions; [da]-long (40 msec voiced
transitions) shifted the phoneme boundary toward voiced and
[da]-short (10 msec), to a lesser extent, toward voiceless. The
fact that two stimuli with the same VOT had different adapting

effects rules out the possibility that both voiced and voiceless
detectors simply look at different ranges of Voice Onset Time
(Eimas and Corbit, 1973; Cooper and Nager, 1975) and indicates,
more generally, that there must be at least a component of the
effect that is not related to the separation cue. Is this other
component simply the F1 transition detector, or is it at an integrative level? Cooper points out, in support of the latter,
that even test stimuli which have no F1 transitions (those with
VOT greater than 20 msec) are perceived as more voiceless after
adaptation with [da]-long and more voiced after [da]-short.

If (and only if) the F1 detector is assumed to give zero
output to stimuli that have no F1 transitions, this fact could
indeed be taken as evidence for adaptation at the integrative
level. Since the two adapters do not differ in separation, only
a higher level of adaptation can explain the differential effect
of [da]-long and [da]-short on stimuli with no F1 transitions.

Cooper's argument does establish the integrative level as
a possible site of adaptation; but it is not conclusive, because
the assumption that there are no F1 cues to voicelessness in
stimuli with no F1 transitions might not be correct. Subjects
in Cooper's study do give 80% voiced responses to some of the
stimuli with no F1 transitions, so there must be some cues to
voiced present. Furthermore, Lisker (1975), using voiced/voice-
less series without any F1 transitions at all (i.e. with flat
F1), has shown that the low onset frequency of F1 is itself a
cue to voiced, whether or not transitions are present.[4] Which
of the two F1 cues, F1 transition duration or F1 frequency onset, or some composite of both, is responsible for adaptation of
the voiced end of the continuum is unclear, since the two cues
are confounded in the test series used to date. Cooper's [da]-
long and [da]-short adaptors also differ in both.

In summary then, as long as there is some (fatiguable) F1
cue to voicedness to be extracted from stimuli with no F1 transitions, we can explain the differential adapting effects of
[da]-long and [da]-short on these stimuli as occurring at a
level where F1 information is being processed independently of
separation information. Adaptation, therefore, need not be
attributed to an integrative level.

In another experiment, Cooper (1974c) used two test continua,

---

[4]As Summerfield (1975a) points out, one advantage of low F1 onset as a cue to voiced is that it neatly explains why the phoneme
boundary in [bi-pi] series is at a longer VOT than in [ba-pa]
series (Summerfield, 1974; Summerfield and Haggard, 1974; Cooper,
1974b). Because the vowel [i] has a very low F1, the onset of
F1 in [pi] is so low that it constitutes a strong cue to voiced,
so that a greater separation cue to voiceless is required to
counter-balance it.

[ba-pa] and [bi-pi], and adapted them in different directions
by repeating a sequence consisting of [da] and [ti]. The [a]
series boundary was shifted toward voiced, and the [i] boundary
towards voiceless. This effect has been replicated by Miller
and Eimas (1975) with [bae-pae] and [bi-pi] test series and a
[da,ti] adapting sequence. Both Cooper and Miller and Eimas
interpret this result to mean that there are several (to some
extent) independent channels where the voicing decision can be
made, each one for a different vowel. Obviously, acceptance of
such vowel-contingent voicing analyzers vastly complicates the
type of model we have been using. Given the results of Summerfield and Haggard (1974) and Summerfield (1974, 1975a), however,
it is clear that very great care must be exercised in the interpretation of complex adaptation results in voicing.

As mentioned earlier, Summerfield and Haggard showed that
the differences in voicing perception in different vowel contexts can be understood in terms of the differential availability of the two cues. Before [i] the F1 detector output is approximately the same for [bi] and [pi]; thus, the separation cue
controls the decision. Similarly, they show that in [a] context
the F1 cue has greater control: that is, over the range [ba-pa]
a greater change occurs in the F1 detector output than in the
separation detector output. Cooper's [da, ti] adapting sequence
will, on the simple model, fatigue both detectors. The [i]
boundary, therefore, shifts toward voiceless because the F1 detector, adapted or not, exerts little control. Similarly the
[a] boundary shifts to voiced because the F1 detector is fatigued and it exerts more control over the decision than separation.

This account predicts that any procedure which fatigues
detectors both for the separation cue and for the F1 cue will
have the effect of shifting the [a] boundary toward voiced and
the [i] boundary toward voiceless, including the other possible
sequence, [di, ta]. Cooper (1974a) reports to the contrary
that [di, ta] in fact shifts the [a] boundary toward voiceless
and the [i] toward voiced, supporting the vowel-contingent hypothesis and arguing against the predictions we have made from
the simple model. Recently an attempt to replicate the vowel-
contingent findings with similar test series has been made by
Pisoni, Sawusch and Adams (1975). These investigators find that
[da, ti] shifts the [a] boundary toward voiced, while [di, ta]
shifts it toward voiceless, in agreement with Cooper's results.
However, no effect on the [bi-pi] series is found in either
case. This clearly constitutes a failure to find a vowel-
contingent effect, Pisoni et al.'s claims notwithstanding. While
this conflict of facts persists, further discussion seems fruit-
less. It is, in any case, clear that Summerfield and Haggard's
independent work on the differential availability of cues in
various vowel contexts introduces great complexity to the interpretation of vowel-contingent effects. The situation undoubtedly

will deteriorate further when other cues like the burst and aspiration are taken into account.

A third type of explanation for vowel-contingency (suggested
by Summerfield and Haggard, 1974) is that at least one of the
cues to voicing is extracted by mechanisms that cover only limited portions of the frequency spectrum. For example, it might
be expected that repetition of the high F1 in [da] will have a
strong effect on the subsequent extraction of F1 information
from [da], but little effect on the processing of the lower frequency [di]. That some, if not all, adaptation effects are
spectrally specific, is a more or less inescapable conclusion
from studies of adaptation of the transition cues to place of
articulation, to which we will turn shortly.

All this seems vastly complicated. But the general implications are clear: adaptation is attributable to the level of
individual acoustic cues, although the possibility of an integrative level remains (Cooper, 1974b). Structurally this formulation is close to the pair of linguistic feature detectors
for voiced and voiceless proposed by Eimas and Corbit (1973).
The difference is that Eimas and Corbit's detectors looked at
different ranges of VOT, while those suggested here pick up two
distinctly different cues. The outputs of these detectors
could be mapped fairly directly into linguistic categories. As
noted before, the variability of at least the separation cue is
small enough in natural speech for this proposal to hold, particularly as several sources of variability, namely, those
occasioned by changes in place of articulation and by the following vowel, are handled by the cue detectors themselves in
terms of their inherent cue strength and availability. The
vowel-contingent effect (Cooper, 1974c) raises the additional
possibility that the extraction mechanisms operate only within
limited bands of the frequency spectrum. Although this increases
the number of detectors required, it would not complicate the
detector-to-phonetic level mapping.

Other types of variability, calling for "active" mechanisms
like reweighting and recalibration, do not affect the plausibility of this account, as these mechanisms operate on the output
of the detectors. What has emerged so far, then is a pair of
passive property detectors, whose outputs require only quanti-
tative, rather than qualitative, adjustment before they can be
given linguistic significance.

PLACE OF ARTICULATION

1. Transition Cues

The place of articulation of a consonant refers to the part
of the vocal tract where it is formed: at the lips for [b], [p]

and [m], behind the teeth for [d], [t] and [n], and at the velum
for [g], [k] and [ŋ]. In initial stop consonants the vocal
tract is completely constricted. When the constriction is re-
leased, a brief burst of noise is emitted, and as the vocal
tract moves toward the configuration that it will take up for
the following vowel, the cavities within it change size rapidly,
giving rise to a pattern of movement in the formant frequencies.
The schematic spectrograms (see Fig. 4) of the voiced stops [b],

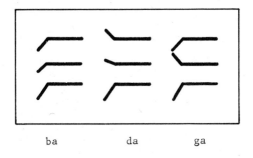

          ba   da   ga

Fig. 4. Schematic spectrograms of [ba], [da], and [ga].

[d] and [g] before a vowel like [a] show the direction of these
frequency transitions at the different places of articulation.
Since the transitions result from the vocal tract moving from
the configuration of the consonant to that of the vowel, the
direction of the transitions is entirely conditioned by the following vowel. The same is true of the relation of the preceding
vowel to the consonant in a VC syllable.
     In spite of this inherent variability across vowel contexts,
however, the transitions in F2 alone are sufficient to perceptu-
ally discriminate labial, dental and velar places of articulation
in synthetic speech (Cooper, Delattre, Liberman, Borst and
Gerstman, 1952). As a result, the transition cues to place have
occupied a control role in theories of speech perception. The
classic contrast is made between two formant synthetic speech
heard as [di] and [du] (Liberman et al., 1967). Here the F2
transition, the sole vehicle of place information, rises to a
high steady state F2 in [di] and falls to a low F2 in [du].
Acoustically, the two [d]'s have very little in common. One way
of rationalizing the direction of transitions is to refer to a
"locus", a frequency to which the formant transition points.
Since the starting position of the vocal tract is much the same
whether [di] or [du] is spoken, the formants may move in different directions, but they should originate from the same locus
frequency, that generated by the cavities of an labiodentally
occluded vocal tract. Perceptual experiments with synthetic

speech have tended to validate this notion (Delattre, Liberman, and Cooper, 1955). Loci are not always easy to see in spectrograms of real speech, but measurements of voiced stop consonant transitions in several V_1CV_2 environments by Öhman (1966), indicate that for a given consonant the initial frequency of the F2 transition varies so much across vowel environments that it may overlap with the F2 values of another consonant. However, if F2 and F3 initial transition frequencies are considered together, the overlap is very nearly eliminated.

Even so, it is unlikely that the transition loci can be considered to provide invariant cue to place. Another source of variability is the vocal tract size of the speaker. A smaller vocal tract, as in a woman or child, will give rise to higher frequency formants and loci. It is therefore possible to synthesize an [ε] (as in bed) suitable to a large vocal tract with the same formant as an [ae] (as in bad) as spoken by a child. Rand (1971) has shown that transitions which give rise to a [d] in one case would give a [b] in the other, suggesting that the listener compensates for the fact that a smaller vocal tract will have a higher frequency locus for [d] transitions. This process of "vocal tract normalization" has also been demonstrated by allowing a precursor phrase carrying information about vocal tract size to influence the perception of a subsequent vowel (Ladefoged and Broadbent, 1957) or stop consonant (Fourcin, 1968). A further complication in the transition cues lies in the effect of speaking rate. Certain articulator movements not only are faster in rapid speech, but there may also be a re-programming of the target positions. This has been observed in vowels (Gay, Ushijima, Hirose and Cooper, 1974), and must therefore be included as a factor capable of changing the slope of transitions.

In the case of voicing, the property detectors amenable to fatigue, if not themselves linguistic, could be mapped onto a linguistic level fairly easily. The far more pervasive variability of the transition cues to place make detectors of this sort unlikely. Instead there is a clear need either for detectors tuned to linguistic features, computed from the signal by some rather complex process, or for detectors capable of extracting transition information in a fairly crude form. The first experimental question is therefore: do the detectors generalize across stimuli that share linguistic attributes like features or phonemes, or across sounds which are spectrally similar.

Adaptation experiments in place of articulation have used stimuli like those shown in Fig. 4 as test material. The continua are generated by changing the onset frequencies of the F2 and F3 transitions to give a range of stimuli from, say, [ba] to [da] to [ga]. Repetition of any of the three full stimuli reliably shifts adjacent boundaries toward the adapted sound

(Cooper, 1974a; Ades, 1973; Bailey, 1975a). The earlier results suggested that the effect could be attributed to selective fatigue of "labial", "dental" and "velar" linguistic
feature detectors: Cooper (1974) demonstrated that [pae] and
[bi] both adapted the [b] end of the [bae-dae] continuum, and
later Cooper and Blumstein (1974) produced the same results with
[mae] and [vae]: all of which contain initial labial consonants. Cooper and Blumstein point out, though, that a detector
tuned to the rising transitions in F2 and/or F3, which characterize initial labials in all environments, could explain the
data equally well.

An attempt to distinguish these alternatives by Ades
(1974a) followed the tradition of the [di-du] contrast. A
[bae-dae] test series was used where both the F2 and F3 transitions in the extreme test [dae] were falling. An adapting
stimulus, [de], was constructed in which F2 was rising and F3
flat. In spite of the opposite orientation of the transitions,
the [de] adapted the [dae] end of the series to a small but
significant extent: Ades therefore argued that at least some of
the adaptation effect is linguistic in nature. However, in
terms of the starting frequencies of the formants, the [de] was
much closer to the [dae] than to [bae]; so if spectral close-
ness, rather than simply direction of transitions, is a factor,
then the transfer of adaptation between [de] and [dae] could
be at an auditory rather than phoneme level.

Experiments by Bailey (1973, 1975a) have made it clear that
adaptation of the transition cues to place is, indeed, heavily
dependent on spectral similarity of the test series and the
adaptor. Bailey (1973) used two [ba-da] test series (Fig. 5),

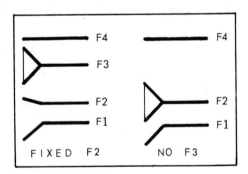

Fig. 5. Two [ba-da] stimulus series used by Bailey (1973).
No F3 adaptors shift the phoneme boundary on the Fixed F2
series, but not vice versa.

one where the discriminating information was carried in F3, F2 being fixed; and the other where the information was carried in F2, there being no F3. [ba] and [da] from the Fixed F2 series have no adapting effect on the No F3 test series, because No F3 test stimuli have no energy in the F3 region whose reception can be distorted by the F3 in Fixed F2 adaptors. On the other hand, No F3 [ba] and [da] do selectively adapt Fixed F2 test items because, although the Fixed F2 stimuli carry no distinctive information in F2, the reception of F2 can be differentially distorted by the F2 transitions in the No F3 adaptors.

The implication is that while adaptation may occur in a given spectral region, it will not transfer to another. Before attempting to characterize the level at which this effect occurs, it is emphasized that the lack of symmetry in Bailey's experiment effectively rules out all explanations of adaptation in terms of levels where [ba] Fixed F2 and [ba] No F3 are represented as the same. Such levels include the syllable, the phoneme and the linguistic feature. If any adaptation at all took place at these levels, then sounds on either series would adapt the other series, whereas the effect works only one way. One might argue that adaptation might occur at a level where one instance of phoneme [b] is distinguished from the other instances of phoneme [b] if they are spectrally dissimilar, but such levels are hardly linguistic. Further support for the lack of linguistic adaptation comes from the failure of the effect to transfer across the extreme vowels [i] and [u]. [bi] has a fatiguing effect on a [bi-di] series, as does [bu] on a [bu-du] series, but, although they share the feature labial and the phoneme [b], [bi] will not adapt [bu-du], nor will [bu] adapt [bi-di] (Bailey, 1975a).

Again, the spectral specificity of adaptation of the transition cues permits us to explain the "vowel-contingent" effect of Miller and Eimas (1975), and Pisoni, Sawusch and Adams (1975): a [bae-dae] series was b-adapted[5] and a [bi-di] series d-adapted by repetition of a sequence containing [bae] and [di]. Rather than accepting vowel-contingent labial, dental and velar analyzers, which involves a dangerous proliferation of detector types, the effect can be attributed to the fact that the F2 transition cues to [di] and the F2 cues to [bae] are over 600 Hz apart, so

---

[5]For the sake of brevity, a [b-d] series is described as "b-adapted" when the phoneme boundary is shifted toward the [b] end of the series, i.e. when detectors responsible for [b] are fatigued.

that they can be adapted in opposite directions by spectrally specific mechanisms, without mutual interference.

What, then, is the probable site of adaptation? The emphasis placed on spectral similarity of the adaptor and test item suggests a very low level of auditory fatigue, so low that a brief period of filtered noise with the same overall power spectrum as, say, the [d] transition might d-adapt a [bae-dae] series. However, it appears that it is the change in spectrum over time that determines the effect: the total energy spectrum of [aeb] is the same as in [bae], yet [aeb] does not adapt a [bae-dae] series (Ades, 1974a). The same point is made in an experiment on non-speech adaptors (See Table 2): both the chirp, the formant transitions alone, and the tweet (the isolated F2 and F3 transitions) have a small but significant adapting effect, but the tweet played backwards, a transformation that preserves the power spectrum but changes the time course of spectral change, has no effect (Ades, 1973).

A related explanation might be sought in the changes in apparent pitch that follow auditory fatigue. Exposure to a 1000 Hz tone causes a 1100 Hz tone to be heard as having a still higher pitch. Thus, repetition of a rising [b] transition might make a neutral, boundary transition appear like a falling [d] transition. However, this cannot be the basis of speech adaptation since the corresponding downward shifts in apparent pitch do not occur (Elliott and Fraser, 1970).

Both these explanations place the phenomenon in what Bailey (1975a) calls the neural spectrogram. It seems instead that adaptation resides in mechanisms that extract transitional information from the spectrum, rather than in the spectrogram itself. In their simplest form, these detectors could respond to changes in frequency from one value to another (perhaps in a given time). Such a configuration accounts for the data presented so far, because detectors of this sort are inherently specific spectrally. An immediate implication of this is that the detectors are unlikely to be "formant-specific"; that is a given transition detector would fail to distinguish a high F2 transition in one stimulus from an F3 transition in another, as long as they were both at the same frequency. It is not yet clear whether adaptation of transition cues in synthetic speech syllable precedes formant identification (i.e. whether or not an F2 can adapt an F3 of the same frequency), but available evidence in non-speech experiments suggests that it does: non-speech stimuli consisting only of the 2nd and 3rd formants, the bleat and the tweet (see Table 2) do have an adapting effect (Tartter and Eimas, 1975; Ades, 1973). Thus adaptation is not formant-specific, in that F2 and F3 can apparently be fatigued by Fl and F2 (where the numbers are defined by counting formants from the bottom upwards).

At some stage, formants presumably must be identified as

Adaptor	CV Syllable	Bleat	Gulp	Chirp	Tweet	Backward Tweet	VC Syllable	Speech-embedded Chirp
/b/ Version								
/d/ Version								
Percent Adapting Effect	"100"	67 a1 46 a2	26 b	47 a1 41 b 76 d	30 d	-5 d	3 e	29 c

Table 2. Size of adapting effects of non-speech stimuli in [b-d] test series, as a percentage of the effects of the b- and d-syllables from which they are derived. (Where possible, the average effect of the [b] and [d] versions has been used). a1) Tartter and Eimas, Experiment 1 (1975). a2) Tartter and Eimas, Experiment 2 (1975). b) Bailey (1975a). c) Tash (1974). d) Ades (1973). e) Ades (1974a).

such, but an experiment by Klatt and Shattuck (1973) shows that mechanisms ignorant of the notion "formant" may play a large part in speech perception. Subjects were required to make a variety of judgements about brief "2-formant" sine wave glissandos, which were located in spectral regions appropriate either to F1 and F2, or to F2 and F3. Even when its intensity was reduced substantially, the component in the F2 region dominated subject's perceptual judgements, whether it was paired with an F1 or an F3 component. The frequently observed pre-eminence of F2 cues may, therefore, not result from its being F2, as defined by a formant counting device, but because it lies in a spectral region which has more weight. This experiment, then, independently verifies the existence of a stage of processing where formants are not identified by a counting procedure. This is the stage to which we might provisionally attribute adaptation effects.

In terms of the model used for the voice distinction (Fig. 3), adaptation has again been placed at a relatively peripheral level, where information from different spectral regions is processed independently. Is this the only level at which mechanisms for place of articulation can be adapted? No definitive answer to this question can yet be given, but the possibility of a higher level has been raised for several reasons.

Firstly, it can be seen in Table 2 that as long as non-speech adaptors contain exactly the same transistions as the test stimuli, then they have a positive adapting effect. Indeed, all such non-speech adaptors have been shown to have significant effects in at least one study. This, in itself, is in agreement with the notion that adaptation occurs in relatively peripheral detectors which register transitions from one frequency to another. However, if this is the only mechanism involved, why are adapting effects of non-speech adaptors always smaller than those of the syllables from which they are derived? The same question may be asked of non-speech adaptors for voicing (Table 1).

One theory, exemplified by Tartter and Eimas (1975), is that there are two levels of adaptation, one auditory and the other phonetic. Syllables adapt at both levels, while non-speech sounds, to the extent that they are not identifiable as phonemes, engage only the auditory level. However, it was argued above that there is no phonetic level in any obvious sense of the term. ([bi] does not adapt detectors for [bu], (Bailey, 1975a) and two versions of [ba] may be constructed, one of which will not adapt mechanisms for the other (Bailey, 1973)). Another type of higher level capable, in principle, of explaining the incomplete adaptation with non-speech is the "acoustic syllable", a concept discussed in Studdert-Kennedy (1975). At this level, the entire syllable is represented in an auditory rather than phonetic form. But this level also fails to predict

the asymmetry in Bailey's Fixed F2/No F3 experiment: if a No
F3 [ba] syllable is acoustically similar to Fixed F2 [ba], and
can thus adapt it, why should a Fixed F2. [ba] not adapt a No
F3 one?
   An alternative is to view the incomplete effects of non-
speech in terms of the response that transition cue detectors
would be likely to have to the material in the so-called neural
spectrogram. For instance, chirps and tweets may excite the
relevant detectors less because they are interpreted not only as
onset transitions, but also as offset transitions, or even
bursts. Or, again, the gulp (see Table 2) may produce only a
small effect (Bailey, 1975a) because the high initial frequency
of F1 gives the appearance of a low frequency burst. (This
postdicts correctly that the b-gulp has a far greater effect
on shifting the phoneme boundary than the d-gulp).
   However, rather more difficult to explain is the fact that
stimuli lacking energy in the F1 region, the bleat and the tweet,
have a smaller effect than the equivalent stimuli which do have
F1 energy, the syllable and the chirp. In an extreme case,
Verbrugge and Liberman (1975) find that the isolated F3 has no
significant adapting effect on a [ra-la] test series where the
[r-l] distinction was carried solely in the slope of the F3
transitions. Tartter and Eimas (1975), however, do find a significant though small effect of the isolated F3 on a [d-g]
series. While these small effects possibly indicate the activity of an additional higher level reached only by the full syllable, other explanations of the weaker effects of non-speech
should be exhausted before a higher level, that cannot be linguistic anyway, is accepted by default. In general, two
strengths of adaptation do not necessarily indicate two levels
of adaptation: it could be that there is just one level, more
engaged by the full syllable than by parts of it. Whether this
is because the full syllable is more "speech-like" than its
reduced derivatives, as has often been claimed (Eimas, Cooper
and Corbit, 1973; Tartter and Eimas, 1975; Verbrugge and
Liberman, 1975), is unclear. This explanation is, however, similar to one we offer in a later section on source effects.

2. The Burst Cue and Integrative Detectors for Place

   More convincing evidence for adaptation at a higher level
comes from experiments where stimuli containing bursts, as well
as transitions, are used. The burst, the brief frication noise
due to the sudden release of the articulators, is a sufficient
cue in many contexts for the perception of the voiceless stops
[p], [t], and [k]. While bursts above about 3000 Hz invariably
signal [t], the appropriate burst frequency necessary to give
[p] and [k] judgements in synthetic speech is heavily determined
by the vowel (Cooper et al., 1952).

We might, then, distinguish two stages in the perception of place. In the first stage, the three cues, F2 and F3 transitions and burst, are extracted independently from the neural spectrogram. (This corresponds to the level of the F1 and separation cues in our voicing model, but differs in that each cue is able to generate information about all three places, labial, dental and velar. In the case of voicing, one cue was responsible for voiced and another for voiceless.) At the second, integrative stage, the three cues are brought together to ultimately produce a perceptual judgement of place.

Experiments where subjects identify synthetic patterns with a large variety of F2 and F3 transitions and bursts indicate that the three cues are, in fact, processed independently (Hoffman, 1958; Harris, Hoffman, Liberman, Delattre and Cooper, 1958). To give an example, the effect of a given burst is the same, regardless of the configuration of the two transitions. Nevertheless, the way in which the cues are summated gives the appearance of quite complex interactions. Hoffman suggests that each cue produces a tendency toward or away from b-, d- or g-likeness, and that each of the three cues are then taken as component vectors to be computed into a resultant vector, in the manner of a parallelogram of forces. Bailey (1975a) points out that his adaptation experiments on transition cues are in broad agreement with Hoffman's notion of independent cue processing, in that the adapting effect is specific to the frequency regions where the cues are carried.

Stevens (1973) has made some explicit proposals about the nature of an integrative level, based partly on the observation that in initial position, labials are characterized by a rapid rise in frequency (low frequency bursts followed by rising transitions), dentals by a fall in frequency (high burst followed by falling transitions), and velars by a spreading of frequency (mid-range burst followed by diverging F2 and F3 transitions. These paradigmatic configurations, involving transitions only, are apparent in Fig. 4. There are several advantages to taking these three patterns as a description of the sufficient stimuli for the three place categories. Firstly doing so unifies the three main sub-cues into time-varying global patterns that are reasonably invariant over different vowel contexts (cf. the increased degree of invariance in place cues when both F2 and F3 loci are taken into account (Öhman, 1966)). Secondly, it explains why, in tape splicing experiments, transitions are more important cues before [a], while bursts have more weight in judgements of [d] and [g] before [i] (Fischer-Jorgensen, 1972). A global property detector for dentals demands overall fall in frequency which is not present in the F2 and F3 transitions in [di]; hence, the poor identification when the high frequency burst is removed (Stevens, 1973). Thirdly, if there are property detectors for rising, falling and

spreading patterns, we have some basis for explaining the discontinuous nature of perception (categorical perception) that
is evident along synthetic series ranging from [b] to [d] to [g],
both in adults (Liberman, Harris, Hoffman and Griffith, 1957;
Pisoni, 1971) and in infants (Eimas, 1974). If we assume that
Stevens' detectors take input from detectors for the individual
cues, it is interesting that his view of the integrative level
is not in conflict with Hoffman's finding that the three sub-
cues act independently. A process like vector addition (Hoffman, 1958) would be expected to produce non-linear changes at
the integrative level in response to linear changes in its inputs, and, thus, generate discrimination peaks.

Experiments that speak to the issue of whether adaptation
occurs at the integrative level have used standard test series
where the stimuli differ only in their transitions and adaptors
with bursts. If a CV cued only with a burst adapts sounds cued
only by transitions, it can be argued that the effect must be
at an integrative level. Such results have indeed been found.
Diehl (1975a) has adapted the [dɛ] end of a [bɛ-dɛ] series with
a [tɛ] consisting of only the [t] burst followed by a steady
state vowel. Similarly, Ganong (1975) has adapted a [bae-dae]
continuum with both [sae] and [tae] lacking in transitions, the
size of the effect being roughly one third of that found with
[sae] and [dae] adaptors which do have transitions. If only a
burst cue is being adapted, and the response to only transition
cues is being tested, as would be dictated by the view that
adaptation occurs only at a level of cue-independence; then this
transfer of adaptation between bursts and transitions could not
occur. In a similar vein, Blumstein and Stevens (1975), using
a [b-d-g] series, could shift the boundaries with either transition-cued CV's or with CV's consisting of transitions and appropriate bursts; but if the burst and transition information
conflicted, as with a [d] burst and [g] transition, no significant effect was seen. Again, only transitions are present in
the test series, so the spectral position of the burst in the
adaptor, they argue, can have an effect only at an integrative
level.

However, before accepting that adaptation can occur at a
level of cue integration, there are objections to the above interpretation of experiments with bursts in the adaptor stimuli.

Firstly, the concept of integrative property detectors as
a site of adaptation is sensitive to the same objections which
can be made against phonetic and linguistic feature levels:
namely that two stimuli, for example, Bailey's [bi] and [bu],
may contain the spectral pattern sufficient to activate an integrative detector for rising frequency and still fail to exhibit transfer of adaptation. Thus, if there is an integrative
level, it must also be spectrally specific. Bailey's Fixed
F2/No F3 experiment makes this same point. Because this

interpretation somewhat weakens the case for distinguishing
between cue-independent and integrative levels, it is worth pursuing the idea that even the experiments where burst-cued stimuli adapt detectors for transition-cued stimuli can be explained
in the same way as the other experiments; by mechanisms that
simply register frequency changes independently in each formant.

For example, when a burst is followed at a short interval
by a steady state vowel, the system might interpret change in
frequency as a transition, either because of a smear in the
neural spectrogram, or because a transition detector can be activated by frequency changes whether or not transitions are
actually present. Data in support of this can be found in Diehl
(1957a), where adaptation of a [bɛ-dɛ] test series was attempted
with [tɛ] and [pɛ] with no transitions, only bursts. Diehl's
[t] burst was at roughly the same frequency as the initial F3
transitions in the extreme [dɛ] test stimulus; on the other hand
the [p] burst was over 900 Hz lower than the F2 transition in
the extreme [bɛ] test stimulus, too far away to be read as part
of a labial transition by a transition detector. Thus, although
the burst-cued [tɛ] and even the [t] burst alone had a d-adapting
effect, neither the burst-cued [pɛ] nor the [p] burst alone had
a b-adapting effect. This asymmetry is particularly striking
given that on this test continuum the [b] end was twice as
amenable to adaptation as the [d] end, when the extreme syllables
were used as adaptors. However, it is quite easily explained if
we assume that transition detectors treat the frequency change
from a burst to a steady state formant as if it were a transition.

By attributing the effect of burst-cued CV's to transition
detectors, we avoid having to postulate a higher integrative
level as the site of transfer of adaptation between bursts and
transitions. A similar interpretation can be made of the effect
of conflicting burst and transition cues (Blumstein and Stevens,
1975). Here the presence of a conflicting burst might interfere
with the extraction of the transition information, or, to put
it another way, the transition detectors might read the burst
as part of the transition. A high frequency [d] burst will make
little difference to the extraction of the falling [d] transitions, as both are part of a generally falling pattern, but a
[g] burst or [b] burst followed by [d] transitions could give
the illusion of discontinuous or smeared transitions.

The issue here is really one of segmentation. To take the
Blumstein and Stevens experiment as evidence for a higher level
of adaptation, it must be assumed that a transition detector
somehow knows that the burst is not part of the transition. Indeed, the notion of global property detectors for place can be
re-interpreted as meaning that there is, in fact, no distinction
to be made between the two cues: after all, one of the reasons
for postulating global property detectors is that in labials,

dentals and velars, the burst+transitions follow the same trajectory as the transitions alone.

In summary, it seems possible, in principle, to reduce all
adaptation effects in place of articulation to a single level.
At this level, information is extracted from various spectral
regions independently. However, to accomodate the effect of
conflicting burst and transition cues it has been suggested that
detectors operate before bursts and transitions are portioned
into distinct segments. In a later section the problem of segmentation, as it relates to feature extraction, is explored in
more detail.

With reference to feature systems in general, transition
detectors for place are rather different from the F1 and separation cues to voicing. Outputs of the detectors for voicing,
while not themselves representing invariant cues to voiced and
voiceless, require only simple readjustment before a linguistic
description of the input is achieved. But detectors for transition cues to place are quite different. Firstly the output of
a given detector cannot be generally associated with a particular linguistic feature. To take an extreme case, a rising
transition around 2500 Hz might act as a cue to [d] if it was
a second formant (as in [di]), or as a cue to [b] if it was a
third formant (as in [ba]); yet both cues would be picked up
by the same detector. Secondly, the normalization required for
changes in vocal tract size and rate of speech must be exceedingly complex, readjusting not only for the starting point of the
transition but also for its duration and overall spectral location.

Of course, this is precisely the problem that makes Stevens'
(1973) global pattern detectors, which pick up particular combinations of the component F2, F3 and burst cues, so attractive.
If rising, falling and spreading patterns really represent acoustic invariants to place, they might take as their input the output of the individual cue extractors which we have taken to be
the site of adaptation. But, as yet, evidence that adaptation
occurs at the integrative level is inconclusive.

STOP CONSONANTS AND SEMI-VOWELS

Semi-vowels differ from stops in that the motion of the
articulators, and therefore the transitional frequency changes,
are less abrupt. Semi-vowel transitions start at roughly the
same frequencies as those for a stop consonant with the same
place of articulation. Therefore, series of syllables ranging,
for example, from [ba] to [wa] can be made simply by increasing
the duration of the transitions while holding their starting
frequencies constant. Typically, transitions in [ba] are over
within about 30 msec, while [wa] transitions may last for about

60 msec. Longer transitions of fixed extent imply a slower
rate of frequency change (in Hz/sec), so both rate and duration
are possible cues. Of the two, it appears that duration is
decisive: when the following vowel is changed, the position
of the [b-w] boundary remains at a constant duration in spite
of wide variation in rate of the transition (Liberman, Delattre,
Gerstman and Cooper, 1956).

As with voicing and place of articulation, identification
boundary shifts have been observed in series ranging from stop
to semi-vowel following repetition of stimuli from the extreme
ends of the series (Bailey, 1975a, b; Diehl, 1975b; Cooper,
Ebert and Cole, 1975). Of more interest are the various kinds
of transfer of adaptation. Firstly, the adaptation of place
cues can transfer between stop and semi-vowel: [wa] may b-adapt
a [ba-da] series, and [ba] w-adapt a [wa-ja] series. Results
of this sort have been obtained by Bailey (1975a, b), though
such cross-series effects are quite small. Following Bailey,
they can be attributed to the close spectral correspondence of
the F2 and F3 transitions of a stop ([b] or [d]) to those of its
corresponding semi-vowel ([w] or [j]): stop and semi-vowel
transitions start at the same frequencies.

Secondly, adaptation of stop/semi-vowel cues has been found
to transfer across place. For example, [b] may d-adapt a [d-j]
series, and [j] w-adapt a [b-w] series. Again, the transfer
effects are generally less than 50% of the full effect found
when the adaptor is taken from the same series as the test items,
and they do not always reach significance (Bailey, 1975a, b;
Cooper, Ebert and Cole, 1975; Diehl, 1975b). Rather than attribute the transfer to phonetic detectors for stop versus semi-
vowel (Cooper et al. 1975; Diehl, 1975b), we can develop the
view, already put forward for the transition cues to place, that
adaptation effects arise independently in each formant (i.e.
each spectral region). The F2 and F3 transitions of [da] are
very different from those of [ba], but the F1 transitions are
identical and could, therefore, be the site of whatever adapting
effect [da] may have on a [ba-wa] series.

It is possible to visualize two types of detector, one for
the extent and direction of transitions (which would play a role
in place judgements), and another for duration of transitions
(which would contribute to the stop/semi-vowel distinction).
However, a further simplification can be achieved if we cease to
regard place judgements and stop/semi-vowel judgements as different at the detector level. For example, all frequency transition adaptation might occur at a level where there are a very
large number of detectors, each one responding when a formant
moves from one fixed frequency, Fi, to another (not necessarily
different) frequency Fj, in a particular time, T. For any given
stimulus, an analysis of its place of articulation would consist
of a decision over some subset of these detectors, while the

outputs of some other subset of the detectors would be used for
an analysis of whether it was a stop or semi-vowel.

Of course, the central problem of speech perception, the
mapping from the detectors to the phonetic categories, remains.
For example, there is no duration of transition, T, such that
all shorter durations are reported as stops and all longer ones
as semi-vowels. Indeed, the same duration may give rise to the
perception of a stop on a [g-j] series and semi-vowel on a [b-
w] series (Liberman, Delattre, Gerstman, and Cooper, 1956;
Cooper, Ebert and Cole, 1975). This in itself does not contra-
dict the above view of adaptation, because various types of
recalibration and reweighting are taken to intervene between
feature extraction and phonetic decision (see Fig. 3). In this
case a perceptual compensation perhaps is made for the fact that
velars are accompanied by longer transitions than labials,
either because of commands to the articulators or because of
the latters' inertial properties. However, an experiment by
Cooper, Ebert and Cole (1975) appears to place some adaptation
after the recalibration process and, indeed, at a linguistic
level. Cooper et al. used a [ga] with 35 msec transitions as
an adaptor on a test series where transition duration ranged
from 15 msec for [ba] to 45 msec for [wa]. Surprisingly, the
effect was to shift the phoneme boundary toward [b], suggesting
that adaptation occurs at a phonetic level where [g] and [b] are
represented as stops, rather than an acoustic level where [w]
and [g] are represented as having long transitions.

This result is hard to evaluate since Cooper, et al. find
a b-adapting effect of similar magnitude after fatigue with the
isolated vowel [a]. They suggest that the rapid amplitude onset of their synthetic [a] may stimulate a burst, and make it
more akin to a stop than a semi-vowel. Because all the test
stimuli have the same initial amplitude at onset, they propose
that the b-adapting effect of the "burst" in [a] must occur at
an integrative level where transition duration and amplitude
onset information are combined. Whether or not this rapid amplitude onset is the source of the b-adapting effect of [ga] is
not clear. In Fig. 4, it can be seen that the initial frequencies of the F2 and F3 transitions are quite close. Because this
proximity at onset could create an apparent (or real) burst,
Cooper et al. constructed another [ga] where the F2 and F3 onsets were more separated. This stimulus too had a b-adapting
effect. This is, I believe, the best evidence there is for
phonetic level adaptation, though it is not completely satisfactory because the second [ga] adaptor may still have burst-
like onset characteristics. As Bailey (1975a) notes, it would
be of interest to know whether a [wa] with relatively short
transition would g-adapt the [g-j] series.

Another, related cue to the stop/semi-vowel distinction is
the rise time of amplitude during the transitions. It is true
of both natural speech and the output of most speech synthesizers

that the amplitude of a voiced sound is dependent on F1 frequency. Thus, when F1 rises to its steady state relatively
slowly, as it does in a semi-vowel, the amplitude envelope shows
a more gradual rise. Diehl (1975b) has used two sawtooth waves
as adaptors, one of which (the "pluck") had very rapid rise time
and the other (the "bow") a more gradual one. The pluck had a
strong b-adapting effect on the [ba-wa] test series. Because
the test stimuli also differed in their amplitude envelopes,
the effect of the pluck could lie in the fatigue of independent
amplitude rise time detectors, though Diehl himself appears to
favour an effect at a phonetic level. However, either explanation is made hazardous by the failure of the bow adaptor to have
a corresponding w-adapting effect.

More convincing evidence for amplitude rise time detectors
derives from the fact that pluck and bow stimuli are themselves
capable of being adapted; Cutting, Rosner and Foard (1975) used
a continuum of sawtooth stimuli with amplitude rise times varying from 0 to 80 msec. Such series are perceived as having a
sharp boundary between pluck and bow categories, and also yield
discrimination peaks (Cutting and Rosner, 1974; Cutting et al.,
1975). As with speech stimuli, repetition of sounds at the
extreme ends of the pluck/bow series shifts the perceptual boundary. Of particular interest is the finding that, when the frequencies of the sawtooth in the test and adapting stimuli are
different, the adaptation effect is weakened; furthermore, a
sine-wave adaptor, especially one of different frequency, caused
an even smaller (but still significant) boundary shift (Cutting
et al., 1975). This suggests that the detectors for amplitude
rise time operate in a frequency specific fashion, even though
rise time is not itself a spectral cue.

Three types of cue to the stop/semi-vowel distinction have
been mentioned. First, the frequency transition detectors
already proposed for place can be extended such that each is
sensitive to a particular duration of a given frequency change.
This permits one to explain the transfer of adaptation across
place and across the stop/semi-vowel distinction, without having to postulate a linguistic level that has been ruled out for
place distinctions. It also accounts for the weakness of the
transfer. Second, the work of Cutting et al. (1975) demonstrates frequency specific detectors for amplitude rise time.
These could be the source of Cooper et al.'s (1975) b-adapting
effect of [a], since the lack of transitions in [a] leads to a
stop-like amplitude rise time of zero. The third cue is the
onset burst, implicated possibly in the ability of [ga] with
semi-vowel-like frequency transition and rise time to adapt the
stop end of a stop/semi-vowel series (Cooper et al., 1975).

As with the work on integrative property detectors for
place (Blumstein and Stevens, 1975), the issue of an integrative
detector for stops versus semi-vowels, combining both

transitional and burst cues, depends on assumptions about segmentation. If a "burst" is responsible for the above adapting
effects of [a] and [ga], the question arises as to whether a
rise time detector can be expected to ignore the burst and pick
up only the remaining amplitude envelope, or whether it will
absorb the burst into a single segment, shared with rise time
proper. It is to the general problem of segmentation that we
now turn.

DO DETECTORS KNOW WHEN TO DETECT?

We have characterized detectors for place and for the stop/
semi-vowel distinction as responding to motions of a formant
from one frequency to another in a fixed time. This account is
incomplete in at least two ways. Firstly, there is no information on the broadness of tuning of the detectors: over what
range of frequencies and durations will a given transition detector respond? Secondly, how is the information in the neural
spectrogram selected by the detector? As we have noted, both
Blumstein and Stevens (1975), and Cooper, Ebert and Cole (1975),
and, to some extent, Diehl (1975a) and Ganong (1975), assume
implicitly that a transition detecting mechanism would be able
to select from the spectrogram only segments that are literally
frequency transitions, so that adjacent bursts would be ignored.
This requires that the signal already be segmented into burst,
transition, and steady-state portions, or that such selection
is an inherent property of the detectors themselves. Although
the status of bursts has received no attention, there is some
work relevant to the segmentation between transitions and steady
states.

Consider the view that transition detectors respond whenever formants move through their field. If this is true, the
same detector would respond to a given transition whether it
was in syllable-final or syllable-initial position; in other
words, adaptation should transfer across syllable position.

There is some evidence for this from an experiment by Tash
(1974), who used as an adaptor the "speech-embedded chirp" (see
Table 2). Speech-embedded chirps are constructed by preceding
the chirp portion of the extreme [bae] and [dae] stimuli in the
test series with steady-state vowels having formant frequencies
the same as the initial formant frequencies of the chirp. Although the chirp is at the end of the adaptor, an adapting effect is found on a CV test series, where the transitions are in
initial position. This implies that detectors for CV's may
also operate for VC's (as long as the transitions are at the
same frequency). There is, however, an alternative interpretation of the result: the initial formant frequencies of the
speech-embedded d-chirp are at precisely the same values as the

formant frequencies at the onset of the test [dae], while the
embedded b-chirp corresponds to the test [bae]. There is,
therefore, the possibility that in speech-embedded chirps it is
the initial part of the vowel that has the adapting effect, not
the final chirp.

That steady state vowels can adapt [b-d] series can be
demonstrated by an analysis of the data of Cooper (1974a, Experiment 3) where adaptation of a [bae-dae] series is attempted with
[ae], and Ades (1974a, Experiment 1), where [aeb] and [aed] were
used. (In the latter case, [aeb] and [aed] both shifted the
phoneme boundary in the same direction, their differential effect being miniscule (see Table 2), so their effects are attributable to the initial vowel [ae].) Overall, there is no significant effect in either experiment, but a close examination
reveals that individual subjects' boundaries are shifted by
[ae] in a direction that depends on the position of their unadapted boundaries. In Fig. 6, the boundary shift caused by
adaptation with [ae] in the studies of Cooper and Ades is plot-
ted against the position of the unadapted phoneme boundary, for
each subject. The graph shows that the more d-ward the unadapted boundary and therefore, by hypothesis, the more b-like the
flat F2 and F3 transitions of [ae], the more the vowel b-adapts
the subject. The correlation is significant in both experiments
($r = 0.76$, $p < 0.025$; $r = 0.92$, $p < 0.01$).

This adapting effect of [ae] clouds an interpretation of
the speech-embedded chirp effect which attributes adaptation to
the final chirp, rather than the initial steady state. But more
importantly, it establishes that the F2 and F3 transitions detectors which contribute to the perception of stop consonants
are engaged, even when the F1 is such as to signal that no stop
consonant is present. <u>This is just what would be expected if
information is extracted from each formant independently.</u> A
similar point is made in an experiment of Bailey (1975a) where a
[b_3-d_3] series is d-adapted by a [ja] whose transitions completely overlap those of [d_3] (see Fig. 7). [d_3] on the other
hand, did not affect the [wa-ja] series, presumably because here
the overlap is only partial. Thus, adaptation may occur as long
as the adaptor contains transitions with the same trajectory as
the information-bearing portion of the test stimulus, even
though the adaptor is a vowel or semi-vowel and the test a consonant.

That adaptation of CV mechanisms is possible with a steady-
state vowel highlights the segmentation problem in a particularly striking way. If each detector is engaged literally whenever
a formant passes from one frequency to another in a time T, then
the sustained vowel [ae] would activate the same detector over
and over again. The [ae] would, in effect, be segmented into
periods of duration T, in every one of which F2 and F3 information would be contributing to adaptation. This seems

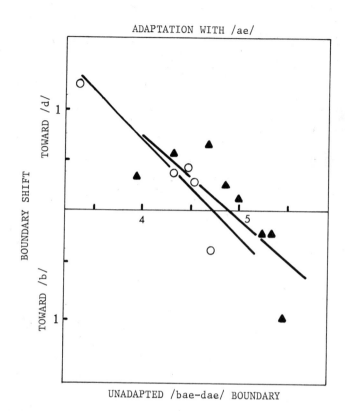

Fig. 6. Boundary shifts of individual subjects along a [bae-dae] continuum, after adaptation with the vowel [ae], as a function of the position of their unadapted boundaries. The scale of the latter in arbitrary stimulus units ranges from [b] (low numbers) to [d] (high numbers). Data from Ades (1974a), circles and Cooper (1974a), triangles; and regression lines of boundary shift on unadapted boundary.

uneconomical. An alternative is that detectors only operate at rapid onsets in amplitude, so that the F2 and F3 trajectories are extracted from only the initial period T of the vowel, and only the initial period carries the vowel's CV-adapting effect. Presumably, another set of detectors, whose activities would be contingent on sudden amplitude offsets, would be responsible for the boundary shifts in VC test series which have been observed following adaptation with VC adaptors by Ades (1974a). That initial and final detectors are distinct is suggested by the fact that there was absolutely no transfer of adaptation, positive or

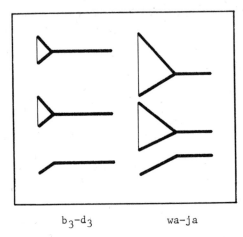

b₃-d₃   wa-ja

Fig. 7. [b-d] and [wa-ja] test series from Bailey (1975a).
[ja] d-adapts the [b-d] continuum, but [d] has no effect on the
[wa-ja] continuum. Note that the [ja] transitions completely
overlap those of [d], but not vice versa.

negative, between CV and VC syllables (Ades, 1974a).

The notions of amplitude onset and offset must be extended
to refer to sudden increases and decreases. The formant transitions in [sae] do not occur at the very onset of the syllable,
but between the frication noise of the [s] and the vowel.
Ganong (1975) has shown that a synthetic [sae], with transitions,
has as strong an adapting effect on a [bae-dae] series as [dae]
itself. The increase in energy at the point where frication
ends and voicing begins must therefore be great enough to activate the transition detectors. All the same, detectors that
respond only at rapid amplitude increases, or decreases, would
clearly be of only limited use in running speech. They would
pick up transitions associated with stops and with consonants
in initial and final position, but would ignore semi-vowels and
liquids ([r] and [l]) in medial position, where the degree of
vocal tract closure is insufficiently great to cause dramatic
changes in the amplitude envelope.

Another possibility that should be considered, then, is that
detectors are enabled not only at amplitude change points, but
also wherever the frequency spectrum shows discontinuities.[6]

---

[6]One way of automatically segmenting the input waveform is to
double differentiate each formant with respect to time. The effect of this would be to highlight discontinuities in the formants (i.e. changes in frequency change).

At present, there exist no data to resolve this issue. Whether detectors are on "free run", responding whenever a formant passes through their field, or whether they are activated only upon some change in the spectrum, remains an important area for future research.

PERCEPTUO-MOTOR ADAPTATION

The variability of the acoustic cues across context is a result of the way speech is produced. We have already mentioned the effects of rate on the separation cue in voicing, the effect of vocal tract size on the spectral position of the formants, and the way in which the transition cues to place are conditioned by adjacent vowels. These and other instances of the lack of invariant cues have led many investigators to propose that perception is mediated by mechanisms that have knowledge of production constraints, and take them into account. Models of this sort have taken various forms; such as, the motor theory of speech perception (Studdert-Kennedy, Liberman, Harris and Cooper, 1970) and analysis-by-synthesis (Stevens and House, 1972). But support for them has been for the most part somewhat circumstantial.

In an effort to find evidence for this perceptuo-motor link, W.E. Cooper and his colleagues have investigated the possibilities, (1) that subjects' repeated utterance of a syllable will lead to adaptation of their perceptual system and (2) that perceptual adaptation will cause changes in subsequent production. If either were the case, it could be argued that there are (fatiguable) mechanisms jointly responsible for speech perception and speech production.

The first type of perceptuo-motor effect, that of production on perception, was discussed by Cooper, Blumstein and Nigro (1975). Phoneme boundaries on a [b-d] series were shifted toward [b] after subjects had repeatedly uttered a sequence consisting of [bae, mae, vae]. This adapting effect was too variable to be significant, which is surprising given that auditory feedback was available in this condition and might have been expected to give rise to some purely perceptual adaptation. Lackner (1974) also found that subjects made few errors in the perception of their own speech when asked to repeat a syllable over and over again, though they made very many errors when listening to recordings of their own repetitions later. To explain the lack of perceptual adaptation when the repeated stimulation is self-produced, Lackner appeals to the notion of "corollary discharge" (see Teuber, 1960), a signal the motor system sends to cancel out self-produced (re-afferent) stimulation.

Corollary discharge might explain why there is little perceptual adaptation from repeated production, but it does not

address the possibility of perceptuo-motor effects themselves.
In a condition where auditory feedback was eliminated by having
the subject whisper the adapting sequence in the presence of
white noise, Cooper, Blumstein and Nigro (1975) found an even
smaller boundary shift on the [b-d] test series than when feedback was available. However, there appears to be a positive
correlation between the boundary shift shown by subjects in this
condition and in the purely perceptual condition.

The results of perceptual adaptation on subsequent production on the other hand are much more clear. In this task, the
subject is adapted by repeated presentation of a syllable in the
usual way and then required to utter a syllable. This work has
been restricted to the voicing distinction, where measurement
of acoustic cues is relatively easy. The basic finding is that
after repetition of [pi] a subject's production of [pi] has a
shorter voice onset time (Cooper, 1974d). This is in the same
direction as perceptual effects: repetition of [p] makes [p]
sound more b-like. Like perceptual adaptation, perceptuo-motor
effects transfer across place. Adaptation with [pi] shortens the
VOT of subsequent [ti] utterances (Cooper and Lauritsen, 1974),
and fatigue with [rəpi] has the same effect on [rəti] utterances
(Cooper and Nager, 1975).

The conclusion drawn from these studies is that adaptation
occurs in mechanisms that both extract cues from the speech signal and also control the timing of articulators in speech production. The most important aspect of the perceptuo-motor
effect is that it only occurs when the adapting stimulus and the
utterance are voiceless. [pi] has no effect on the VOT of subsequent [bi] utterances, and repetition of [bi] appears to have
no effect on the VOT of either voiced or voiceless sounds. This
suggests that perceptuo-motor adaptation occurs only at the level
of the separation cue, discussed in the section on perception of
voicing. Indeed, it supports the simple model described earlier
in several aspects.

Firstly, the uni-directional nature of the effects vindi-
cates the view that adaptation occurs at a level where the separation cue to voiceless and the Fl cues to voiced are processed
independently. If the cues were integrated before adaptation,
then fatigue with [bi] would be expected to increase the VOT of
voiceless utterances. Secondly, the same fact supports our
simplifying assumption, derived form the notion of a threshold
for judgements of temporal order (Hirsh, 1959; Stevens and Klatt,
1974) that while separation is a cue to voicelessness, the lack
of it (as in [bi]) is not a cue to voiced.

Cooper and Nager (1975) point out that the reason why the
production of voiced stops in unaffected (in VOT) by adaptation
is that the timing of the onset of voicing in voiced stops requires no central control. These very short VOT's are the
result of the mechanical coupling of supraglottal and subglottal

cavities: the reduction of intra-oral pressure accompanying the release forces air to flow from the subglottal cavity across the larynx. This finds a correlate in our perceptual model, to the extent that the separation cue does not contribute towards the cues for voicedness. In contrast, accounts of voicing that assume detectors for separate ranges of voice onset time (Eimas and Corbit, 1973; Cooper and Nager, 1975) require that a rather post hoc asymmetry be introduced into the model in order to explain why there are no VOT effects on the production of voiced stops.

Finally, it is probably not a coincidence that the separation cue, which we argue to be the site of these perceptuo-motor effects, is the same cue implicated by Summerfield (1974, 1975a) in the perceptual recalibration for the apparent rate of speech. This is particularly gratifying because the articulatory link with perception originally was proposed so that the perceptual mechanism would be able to cope with the variability of acoustic cues by taking production conditions into account.

SOURCE EFFECTS

In this final section, we review a class of experiments that threaten the entire edifice of detectors developed so far. These experiments suggest that the activities of detectors depends on variables that seem totally irrelevant to feature extraction. Factors like overall intensity, fundamental frequency (pitch) and the spatial location of a syllable are unrelated both to its linguistic description and to the acoustic properties for which we have supposed there are detectors. Yet adaptation is weakened when test items and adaptor differ on these dimensions. Further, all three dimensions seem to give rise to contingent effects.

The first experiment of this kind shows that fatigue incurred by repetition of a male voice does not transfer to test items uttered by a female speaker (Lackner, Goldstein and Tuller, forthcoming). The method used here did not involve phoneme boundary measurements, but was an extension of the Verbal Transformation Effect (VTE) (Warren and Gregory, 1958; Warren, 1968), in which the perception of a repeated sound appears to undergo systematic changes. In their further development of this task, Goldstein and Lackner (1974) and Lackner and Goldstein (1975) present a repeated natural speech adaptor followed by one test item. The subjects' task is to report the last two sounds in the sequence. Under conditions where the penultimate and test item are uttered by the same speaker, the probability and type of misperception of the test syllable is correlated with misperception of the penultimate item. But no such relation occurs when the adapting sequence is spoken by a male and the test item

by a female speaker (Lackner, Goldstein and Tuller, forthcoming).
      Male and female voices differ in the spectral location of
their formants, so the failure of transfer of adaptation in VTE
could be attributed to the spectral specificity of adaptation
effect (Bailey, 1973). Accordingly, Ades (forthcoming) used two
synthetic [b-d] series that were identical except in fundamental
frequency, which was at a low pitch suitable to a male speaker
in one series and at a high pitch in the other. An adapting
sequence consisting of a high pitched [b] and low [d] shifted
the phoneme boundary of the high series toward [b] and the low
series toward [d], simultaneously. (The converse effects with
a [d] high, [b] low adaptor sequence were also observed.) This
pitch contingent effect could not have occurred unless separate
mechanisms are responsible for the [b-d] distinction in high and
low pitched voices respectively.
      Another contingent effect, possibly of the same sort, can
be obtained with ear of input. When the adapting sequence is
presented to one ear and the test items to the other, transfer
is incomplete (Ades, 1974b; Lackner and Goldstein, 1975). Furthermore, it is possible to simultaneously shift the phoneme
boundary in one direction in one ear and in the opposite direction in the other ear, by presenting [bae] to one ear and [dae]
to the other simultaneously (Ades, 1974b). Warren and Ackroff
(1974) report an analogous finding using the VTE paradigm.
These experiments could be interpreted in terms of speech related property detectors which received more input from one ear
than the other (Ades, 1974b), but Darwin (1976) suggests that
such adaptation effects reflect detectors that are specific to
the spatial localization of the speaker. However, recent attempts of my own to find localization-contingent effects where
spatial position is not cued by interaural intensity differences
but by a 0.9 msec delay in interaural onset, have not led to
clear results.
      A third, highly counter-intuitive demonstration of an adap-
tion effect contingent on a seemingly irrelevant variable, is
Ganong's (forthcoming) finding of an intensity contingent adaptation. Here two [bow-gow] series were used as test material,
identical except for a 35 dB intensity difference. Fatigue with
a [b]-soft, [d]-loud sequence simultaneously shifts the identification of the soft series toward [b] and the loud series
toward [g]. This result implies that a loud adaptor will have
less effect on a soft series than a soft adaptor. In a second
experiment, Ganong found that a given adaptor has the same effect
on loud and soft series, while Hillenbrand's (1975) data indicate
that a louder adaptor has a greater effect than a soft one.
This three-way empirical impasse awaits clarification.
      A clue to why these puzzling effects should occur can per-
haps be found in the tendency for the auditory system to group
sounds together according to certain criteria, and then to process each group independently. Other examples of this are

auditory stream segregation (Bregman and Campbell, 1971), and
the perceptual mislocation of an extraneous click inserted into
a sentence (Fodor, Bever, and Garrett, 1974). The advantage in
assigning sounds to their respective streams at an early stage
is that the system may then use its knowledge of the constraints
that operate within streams. In recent experiments at Haskins
Laboratories, subjects have had to identify the final consonant
in the VC which is followed, at various time intervals, by a CV
(i.e. [ɛb, gɛ]). When this interval is very short the VC consonant is misperceived, and may not be heard at all. This cannot be an ordinary masking effect because the masking effect is
eliminated (Dorman, Raphael, Liberman and Repp, 1975) when the
CV has a pitch suitable for a different speaker than the VC.
Apparently, the silent interval is required for the perception
of the stop consonant, reflecting the vocal tract constraint
that there must be closure of between the first stop consonant
and the second. However, when the second consonant is uttered
by a different speaker, no such constraint applies. The masking
effect is also eliminated when the VC and CV are presented to
different ears (Liberman, personal communication). Perhaps the
same source effects that influence adaptation also control the
presence of this "backward masking".

If the contingent adaptation effects reflect the action of
source specific mechanisms, we would expect that any variable
capable of releasing the "masking" in the [ɛb-gɛ] experiments,
should also give rise to a contingent effect. But the implications for detector theories are unclear. One possibility is
that the detectors are not only tuned to particular acoustic
cues, but also to a given intensity, pitch, and spatial localization (Darwin, 1976). If this seems unsatisfying, an alternative might be that each incoming sound is tagged according to
its source, and that detectors, though capable of extracting
cues from any source, are assigned to one source; then cannot
be engaged by stimuli from another. In either case, unless the
contingent effects we have ascribed to source differences can
be given another explanation, they add considerable complication
to the ideas so far developed.

Whatever their theoretical import, the source effects make
the interpretation of even simple adaptation experiments much
more difficult. "Vowel-contingent" adaptation, for example,
might include components contingent not only on the vowel or the
spectral position of the formants, but also on the apparent vocal tract size of the speaker; though whether vocal tract size
changes can be themselves generate source effects as defined by
the [ɛb-gɛ] experiment is not yet known. However, one manipulation which <u>does</u> cause release from masking in that paradigm
suggests a disquieting interpretation of the non-speech adaptation effects. Dorman, et al. (1975) trained subjects to identify tweets (isolated second formant transitions) as rising or

falling and, replacing the VC by the tweet portion of the consonant, found identification of the tweets essentially unaffected by the presence of the following CV, whatever the time
interval between them.   There is, thus, the possibility that
non-speech sounds may be less effective adaptors than the entire
syllable, because they are tagged as originating from a different source.   This could, perhaps, be taken as an explication of
the speech/non-speech distinction in adaptation; and as the ori-
gin of the smaller adapting effects of all non-speech sounds
(Tables 1 and 2).
        Finally, a further type of experiment sensitive to the same
source variables are those on the Precategorical Acoustic Store
(PAS) suffix effect (Crowder, 1972), whereby the recall of the
last members of a list of items is worsened by the addition of
an irrelevant item, the suffix, to the end of the list.   The
power of the suffix to disrupt recall is reduced when it differs
from the recall list in ear of entry (Morton, 1970), spatial
localization, as defined by the spatial position of loudspeakers,
(Crowder, 1972), intensity (Morton, Crowder and Prussin, 1969),
or when the suffix originates from a different speaker than the
recall list (Crowder, 1972).   Since these are just the variables
that seem to disrupt adaptation effects, there is the intriguing
possibility that the features are extracted from material in
PAS.   Acoustic cues are extended in time, so some form of memory
in which to hold the neural spectrogram while features are extracted would not be surprising; though it would not seem to be
a requirement of the detectors we have discussed.
        Crowder (1972) points out that variables which control the
amount of disruption caused by the suffix are also the same ones
that control the disrupting effects of competing messages in
multi-channel listening tasks.   Listeners are, of course, capable
of processing more than one auditory message at a time (e.g.
Lackner and Garrett, 1972), and it is hard to see how this would
be possible unless the detectors for acoustic cues are sensitive
to differences between sources (Darwin, 1976).

CONCLUSION

        For the sake of parsimony, and with varying degrees of suc-
cess, we have presented the case that all adaptation effects
occur at one level, that of individual acoustic cues.   The adapted level appears to extract acoustic information from something
akin to a neural spectrogram, though it is unclear as yet whether
the spectrogram has already been segmented into portions of
burst, steady state, transition, silence, etc., or whether this
is a consequence of the feature extraction itself.   Compared to
other formulations of speech perception, the adaptation level
corresponds most closely to that of Fant's (1962, 1968) acoustic

features, except that Fant describes the acoustic correlates of place in terms of static configurations of the vocal tract, rather than of the motion from one configuration to another which transition detectors imply. The point, however, is that the output of the adaptation level would require considerable processing before it could be mapped into linguistic features or phonemes.

Several alternative sites of adaptation have been ruled out, even as components in the effect. The phonetic and linguistic distinctive feature level is disallowed by the failure of one item to adapt detectors for another with the same linguistic content when they differ too much acoustically (Bailey, 1973, 1975a). The syllable, interpreted linguistically (i.e. all productions of [ba] are the same) or acoustically, is ruled out by the experiments diagrammed in Figs. 5 and 7 (Bailey, 1973, 1975a): if one stimulus is sufficiently close linguistically or acoustically to a second stimulus to adapt it, then the second should adapt the first; whereas, in fact, the effects are asymmetrical.

Evidence for integrative levels, which receive input from more than one acoustic feature (Cooper, 1974b; Blumstein and Stevens, 1975; Cooper, Ebert and Cole, 1975), is somewhat stronger than for literally linguistic levels, but far from conclusive. In addition, to explain the asymmetrical adaptation in Bailey (1973, 1975a) integrative detectors for place would have to be specific to the spectral location of all their component cues.

Of course, not many experiments have looked for integrative detectors; so it is not really surprising that the evidence for them is so sparse. We have argued that the level of the component cues is the sole site of adaptation, partly in order to show what kinds of assumptions have to be made if integrative levels are to be accepted. But, in case these assumptions can be met, it is worth asking whether integrative levels of adaptation could explain all the effects discussed so far, or whether adaptation at the lower level would still have to be postulated. Two experiments are relevant here. Firstly, the perceptuo-motor effect (Cooper, 1974d) cannot be explained by an integrative level, because repetition of [bi] has no effect on the production of [pi]; the effect is restricted to the separation cue to voiceless. Secondly, Tartter and Eimas find that the isolated F3 of [gae] can shift the [d-g] boundary toward [g]: they point out that the F3 adaptor, which contains only a rising transition, does not satisfy the conditions for an integrative detector for velar stops, which would only respond to a "spread" of energy (rising F3 and falling F2)(Stevens, 1973).[7]

---

[7]Though see Maffei et al. (1973) for a case where a unit is fatigued by a stimulus that does not activate it.

Thus, if conclusive evidence for fatiguable integrative detectors could be found, it would be necessary to introduce them as a second site of adaptation, rather than the sole site, at least for transition cues to place and for the voicing distinction.

Spectral specificity is a pervasive property of the adapted level: transfer of adaptation of consonants across different vowel environments is either incomplete (Ades, 1974a; Cooper, 1974a) or non-existent (Bailey, 1975a), and vowel-contingent effects abound. This is not surprising for the cues to place of articulation, where the frequency at which information is conveyed is inherent in the cues themselves. But the work of Cutting et al. (1975) on amplitude rise time suggests that the same principle of frequency dependence extends to envelope cues as well.

To explain why adaptation effects seem to be frequency specific, it is worth remembering that the first operation that the auditory system performs is to resolve the acoustic waveform into the frequencies of which it is composed. The pertinent question is: at what stage in speech processing, if ever, is a representation of acoustic events in terms of the frequency at which they are conveyed discarded in favor of a frequency-independent representation? There is no answer to this at present, but it is obvious that frequency information must be maintained up to the level of processes like vocal tract normalization (Rand, 1971), which need formant frequency information as input. Indeed, given the model in Fig. 3, which locates cue extraction before normalization, cue extraction, and therefore adaptation, has to be frequency specific, at least for frequency cues.

Adaptation in single cells of animal visual systems is similarly restricted to lower levels (Hubel and Wiesel, 1965; Maffei, Fiorentini and Bitsi, 1973). This analogy is by no means fortuitous. The transformation from a frequency specific representation of, say, a stop versus a semi-vowel, to a representation of stop versus semi-vowel that is insensitive to the frequency location of the original cues, is a generalizing transformation that decreases specificity. It was precisely the same type of transformation between a level sensitive to visual events within small fields and a higher level responding to the same event over a much larger field ("hypercomplex cells of higher order", Hubel and Wiesel, 1965) that appears to present a barrier to adaptation in vision. Quite different is the transformation of increasing specificity between the level of independent cues and the integrative level. The above arguments against adaptation at higher levels do not therefore apply to integrative levels that are frequency specific.

It is not so clear, however, that the separation cue or, indeed, the Fl cue(s) to voicing are frequency dependent at the adapted level, because of the extreme complexity associated with the vowel-contingent voicing effects. More importantly, the separation cue is capable of perceptuo-motor adaptation (Cooper, 1974d). The perceptuo-motor effect in voicing should not be spectrally specific; that is, it should occur just as strongly when the perceptual adapting stimulus and the subjects' utterance contain different vowels. The reason for this is that the mechanism that controls the onset of voicing by adducting the vocal folds some time after consonantal release, should not be influenced by the shape the vocal tract is assuming for the vowel. The issue here is that if the perceptual adaptation of the separation cue is vowel specific and the perceptuo-motor effect is not, two levels of adaptation would be demanded.

Perceptual adaptation effects on production have been found in only one cue, but their existence is paradoxical, given what we have termed the source-contingent effects. Here adaptation brings out with great clarity one of the classic objections to theories of speech perception which implicate speech production mechanisms. According to the motor theory of speech perception (Studdert-Kennedy, Liberman, Harris and Cooper, 1970), the acoustic signal is mapped, by an as yet unknown process, perhaps via some linguistic representation, into something roughly equivalent to motor commands for the vocal apparatus; these instructions are themselves taken to be the objects of perception. The perceptuo-motor adaptation effects give strong support to this theory. But the involvement of the listener's own production system clashes with his ability to decode sounds from more than one source simultaneously, that is with source-contingent adaptation effects and multi-channel listening in general. The analysis-by-synthesis model (Stevens and House, 1972) differs from the motor theory in that the listener can be regarded as creating a model of the speaker's vocal tract as an aid to speech perception. In principle, therefore, several sources could be decoded by building a model of the vocal tract of each. However, this account would evade the fact discovered by Cooper and his colleagues that perceptual adaptation has an effect on the listener's own production, not merely on his model of the speaker's. Of course, some compromise theory which reconciles perceptuo-motor and source-contingent adaptation might exist, but we must face the possibility that one or the other of these effects is either an artifact or has been misinterpreted.

In conclusion, it is hoped that this review has clarified the nature of adaptation experiments in speech and justified their rapid development in several laboratories. Studdert-Kennedy (1975) remarked that adaptation would be of little value in speech research if it was merely sensitive to a linguistic level. We might add that the unique contribution of the technique is that it permits us to probe the crucial early stages of speech perception with some precision. The mapping from this level into the phonetic level must be quite complex and the

involvement of "active" processes (Studdert-Kennedy et al., 1970;
Stevens and House, 1972), and of the perceiver's knowledge of
speech production (Fodor, Bever and Garrett, 1974) remains obscure. But we can expect adaptation experiments to help define
the level of representation upon which these mechanisms operate.

ACKNOWLEDGEMENTS

    This paper was written while the author held a Research
Fellowship from the Medical Research Council. The author thanks
S. Brady and C.J. Darwin for helpful discussion and comments on
the manuscript.

References

Abbs, T.H. and Sussman, H.M. (1971) Neurophysiological Feature Detectors and Speech Perception: A Discussion of Theoretical Implications, J. Speech Hearing, Res., 14, 23-36.

Ades, A.E. (1973) Some Effects of Adaptation on Speech Perception, Quarterly Progress Report, Research Laboratory of Electronics, MIT, No. 111, 121-129.

Ades, A.E. (1974) How Phonetic is Selective Adaptation? Experiments on Syllable Position and Vowel Environment, Percept. and Psychophys., 16, 61-66.

Ades, A.E. (1974b) Bilateral Component in Speech Perception? J. Acoust. Soc. Amer., 56, 610-616.

Ades, A.E. (Forthcoming) Source Effects in Speech Adaptation.

Bailey, P.J. (1973) Perceptual Adaptation for Acoustical Features in Speech, Speech Perception, 2.2, 29-34. (Progress Report of the Department of Psychology, The Queen's Univ. of Belfast.)

Bailey, P.J. (1975a) Perceptual Adaptation of Speech: Some Properties of Detectors for Acoustical Cues to Phonetic Descriptions, Doctoral dissertation, Cambridge University.

Bailey, P.J. (1975b) Preliminaries to an Account of Formant Transition Perception, Speech Perception, 2.4, 55-59. (Progress Report of the Department of Psychology, the Queen's University of Belfast.)

Barlow, H.B., Hill, R.M. and Levick, W.R. (1964) Retinal Ganglion Cells Responding Selectively to Direction and Speed of Image Motion in the Rabbit, J. Physiol., 173, 377-407.

Blakemore, C. and Campbell, F.W. (1969) On the Existence of Neurons in the Human Visual System Selectively Sensitive to the Orientation and Size of Retinal Images, J. Physiol., 203, 237-260.

Blumstein, S.E. and Stevens, K.N. (1975) Property Detectors for Bursts and Transitions in Speech Perception, J. Acoust. Soc. Amer., 57, S52:Y10.

Bregman, A.S. and Campbell, J. (1971) Primary Auditory Stream Segregation and Perception of Order in Rapid Sequences of Tones, J. Exp. Psychol., 89, 244-249.

Chomsky, N. and Halle, M. (1968) The Sound Pattern of English, New York: Harper and Row.

Cole, R.A. and Scott, B. (1974a) Toward a Theory of Speech Perception, Psychol. Rev., 81, 348-374.

Cole, R.A. and Scott, B. (1974b) The Phantom in the Phoneme: Invariant Cues for Stop Consonants, Percept. Psychophys., 15, 101-107.

Cooper, F.S., Delattre, P.C., Liberman, A.M., Borst, J.M. and Gerstman, L.J., (1952) Some Experiments on the Perception of Synthetic Speech Sounds, J. Acoust. Soc. Amer., 24,

597-606.

Cooper, W.E. (1974a)   Adaptation of Phonetic Feature Analysers for Place of Articulation, J. Acoust. Soc. Amer., 56, 617-627.

Cooper, W.E. (1974b)   Selective Adaptation for Acoustic Cues of Voicing in Initial Stops, J. Phonetics, 2, 303-314.

Cooper, W.E. (1974c)   Contingent Feature Analysis in Speech Perception, Percept. Psychophys., 16, 201-204.

Cooper, W.E. (1974d)   Perceptuo-motor Adaptation to a Speech Feature, Percept. Psychophys., 16, 229-234.

Cooper, W.E. (1975a)   Selective Adaptation to Speech, in E. Restle, R.M. Shiffrin, J.N. Castellan, H. Lindman and D.B. Pisoni (Eds) Cognitive Theory, Potomac, Md.: Erlbaum Press.

Cooper, W.E. and Blumstein, S.E. (1974)   A 'Labial' Feature Analyser in Speech Perception, Percept. and Psychophys., 15, 591-600.

Cooper, W.E., Blumstein, S.E. and Nigro, G. (1975)   Articulatory Effects on Speech Perception: A Preliminary Report, J. Phonetics, 3, 87-98.

Cooper, W.E., Ebert, R.R. and Cole, R.A. (1975)   Perceptual Analysis of Stop Consonants and Glides, J. Exp. Psychol. (in press).

Cooper, W.E. and Lauritsen (1974)   Feature Processing in the Perception and Production of Speech, Nature, 252, 121-123.

Cooper, W.E., and Nager, R.M. (1975)   Perceptuo-motor Adaptation to Speech: An Analysis of Bisyllabic Utterances and a Neural Model, J. Acoust. Soc. Amer., 58, 256-265.

Crowder, R.J. (1972)   Visual and Auditory Memory, in J.F. Kavanagh and I.G. Mattingly, Language by Ear and by Eye, Cambridge, Mass.: MIT press.

Cutting, J.E., and Rosner, B.S. (1974)   Categories and Boundaries in Speech and Music, Percept. Psychophys., 16, 564-570.

Cutting, J.E., Rosner, B.S. and Foard, C.F. (1975)   Rise Time in Non-Linguistic Sounds and Models of Speech Perception, Haskins Laboratories Status Report on Speech Research, SR-41, 71-93.

Darwin, C.J. (1976)   The Perception of Speech, in E.C. Carterette and M.P. Friedman (Eds), Handbook of Perception, New York: Academic Press.

Delattre, P.C., Liberman, A.M. and Cooper, F.S., (1955)   Acoustic Loci and Transitional Cues for Consonants, J. Acoust. Soc. Amer., 27, 769-773.

Diehl, R.L. (1975a)   The Effect of Selective Adaptation on the Identification of Speech Sounds, Percept. Psychophys., 17 48-52.

Diehl, R.L. (1975b)   Feature Analysers for the Phonetic Dimension Stop vs Continuant, J. Acoust. Soc. Amer., 57, S53-Yl2.

Dorman, M.F., Raphael, L.J., Liberman, A.M. and Repp, B. (1975)
    Some Masking-like Phenomena in Speech Perception, J.
    Acoust. Soc. Amer., 57, S48:X6.
Eimas, P.D. (1974) Auditory and Linguistic Processing of Cues
    for Place of Articulation by Infants, Percept. Psychophys.,
    16, 513-521.
Eimas, P.D., Cooper, W.E. and Corbit, J.D. (1973) Some Proper-
    ties of Linguistic Feature Detectors, Percept. Psychophys.,
    13, 247-252.
Eimas, P.D. and Corbit, J.D. (1973) Selective Adaptation of
    Linguistic Feature Detectors, Cog. Psychol., 4, 99-109.
Eimas, P.D., Siqueland, E.R., Jusczyk, P. and Vigorito, J.
    (1970) Speech Perception in Infants, Science, 171, 303-
    306.
Elliott, D.N. and Fraser, W.D. (1970) Fatigue and Adaptation,
    in Foundations of Modern Auditory Theory, Vol. 1, J.V.
    Tobias (Ed), New York: Academic Press.
Fant, C.G.M. (1962) Descriptive Analysis of the Acoustic
    Aspects of Speech, Logos, 5, 3-17.
Fant, C.G.M. (1968) Analysis and Synthesis of Speech Processes,
    in Manual of Phonetics, B. Malmberg (Ed.), Amsterdam:
    North Holland.
Fant, C.G.M. (1970) Automatic Recognition and Speech Research,
    Speech Transmission Laboratory, Quarterly Progress and
    Status Report, 1/1970, 16-31. Royal Institute of Techno-
    logy, Stockholm. Also in Fant, C.G.M. (1973), Speech
    Sounds and Features, Cambridge, Mass.: MIT Press.
Fischer-Jørgensen, E. (1972) Perceptual Studies of Danish Stop
    Consonants, Annual Report (Institute of Phonetics, Univer-
    sity of Copenhagen), 6, 75-176.
Fodor, J.A., Bever, T.G. and Garrett, M.F. (1974) The
    Psychology of Language, New York: McGraw Hill.
Fourcin, A.J. (1968) Speech Source Inference, IEEE Trans. Audio
    Electroacoust. AU-16, 65-67.
Ganong, W.F. (1975) An Experiment on "Phonetic Adaptation",
    Quarterly Progress Report, Research Laboratory of Elec-
    tronics, MIT, No. 116, 2-6-210.
Ganong, W.F. (Forthcoming) An Acoustic Component of Phonetic
    Adaptation.
Gay, T., Ushijima, T., Hirose, H. and Cooper, F.S. (1974)
    Effect of Speaking Rate on Labial Consonant-Vowel Articu-
    lation, J. Phonetics, 2, 47-63.
Goldstein, L.M. and Lackner, J.R. (1974) Alterations of the
    Phonetic Coding of Speech Sounds During Repetition, Cogni-
    tion , 2, 279-297.
Harris, K.S., Hoffman, H.S., Liberman, A.M., Delattre, P.C. and
    Cooper, F.S. (1958) The Effect of Third Formant Transi-
    tion of the Perception of Voiced Stop Consonants, J.
    Acoust. Soc. Amer., 30, 122-126.

Hillenbrand, J.M. (1975) Intensity and repetition effects on selective adaptation to speech. Research on Speech Perception, 2, 57-137. (Progress Report of the Department of Psychology, Indiana University).

Hirsh, I.J. (1959) Auditory Perception of Temporal Order, J. Acoust. Soc. Amer., 31, 759-767.

Hoffman, J.S. (1958) Study of Some Cues in the Perception of Voiced Stop Consonants, J. Acoust. Soc. Amer., 30, 1035-1041.

Hubel, D.H. and Wiesel, T.N. (1965) Receptive Fields and Functional Architecture in Two Nonstriate Visual Areas (18 and 19) of the Cat. J. Neurophys., 28, 229-289.

Jakobsen, R., Fant, G. and Halle, M. (1952) Preliminaries to Speech Analysis: The Distinctive Features and Their Correlates, Massachusetts Institute of Technology, Acoustic Laboratory, Technical Report 13, (9th edition published by MIT Press, Cambridge, Mass., 1969).

Klatt, D.H. (1973) Voice-Onset Time, Frication, and Aspiration in Word-initial Clusters, Quarterly Progress Report, Research Laboratory of Electronics, MIT, No. 109, 124-135.

Klatt, D.H. and Shattuck, S.R. (1973) Perception of Brief Stimuli that Resemble Formant Transitions, Paper presented at the 86th meeting, Acoustical Society of America, Los Angeles, Calif.

Kuhl, P.K. and Miller, J.D. (1975) Speech Perception in the Chinchilla: Phonetic Boundaries for Synthetic VOT Stimuli, J. Acoust. Soc. Amer., 57, S49:X13.

Lackner, J.R. (1974) Speech Production: Evidence for Corollary-discharge Stabilization of Perceptual Mechanisms, Percept. and Motor Skills, 39, 899-902.

Lacker, J.R. and Garrett, M.F. (1972) Resolving Ambiguity: Effects of Biasing in the Unattended Ear, Cognition, 1, 359-372.

Lackner, J.R. and Goldstein, L.M. (1975) The Psychological Representation of Speech Sounds, Quart. J. Exp. Psychol., 27, 173-185.

Lackner, J.R., Goldstein, L.M. and Tuller, B. (Forthcoming) Further Observations on the Psychological Reality of Speech Sounds.

Ladefoged, P. and Broadbent, D.E. (1957) Information Conveyed by Vowels, J. Acoust. Soc. Amer., 29, 98-104.

Liberman, A.M., Cooper, F.S., Shankweiler, D.P. and Studdert-Kennedy, M. (1967) Perception of the Speech Code, Psychol. Rev., 74, 431-461.

Liberman, A.M., Delattre, P.C., Gerstman, L.J. and Cooper, F.S., (1956) Tempo of Frequency Change as a Cue for Distinguishing Classes of Speech Sounds, J. Exp. Psychol., 52, 127-137.

Liberman, A.M., Harris, K.S., Hoffman, H.S. and Griffith, B.C. (1957) The Discrimination of Speech Sounds within and

Across Phoneme Boundaries, J. Exp. Psychol., 53, 358-368.

Liberman, A.M., Harris, K.S., Kinney, J. and Lane, H. (1961) The Discrimination of Relative Onset Time of the Components of Certain Speech and Non-Speech Pattern, J. Exp. Psychol., 61, 379-388.

Lisker, L. (1975) Is is VOT or a First Formant Transition Detector? J. Acoust. Soc. Amer., 57, 1547-1551.

Lisker, L. and Abramson, A.S. (1964) A Cross-language Study of Voicing in Initial Stops: Acoustical Measurements, Word, 20, 384-422.

Maffei, L., Fiorentini, A., and Bitsi, S. (1973) Neural Correlate of Perceptual Adaptation to Gratings, Science, 182, 1036-1038.

Miller, J.D., Pastore, R.E., Wier, C.C., Kelly, W.J. and Dooling, R.J. (1974) Discrimination and Labelling of Noise-buzz Sequences with Varying Noise-lead Times, J. Acoust. Soc. Amer., 55, 390 (A).

Miller, J.D. and Eimas, P.D. (1975) Studies on the Selective-tuning of Feature Detectors for Speech, Developmental Studies of Speech Perception, 3, 103-116 (Progress Report of the Walter S. Hunter Laboratory of Psychology, Brown University).

Morton, J. (1970) A Functional Model for Memory, in D.A. Norman (Ed) Models of Human Memory, New York: Academic Press.

Morton, J., Crowder, R.G., and Prussin, H.A. (1969) Experiment and Theory in Short-term Memory, unpublished paper.

Nabelek, I. and Hirsh, I.J. (1969) On the Discrimination of Frequency Transitions, J. Acoust. Soc. Amer., 45, 1510-1519.

Ohman, S.E.G. (1966) Coarticulation in CVC Utterances: Spectrographic Measurements, J. Acoust. Soc. Amer., 39, 151-168.

Pisoni, D.B. (1971) On the Nature of Categorical Perception of Speech Sounds, Doctoral Dissertation, University of Michigan.

Pisoni, D.B., Sawusch, J.R. and Adams, F.T. (1975) Simple and Contingent Adaptation Effects in Speech Perception, Research on Speech Perception, 2, 22-55 (Progress Report of Department of Psychology, Indiana University).

Rand, R.C. (1971) Vocal Tract Size Normalization in the Perception of Stop Consonants, Haskins Laboratories Status Report on Speech Research, SR-25/26, 141-146.

Stevens, K.N. (1973) Potential Role of Property Detectors in the Perception of Consonants, Quarterly Progress Report, Research Laboratory of Electronics, MIT, No. 110, 155-168.

Stevens, K.N. and House, A.S. (1972) Speech Perception, in J.V. Tobias (Ed), Foundations of Modern Auditory Theory, Vol. 2, New York: Academic Press.

Stevens, K.N. and Klatt, D.H. (1974) The Role of Formant Transitions in the Voiced-Voiceless Distinction for Stops, J. Acoust. Soc. Amer., 55, 653-659.

Strange, W. and Halwes, T. (1971) Confidence Ratings in Speech
    Perception Research: Evaluation of an Efficient Technique
    for Discrimination Testing, Percept. Psychophys., 9, 182–
    186.
Studdert-Kennedy, M. (1975) Speech Perception, in N.J. Lass
    (Ed), Contemporary Issues in Experimental Phonetics,
    Springfield, Ill: Thomas.
Studdert-Kennedy, M., Liberman, A.M., Harris, K.S. and Cooper,
    F.S. (1970) Motor Theory of Speech Perception: A Reply
    to Lane's Critical Review, Psychol. Rev., 77, 234–249.
Summerfield, A.Q. (1974) Toward a Detailed Model for the Per-
    ception of Voicing Contrasts, Speech Perception, 2.3, 1–
    26. (Progress Report of the Department of Psychology,
    The Queen's University of Belfast.)
Summerfield, A.Q. (1975a) Cues, Contexts and Complications in
    the Perception of Voicing Contrasts, Speech Perception
    2.4, 99–129. (Progress Report of the Department of
    Psychology, The Queen's University of Belfast).
Summerfield, A.Q. (1975b) Aerodynamics Versus Mechanics in
    the Control of Voicing Onset in Consonant Vowel Syllables,
    Speech Perception, 2.4, 61–72, (Progress Report of the
    Department of Psychology, The Queen's University of Belfast)
Summerfield, A.Q., and Haggard, M.P. (1974) Perceptual Pro-
    cessing of Multiple Cues and Contexts: Effects of Following
    Vowel Upon Stop Consonant Voicing, J. Phonetics, 2, 279–
    295.
Tarrter, V.C. and Eimas, P.D. (1975) Role of Auditory Feature
    Detectors in the Perception of Speech, Developmental
    Studies of Speech Perception, 3, 66–81 (Progress Report of
    the Walter S. Hunter Laboratory of Psychology, Brown
    University).
Tash, J.D. (1974) Selective Adaptation of Auditory Features
    in Speech Perception, Research on Speech Perception, 1,
    33–81, (Progress Report of the Department of Psychology,
    Indiana University).
Teuber, H.L. (1960) Perception, in J. Field, H. Magoun and
    V. Hall (Eds), Handbook of Physiology: Section I, Neuro-
    physiology, Vol. III, Washington D.C.: American Physio-
    logical Society.
Verbrugge, R.R. and Liberman, A.M. (1975) Context-conditioned
    Adaptation of Liquids and their third Formant Components,
    J. Acoust. Soc. Amer., 57, 552:Y11.
Warren, R.M. (1968) Verbal Transformation Effect and Auditory
    Perceptual Mechanisms, Psychol. Bull., 70, 261–270.
Warren, R.M. and Ackroft, J.M. (1974) Dichotic Verbal Trans-
    formations: Evidence of Separate Neural Processors for
    Identical Stimuli, J. Acoust. Soc. Amer., 56, 554.
Warren, R.M. and Gregory, R. (1968) An Auditory Analog of the
    Visual Reversible Figure, Amer. J. Psychol., 71, 612–613.

Whitfield, I.C. and Evans, E.F. (1965) Responses of Auditory
    Cortical Neurons to Stimuli of Changing Frequency, J.
    Neurophys., 28, 655-672.

NEUROPSYCHOLOGICAL ASPECTS OF ORTHOGRAPHIC REPRESENTATION

John C. Marshall

Department of Psychology
University of Edinburgh

Introduction

The vast majority of the world's languages have never been
committed to writing; in societies which are literate, all normal children learn to speak (and to comprehend speech) before
they learn to write and read; many children in literate societies experience great difficulty in learning to read and write
without manifesting equivalent difficulties with the spoken
language.

Given these facts, it is not entirely unreasonable to think
of speech as the primary 'vehicle' for expressing linguistic
form, and to suppose that writing is "only a more or less im-
perfect reflection" of speech (Sturtevant, 1917). A writing
system--or orthography--then becomes by definition a mapping of
a level (or of elements from a variety of levels) in the structural description of a spoken language. Orthographies are thus
bounded at two ends of the chain of possible visual communications. They must not represent conceptual form (except via
levels of description which are required to characterize the
spoken language). ∎ is a pictographic, not orthographic,
representation of "Petrol and oil available to midnight". The
symbol maps indifferently onto all paraphrases of its 'content'.
At the 'peripheral' end of the communication process, orthographies must not represent acoustic form (except indirectly via
a higher linguistic level). The output of a sound spectrograph
is 'visible speech', not writing. It should be stressed, however, that visible speech is just as 'conventional' as orthographic representation. The output of a speech intonation
spectrometer (Jeffrey and Longuet-Higgins, 1975) displays a
quite different set of characteristics of the speech wave from
those shown by the sound spectrograph. The conventions--or
putative significant elements of speech, as they would be called
--are imposed by the machine (or rather by its designer) in much
the same way that orthographic conventions are imposed by their
designers (or more usually by many generations of designers).

In short, orthographies notate linguistic form, not conceptual or acoustic form. It would be possible in principle for
an orthography to mark all levels of linguistic form. In such
a case, however, it would be more usual to call the

representation a derivation in the theory of formal grammar, and,
more importantly, it might be somewhat inefficient to read (and
to print) novels in this form. The major writing systems with
which we are familiar therefore tend to pick one (or two or
three) levels and provide a (more or less) consistent depiction
of those levels. The three most popular levels are 1: Morphem-
ic (e.g. Chinese), 2: Syllabic (e.g. Japanese Kana), and
3: Phonemic (e.g. English). In recent years, much thought has
been devoted to the question "What are the formal properties of
an optimal writing system for a given language?" (Halle, 1969).
By an optimal orthography, Halle means "....the one that is most
readily learned and once learned is utilized with the fewest
errors by normal subjects." Halle's question is made particularly interesting by the implication that the peculiar form of
a given spoken language may, in part at least, determine which
of its levels should be represented in its writing system.
That is, what is good for English may not be good for Chinese
(and vice-versa). What arguments, then, could be put forward
for there being 'natural' relationships between particular
spoken languages and particular orthographies?

In languages which have strong phonological constraints
upon morpheme shapes and where most words are monomorphemic
(e.g. classical Chinese), severe problems of homophony can arise.
Chao (1968) notes that 116 distinct characters ('words') are to
be found under the syllable hsi ([śi]) in Goodrich's pocket
dictionary. This enables Chao to write a short story which
would consist, when spoken, of nothing but repetitions of hsi
(in each of four tones, admittedly). If we assume that the contexts in which the spoken language is used can provide more cues
to the disambiguation of homonyms than is typically the case
with written material, one can see that alphabetic representations may not always be the optimal form of speech for the eye.
One cannot ask the printed page "Do you mean 'funny ha-ha' or
'funny peculiar'" (Klima's discussion of Li Jiang, an extant dia-
lect of Southwest Mandarin develops this point beautifully
(Klima, 1975)). In like vein, Chomsky and Halle (1968) have
argued that the productivity of certain derivational processes
in English (e.g. nation - national; electric - electricity;
bomb - bombard) makes the lack of a simple one-to-one relationship between grapheme and phoneme a desirable feature of English
orthography. If different signs were used for the a in nation
and the first a in national (in order to map the surface phonology more consistently) the result would be to obscure the
crucial morphological relationship between the words.

We must not assume that, say, the Pitman Initial Teaching
Alphabet will provide a better representation of English than
our present orthography. The consistent mapping of sound is not
an end in itself, as can easily be seen by considering a lower
level than phonology. No one would argue that--for readers

rather than phoneticians--the International Phonetic Alphabet is necessarily the optimal orthography for all the world's languages. The last thing one wants a script to reflect is predictable phonetic variation of the type /p/ as aspirated in pit but unaspirated in spit. The reader's goal is to comprehend the text, and the best way to achieve that goal is not necessarily via specifying a configuration of articulators or of articulatory outputs.

From Alphabets to Meaning

In his remarks on 'performance' models for language, Chomsky (1964) has suggested that "the process of coming to understand a presented utterance can be quite naturally described, in part, as a process of constructing an internal representation (a 'percept') of its full structural description." Could we analogously regard the process of understanding a presented 'writtenance' as the construction of an internal representation of its full structural description? Yes, but .... a number of provisos must be entered before one could accept the paradigm for either the written or the spoken language.

A century of psycholinguistic experimentation has taught us to distinguish between 1: What is formally in the signal (that which could, in principle, be extracted); 2: What is psychologically in the signal (that which is, in fact, extracted by normal subjects under normal conditions); 3: What is 'para-perceptually' in the signal (that which is imposed upon the signal by the knowledge that the subject brings to the stimulus situation). Only confusion results from conflating these three aspects of percept formation.

What then, is English orthography as a formal system? It is alphabetic (albeit in a very messy fashion). That is, there is a simple relationship between the letter sequence c + a + t and the phoneme sequence /k + ae + t/, although for the language as a whole the mapping from grapheme-to-phoneme is many-to-many rather than one-to-one. This latter condition is found, to a first approximation in, e.g., Finnish. Where written English departs from an accurate alphabetic mapping of sound, e.g. damn, the departure is often motivated by regular morphophonemic alternation, e.g. damn - damnation (Weir and Venezky, 1968). Within the framework of generative phonology, Chomsky and Halle (1968) can therefore argue that English orthography is an excellent notation provided that one accepts that the system specifies underlying phonologic representations and does not overly concern itself with phonetic realizations which can be derived by general phonological rules. As they point out, however, this does mean that the orthography is "designed for readers who know the language." The pedagogical applications of the theory

(C. Chomsky, 1970) accordingly stress the desirability of increasing the child's vocabulary and of making him 'aware' of
the structure of his language (Klima, 1972). Dale (1972) writes:
".... the child who misspells president as presedent needs to
have pointed out that it is related to preside. The child who
misspells really as relly needs to think of reality to get it
right. Apon is more likely to be written upon if the child
realizes that it is a combination of up and on. Immagrate
will become immigrate if it is connected with migrate."
     Other levels are also represented (although sometimes a re-
stricted subset of elements from a given level will be selected).
Word-boundaries are marked by space (black bird versus blackbird)
and sentences by initial capitalization and terminal period.
Some syntactic variables are marked; e.g. capitalization for
proper nouns (and, in German, capitalization for all nouns).
Aspects of phrasal structure are represented, e.g. restrictive
and non-restrictive relatives in The Chinese who are industrious
.... versus The Chinese, who are industrious, ...; punctuation
also serves to distinguish possessive from plural as in horse's
versus horses. Further disambiguation on the phrase level is
provided by judicious use of the hyphen, e.g. two-pound weights
versus two pound-weights.
     All of the above (and much more) is formally in the ortho-
graphy, but the psychologically relevant question is 'How much
of this information is available to and actually used by the
reader?'
     In the 1960's the alphabetic nature of English attracted
the most interest and a very strong conjecture concerning the
assignment of meaning to print gained considerable support. The
conjecture was that ".... written material must (my emphasis) be
coded into phonological form to be comprehended" (Laberge, 1972).
The precise phonological form in question (e.g. underlying representation, surface phonemes, phonetic realization, distinctive features) was never specified, but nonetheless it was held
to be obligatory that some phonologic representation or other
be assigned prior to the retrieval of syntactic and semantic
information appertaining to the visual stimulus.
     This unlikely sounding--and hence interesting--hypothesis
was accepted by large numbers of psychologists on the basis of
two lines of evidence, one old and one new. The old evidence
was that electromyographic techniques can sometimes detect
(in some subjects) motor activity of the speech musculature
during 'silent' reading; the new evidence was that (in some
experimental settings) the error matrices for visually presented
letters in immediate recall tasks showed patterns of confusion
along phonological rather than visual dimensions (see Conrad,
1972, for a fuller, and fairer, account of these studies). The
most notable aspect of this work is, of course, its total irre-
levance to the hypothesis it purportedly supports. This can

easily be seen by considering the hypothesis in question, (a),
in relation to its two most obvious rivals, (b) and (c).

(a) Stimulus → Visual Form → Phonologic Form →
                                Semantic Form → (Response)

(b) Stimulus → Visual Form → Semantic Form →
                                Phonologic Form → (Response)

(c) Stimulus → Visual Form →(
(→Phonologic Form →)
↑ ↓
(→Semantic Form   →)
) →(Response)

Figure 1

That some people twitch their tongues when reading to themselves is compatible with all three diagrams; similarly the
possibility of phonological confusions arises whatever the order
in which the various internal representations are assigned to
the visual stimulus. And indeed it is far from clear what kind
of evidence from normal subjects could unambiguously determine
the underlying order of encodings. These 'three-box-trick'
models have retained their popularity (Meyer, Schvaneveldt and
Ruddy, 1974) but the crucial experiments which claim to support
version (a) rather conspicuously fail to rule out the parallel-
processing version (c). One of the most ingenious such experiments is that of Rubenstein, Lewis and Rubenstein (1971). In a
lexical decision task, they claim that reaction times for rejecting (as non-words) letter sequences which are homophonous
with real words (e.g. rume → room) are longer than rejection
times for orthographically legal non-homophonous nonsense syllables (e.g. pake); it is also claimed that acceptance times
for homophonous letter-strings (e.g. maid ↔ made) are longer
than those for non-homophonous strings (e.g. lamp). The first
of these results does indeed fit hypothesis (a) if the hypothesis
is supplemented by a routine which computes the spelling patterns of items located (via a phonologic representation) in
semantic memory; hypothesis (c), however, would provide a far
more parsimonious explanation. The reliability of the second
result is in some doubt (Clark, 1973) but, if correct, is not
beyond the scope of hypothesis (c).
    Furthermore, the 'dual-encoding' hypothesis, as (c) has
come to be called, is strongly supported by the dissociations
that have been observed in cases of acquired dyslexia. Thus
brain-injured subjects have been studied who do indeed appear
to assign meaning to individual words solely via a phonological
coding of the visual stimulus (Marshall and Newcombe, 1973;

(Holmes, 1976), but the reverse dissociation--the assignment of phonological form via a semantic representation of the visual stimulus--is seen in other patients (Marshall and Newcombe, 1966).

That is, the subject with 'surface dyslexia' (Marshall and Newcombe, 1973) who

1: Can read (some nonsense syllables)
2: Whose errors are typically phonologically similar to the stimulus,
3: Whose errors are very frequently phonologically possible but non-existent lexical forms, and
4: Whose semantic reading of the visual stimulus is determined by the (frequently erroneous) phonology of the response (e.g. listen →/lɪstən/, → "it's that boxer, isn't it?"; begin → /bɛgɪn/ → "collecting money .... when you ask someome")

may be interpreted as having lost the ability to assign meaning directly to the visual stimulus, and as having an impaired ability to code grapheme sequences into phonologic representations. But contrariwise, the subject with 'deep dyslexia' (Marshall and Newcombe, 1973) who

1: Cannot read nonsense syllables,
2: Whose errors are often semantically similar to the stimulus,
3: Whose errors are (almost) never non-existent lexical forms, and
4: Whose semantic misreading of the stimulus is sometimes preceded by a (partially) erroneous visual analysis of the stimulus (e.g. sympathy → orchestra; perfect → scent, allegory → lizard)

may be interpreted as having lost the ability to assign phonologic form directly to the visual stimulus, and as having an impaired ability to analyze the visual configuration, and an impaired ability to select specific items within restricted domains of semantic memory. It is difficult to see how the patient who presented with nice produces the circumlocutory utterance "Name ... in France ... South of France" (Marshall and Newcombe, 1966), or presented with cowards, says ".... place in the Isle of Wight" (Shallice and Warrington, 1975) could have arrived at a semantic reading via a phonological form which he so clearly fails to articulate. An illustrative set of semantic misreadings from English-, French-, and German-speaking patients of this latter type is presented in Figure 2. In all cases the subject has been presented, on any one trial, with a single word. The responses are made, under no time pressure, with the stimulus in full view of the subject.

Hypothesis (a) is further embarrassed by the strong syntactico-semantic bias which is typically displayed in the reading performance of the 'deep' dyslexic: Lexical items (particularly concrete nouns) are far easier for the patients to read than

are grammatical formatives (free-standing function words of
various types). A consequence of this bias is that such subjects often read such words as knot, oar, witch, and bee successfully while failing on the homophonous forms not, or, which,
and be, despite the fact that the latter have a substantially
greater frequency of occurrence (Gardner and Zurif, 1974;

Beringer & Stein (1930)

Reichstag → Berlin
Indien   → Elephant
Fuchs   → Hase

Low (1931)

Dad   → Father
child → girl
vice → wicked

Goldstein (1948)

era   → time
wed   → marry
black → dark

Marshall & Newcombe (1966)

drama → play
sick   → ill
soccer → football

Lhermitte, Lecours & Ouvry
                    (1967)

Espagne → Italie
Helene → Yvonne
nausée → peur

Weigl & Bierwisch (1970)

Strickjacke → Mieder
Feigen   → Datteln
Petersilie → Radieschen

Andreewsky (1974)

paille   → fourrage
incendie → feu
instruit → étudier

Shallice & Warrington (1975)

little → small
air   → fly
am   → be

Figure 2

Patterson and Marcel, 1976). Patterson and Marcel (1976) have
also provided more direct evidence that the subject with 'deep
dyslexia' can access the internal lexicon despite a severe impairment in phonological encoding. The patients they describe
are reasonably accurate in performing a lexical decision task—
is this letter-string a word or not?—but, unlike the control
subjects, the dyslexics show no differences in speed or accuracy
of rejection between non-words which are homophonic with real
words (e.g. frute, rair) and non-words which are not homophonic
(e.g. brug, lail). The patients are also very severely impaired, relative to controls, when asked to decide whether or
not two written words rhyme with each other. When the correct
decision can be made on the basis of visual similarity alone,
(walk-talk = rhyme; bale-crow ≠ rhyme) the patients perform
fairly well, but when the correct decision cannot be made on

visual criteria (<u>newt-mute</u> = rhyme; <u>leaf-deaf</u> ≠ rhyme) they
perform very poorly indeed. (Closely similar results are also
reported by Saffran and Marin, 1976).

   Studies of normal subjects also indicate that conversion to
phonological form may be an optional strategy. Thus Baron
(1973) has shown that in a task where one is required to classify short phrases as sense or nonsense, subjects take no longer
to reject "homophone phrases" (<u>It's knot so</u>) than they do to
reject "true nonsense" (<u>I am kill</u>). When subjects are instructed
to respond 'Sense' if the visual stimulus has a meaningful homophonous reading, then acceptance is faster for <u>It's not so</u> than
for <u>It's knot so</u>. (These results are not prima facie consistent
with Rubenstein <u>et. al</u>'s data on reaction times to words like
<u>maid</u>, but that part of their experiment is precisely the one
that is least likely to be statistically reliable.) The notion
that assignment of phonological form is optional suggests that,
when semantic and phonological representations are being constructed in parallel, there might be a race to see which representation can be completed first. Because there is, by definition, in an alphabetically written language <u>some</u> relationship
between the internal letter structure of a word and the internal
structure of its phonological representation, one might suppose
that the phonological form is computed, that is, assigned by
rule. For example, <u>c</u> is pronounced /s/ when followed by <u>e</u>, <u>i</u>,
or <u>y</u>, and is pronounced /k/ in all other contexts (with some
exceptions); <u>g</u> is pronounced as /dz/ when followed by <u>e</u>, <u>i</u>, or
<u>y</u>, and as /g/ in other contexts (with rather more exceptions).
But there is, in general, no relationship between the internal
structure of the written (or spoken) word <u>qua</u> graphemic (or
phonologic) sequence and the internal structure of its semantic
representation. Semantic structure must accordingly be directly
addressed, not computed (in the above sense of the word).

   Even in the absence of explicit articulatory movements,
reading (for meaning) via a phonologic code (a possibility which
is allowed for in the dual-coding model) should be considerably
slower than direct visual reading. In the first case, a computational routine (which is probably intrinsically slow given
the context-sensitive nature of English orthography) must be
followed by direct addressing of semantic structure from the
phonologic code; in the second case, only one stage is required
--the direct addressing of semantic structure from the output
of the visual analyzing system. If phonological coding is
intrinsically slow (as the results of Baron and McKillop, 1975,
suggest), one might inquire as to why this subsystem is used at
all by the normal adult reader. One answer (apart from the obvious one of facilitating the comprehension of words which are
in one's spoken but not one's written vocabulary) might be that
the phonological route to meaning provides an independent check
upon the accuracy of the semantic representation obtained by

direct addressing from visual analysis. No process operates
without error, hence an error-catching device of the above nature could have considerable utility (and this is presumably
why, in natural languages, the dimension of phonological similarity between words is orthogonal to the dimension of semantic
similarity). Saffran and Marin (1976) report that in the course
of (partial) recovery from deep dyslexia, their patient did
indeed try to block errors by sounding out the first letter of
a word or fixing her lips in the position of the initial phoneme.

It seems likely that, in order to obtain a phonological
representation of a written English word, the visual code must
be marked for vowel and consonant sequences and that routines
for syllabification must be applied to this analysis (cathouse
= cat + house, cathode ≠ cat + hode) before grapheme-phoneme
conversion rules can be applied (Hansen and Rodgers, 1968). The
visual code, however, can 'call' the semantic code without these
latter intervening analyses. Experimental manipulation should
therefore be able, in principle, to 'knock out' the internal
visual representation at a point where the semantic code has
been called but the pre-analyses necessary for the eventual construction of a phonologic code have only just begun. In such a
situation any error in the semantic code could not be blocked
or corrected by the second semantic code which would normally
have 'arrived' via the phonological route. The upshot of this
should be an experimental analogue of deep dyslexia; that is,
neurologically-normal subjects should produce errors of the
type illustrated in Figure 2. Precisely this result has been
obtained by Allport (1976) in an experimental design in which
tachistoscopically exposed arrays of unrelated words are followed after brief delays by a patterned masking stimulus. Some
of the errors made by Allport's subjects are shown in Figure 3.

Allport (1976)

calf	→	lamb	jet	→	air
cat	→	dog	mast	→	sail
colt	→	foal	pie	→	tart
swine	→	pig	chive	→	shallot
glove	→	coat	spice	→	chutney

Figure 3

Such errors are, of course, commonplace when normal adults
(and children) are reading continuous text (Morton, 1964; Weber,
1968), but apart from the occasional report of 'associative'
errors in the literature on 'subliminal perception' (Dixon, 1956),

Allport's data are the first to indicate that one can "... inter-
rupt or pre-empt the operation of the grapheme-phoneme translation process" (Allport, 1976) per se. The occurrence of semantic errors when text is being read may simply reflect the
tradeoff between 'contextual' and stimulus information without
necessarily implying that the array seen by the subject on fixation n + 1 masks the internal representation which was inputted
on fixation n.

To return, then, to a distinction drawn at the beginning of
this section, the fact that English orthography is (roughly) alphabetic does not entail that a subject who knows the relationship between sight and sound will necessarily use that knowledge
when assigning meaning to print. Psycholinguists once advanced
a similar conclusion about the notorious passive; the fact that
speakers of English know that be + en and a by-phrase may signal the inversion of logical subject and logical object in
surface structure does not imply that this knowledge is used
when speakers assign a semantic representation to the sentence
"The burgundy was bought by Mary" (Wales and Marshall, 1966).

From Syllabaries and Ideographies to Meaning

There seems little doubt, then, that the dual-coding hypothesis provides a general framework within which studies of the
reading of English may profitably be organized. But an interesting question now arises: 'Does the hypothesis have universal
application?' To what extent may the model apply to all scripts?
Does reading draw upon an innate schematization of dual-coding,
with the 'fine-tuning' of the system being determined by such
factors as the particular form of script learned and the teaching methods whereby it is learned?

Certainly, one would expect to find a relationship between
type of script and the most efficient strategy for assigning
meaning to that script. This relationship is highlighted by
reports of dissociated performance between scripts consequent
upon brain-injury. Lyman, Kwan and Chao (1938) have described
a bilingual (and 'bi-scriptal') Chinese patient with a left
occipito-parietal tumor whose ability to read English was de-
cidedly superior to his Chinese ('ideographic') reading ability.
In English, he "could read many of the words right off, but
when he could not do this, he would spell the letters out loud
and from the sound of the letters he would get the word. For
example, given simple, the patient responded "s-i-m-p-l-sim...
I can't even spell it, doctor .... simple." The subject made
"only one actual mistake in reading 20 single words ('dry'
instead of day) and he understood the content of a simple
English text." 'Literal' (i.e. non-semantic) errors were also
made when writing English spontaneously and to dictation

(e.g. "intervals" → <u>tinteveeds</u>; "be" → <u>de</u>; "persecution" → <u>per-cisution</u>; "nursing" → <u>nersing</u>). But when reading (or writing) Chinese, numerous semantic substitutions were made. Some examples are given in Figure 4.

a: (pronoun plural ending → He)

(He → you)

b: ((go) to → (go) out)

(sell → shop)

c: (festival → many guests)

(start → repeat)

Figure 4

Lyman, Kwan & Chao (1938)

a: Reading
b: Spontaneous writing
c: Writing to dictation

On the assumption (perhaps erroneous) that Chinese is purely ideographic (that is, all the signs of the script specify the morphemes of the spoken language with no direct reference to the phonemic or syllabic substructure of the morpheme), one might argue that Chinese must be read via a direct sign-to-meaning code. The argument would, however, be fallacious. In principle, the visual configuration <u>as a whole</u> could be assigned a phonologic representation and that phonologic representation could address the meaning of the word (Erickson, Mattingly and Turvey,

1973). The fallacy, again, is to confuse the formal nature of
the script with the psychology of script-processing. To say
that phonologic structure cannot be computed by decomposition
from morpheme writing is not to say that sound-structure cannot
be directly assigned. The data presented by Lyman et. al (1938)
suggest that Chinese is not read via an intermediate phonological encoding (by this patient at least), but this now becomes
an empirical claim, not a logical consequence of the nature of
the script itself; conversely, for Lyman et. al's patient,
English (which, as we have seen from other studies, can be read
without phonological mediation) appears to be read and comprehended via a phonological encoding.

Further light is thrown upon the issue by considering the
nature of reading disorders in Japanese. The Japanese child
learns to read in a syllabary, Kana. (I shall ignore for the
moment the distinction between hiragana and katakana.) To a
very good approximation each complex character in the script
maps uniquely onto a syllable (Vowel, or Consonant + Vowel) in
the spoken language. The simplicity of the system--in particular the lack of context-sensitive determinants of phonologic
form--has been held responsible for the rarity of developmental
reading problems in Japan (Makita, 1968). After a few years of
schooling, the child is gradually exposed to Kanji. This script
is derived from Chinese ('ideographic') characters, but in
Japanese is only used for representing lexical formatives (e.g.
base nouns, adjectives, adverbs and verbs). It is not used for
grammatical formatives, either bound or free-standing. Each
normal, adult, educated Japanese is thus bi-scriptal. He can
write the entirety of any sentence in Kana (although it would
be childish to do so), and he can write a (formally) mixed
script with grammatical elements in a syllabary and 'content
words' in a 'morphography'.

Japanese patients have been observed with relatively well-
preserved oral reading (and writing) of Kana but severe impairment of Kanji (Imura, 1943; Sasanuma and Monoi, 1975).
In patients who manifest an impairment of the ability to understand the spoken language, it is usually found that the comprehension of both scripts is markedly impaired; Sasanuma and
Monoi (1975) therefore suggest that the condition is analogous
to the syndrome of 'isolation of the speech area' as described
by Geschwind, Quadfasel and Segarra (1968). The failure of comprehension when sentences or multi-character words are being
read by these patients shows up most strikingly in the preva-
lence of on-kun confusions. Many Kanji characters have two
readings, an on-reading (derived from the Chinese pronunciation
of the character at the time it was borrowed into Japanese), and
a kun-reading which is the native Japanese pronunciation. The
two readings are associated with different meanings, and only
the context (or the concatenation of characters) can determine

which reading is appropriate. In oral reading (and in writing) on responses where only the kun interpretation is valid (and vice-versa) are frequently made by the subject with so-called Gogi ('word-meaning') aphasia. The best English analogue I can think of would be a patient who read Kings X as "Kings Christ" and Xmas as "Cross-mas". (Edgerton, 1941, provides an excellent outline of the ideographic element in English orthography.)

Greater impairment of Kanji- relative to Kana-reading can also be seen in the syndrome of conduction aphasia. We can think of these patients as having an impairment of a phonemic response buffer (in the sense of Morton, 1970). Memory-load (or better perhaps, output organization) during reading aloud will accordingly be eased for the conduction aphasic by virtue of the one-to-one mapping between characters in Kana and syllables in the output (response) code. Such facilitation will not be possible with the reading of Kanji, for there is here no relationship between the internal decomposition of the visual stimulus and the constituent (syllabic) parts of the appropriate (oral) response. Yamadori and Ikumura (1975) have presented data from a patient with conduction aphasia which is consistent with this interpretation. When the subject was reading aloud words written in Kanji, errors and failures to respond increased dramatically as a function of the number of syllables (from one to four) required in the correct response. Over the same syllable range no decrement in performance was observed when the words to be read were written in Kana (and only a small decrement was seen for five-syllable Kana forms). This implies that the syllabary is indeed being used as a syllabary; that is, the formal structure of the code is incorporated into the processing-routines whereby the reader copes with it.

A similar conclusion may be drawn from a study by Sasanuma (1974). Sasanuma's patient displayed a relatively 'pure' reading disorder without significant impairment of writing or other aphasic manifestations. When reading Kana the subject would slowly and laboriously sound out each syllable; "....when he had finally succeeded in vocalizing every syllable of the word (with much trial and error) and obtained thus the sound shape of the word as a whole, then all at once he could grasp the word's meaning." (This kind of strategy is, of course, adopted by a subclass of dyslexic readers of alphabetic scripts, e.g. appauvrissait → "ap...appauv....pauvri...appauvriss", Dubois-Charlier, 1971). When attempting to read Kanji, Sasanuma's patient would sometimes read the word quickly and correctly as a unit; more often, however, he could produce no vocal response at all. The strategy of spontaneously moving "his right index finger over and over to trace the strokes of each character, as if trying to activate the association between the kinesthetic pattern of the word and its sound pattern or its meaning" was of little or no help. Very occasionally, he made a semantic error

when reading Kanji (e.g. <u>cold</u> → 'winter'; <u>Kyoto</u> → 'Kansai'.
Kansai is the name of the western part of Japan where Kyoto city
is situated); similar semantic errors were occasionally made
when the patient was asked to name pictures (e.g. <u>socks</u> →
'gloves'; <u>dice</u> → 'mah-jong').

We can compare Sasanuma's case with a dyslexic subject
(J.C.) who speaks (and reads) English (Marshall and Newcombe,
1973; Holmes, 1973). The two subjects are initially similar in
that neither displays any gross impairment in the expression or
reception of the spoken language. Like Sasanuma's patient,
J.C. frequently adopts the strategy of sounding out the constituents of the written word, e.g. <u>porridge</u> → "pʌ...'pʌr...
pə'rog...'prɔdzd....prəidzd...prɔdzd...pə'rɔdz...'preidzd...
'prɔdzd...prəidzd...". As Holmes (1973) writes, the subject
tries out various sequences until he <u>hears</u> one that has a match
in his lexicon. Sometimes, this leads him to give false responses which are lexical items and to accept these as correct.
Although J.C. often manages no more than a set of neologisms,
when his response <u>is</u> a word he assigns a correct semantic interpretation to the acoustic event. (The interpretation is, however, frequently erroneous vis-a-vis the visual stimulus which
provoked the acoustic response.) There are some words, however,
that J.C. reads without too much hesitation and certainly without overt practice 'try-outs'. Representative examples (plus
the subject's own commentary) include: <u>elephant</u> → "elephant...
I can't read it but it has to be 'elephant' ... only thing it
can be"; <u>sick</u> → "er! ... sick...that's what I will be." Some
of these fast responses are incorrect, e.g. <u>sauce</u> → "sausage
...I'm not reading it...I'm only recognizing it." Finally,
J.C., who is perfectly aware of what he is doing, confides in
the experimenter: "... you see, some of those words I recognize straight away...I don't read them, I recognize them ...
like 'telephone' is a big word but I recognize it.'" (Holmes,
1973). Unlike Sasanuma's subject, J.C. <u>never</u> makes an overt
semantic error, although he sometimes comes close to it in the
sense of producing an appropriate circumlocution immediately
prior to his 'recognition' reading, e.g. <u>lieutenant</u> → "well, I
think I know what that is, it's a rank .... er /lu'tɛnənt/,
isn't it." In such a case, the outright semantic error
<u>lieutenant</u> → 'rank' could be blocked by the phonological en-
coding of a very small subset of elements in the visual stimulus.

We might draw the conclusion that two (at least) strategies
can be applied to a single script (English) but that these same
two strategies are differentially utilized in Japanese. Signal-
to-meaning coding is applied preferentially to the script that
is (formally) most suitable for its efficient operation (Kanji);
signal-to-sound (and then meaning) coding is preferentially
applied when the script (Kana) harmonizes with the strategy.

But a stronger claim than this may be justified. Could it be
that, for subjects who have learnt both scripts, Kana and Kanji,
each one demands the application of the strategy which is most
appropriate? There is some evidence to this effect. Let us
return to alphabets. We have seen that English, French and
German, although formally alphabets, can be read as if the orthographic systems were ideographic. We might, then, expect that
Japanese patients who are analogous to the type of subject
whose paralexic errors are illustrated in Figure 2 should produce semantic errors when reading either Kana or Kanji. If an
alphabet can be read as if it were ideographic, it should be
possible for a syllabary to be read likewise.

But the available evidence (although admittedly limited)
suggests that this does not happen. There are many studies in
which the ability to process Kanji is fairly well-preserved relative to performance in Kana (Asayama, 1914; Kotani, 1935;
Ohashi, 1965; Sasanuma and Fujimura, 1971; Yamadori, 1975). In
some of these cases, it is reported that semantic errors occured
when the patient was attempting to read Kanji (e.g. school →
classroom; right → left, Ohashi, 1965; hospital → doctor,
Yamadori, 1975). I know of no report, however, in which a
Japanese patient has made semantic errors when reading Kana;
here the error types appear always to be visual or phonological
in nature. Within the 'two-script' system of Japanese writing,
we seem to have an analogue of the 'two languages and two
scripts' situation seen in Lyman et. al's (1938) bilingual
Chinese patient.

There are, of course, additional complications in the
Japanese studies due to the association between grammatical
class and (adult) script type. We know from studies of alphabetic orthographies that there is a correlation between the
likelihood of a patient with deep dyslexia making semantic
errors on 'content words' and showing a severe dissociation in
reading ability between content words and grammatical formatives
(Marshall and Newcombe, 1956; Böttcher, 1974). In Japanese,
type of script may be conflated with this syntactic distinction.
Fortunately, there is a way in which the two variables may be
(partially) teased apart. Japanese really has three scripts
not two. In addition to Kanji there are two physically distinct
syllabaries--hiragana and katakana. Hiragana is used for native
words and katakana for the transcription of imported Western
words (which are, of course, usually regularized to conform with
the phonological structure of Japanese). Nouns such as camera,
television and necktie are normally written in Katakana in adult
reading material. Sasanuma and Fujimura (1971) have used the
distinction between syllabaries in order to demonstrate that the
syndrome of preservation of Kanji processing relative to syllabary processing is real rather than artifactual. They selected two groups of aphasic subjects, one group with 'simple

aphasia', that is aphasia without additional apraxic or dysar-
thric impairment, and a second group with aphasia and apraxia
of speech. The spoken language of this second group was characterized by errors in phoneme-sequencing, and distortions of
phonetic realization and prosodic form. When Kanji stimuli
were used, the two groups did not differ on a reading comprehension test (matching a picture to a tachistoscopically exposed word). Group two did, however, show a severe impairment
relative to group one when the same words were exposed in hiragana script. This result is ambiguous. All the stimuli were
(native) concrete nouns, and one could therefore argue that the
native words represented in hiragana would not have been frequently seen in that form since childhood. But the group two
subjects also showed considerable impairment relative to group
one on the task of matching to pictures a set of frequently
seen imported nouns represented in Katakana (although the extent
of their relative impairment was not as great as with the hiragana stimuli).

Further evidence which may speak to the separateness of the
brain-mechanisms underlying 'direct' and 'phonologically-media-
ted' reading and writing has been obtained from English-speaking
patients. Velletri-Glass, Gazzaniga and Premack (1973) have
shown that some very severely brain-damaged subjects with global
aphasia can learn to communicate in the ideographic language
that Premack devised for teaching to non-human primates.
Velletri-Glass et. al think of their technique as mapping the
"primordial cognitive system"--which is not located in the major
language and speech areas of the brain--onto a new code. Similar results have been reported by Baker et. al (1975). A
severely-impaired subject who obtained scores of near zero on
the auditory comprehension, naming, reading comprehension, and
writing subtests of the Boston Diagnostic Aphasia examination
was studied. He observed others using an arbitrary ideographic
communication system, the basic syntactic properties of which
were modelled upon English; he was slowly drawn into the 'game'
and after only eight hours of instruction and playing the
patient was having considerable success in transmitting and receiving "information involving direct and indirect objects,
antonymic contrasts of verbs and of prepositions, judgments on
the truth value of statements, and shifts in sentence modality."

Baker et. al stress the syntactic and semantic productivity
of their subject's proficiency. He can "...deal appropriately
with novel messages," they claim. Yet a certain air of mystery
surrounds this point. If such patients can communicate efficiently in an ideographic system, why cannot they use English
orthography as if it were an arbitrary representation of mor-
pheme-shapes? The null hypothesis for the above studies (and
for the earlier demonstration by Rozin et. al, 1971, which
purports to show that American children with reading problems

can easily learn to read English represented by Chinese characters) must be: A small set of stimulus-response associations has been acquired which in no way parallels natural language abilities. A convincing falsification of the null hypothesis could be highly embarrassing for almost any current attitude to the relationship between language and thought. Baker et. al find themselves claiming that their patient may be "...in the paradoxical position of retaining cortical capacity for communication using symbols while having lost, at least temporarily, the ability to handle natural language." How could the paradox be resolved?

We know that the majority of normal right-handed subjects show a right visual field advantage for the perception and comprehension of written language. A substantial component of the RVF advantage is probably due to the relatively direct anatomical connections between the left temporal/right nasal hemiretinae and the left hemisphere areas which are specialized for language (McKeever, 1974). The RVF advantage for alphabetic material does not decrease in magnitude when Chinese characters (and subjects) are used (Kershner and Gwang-Rong Jeng, 1972). But Sugishita et. al (1976) have shown that the partially disconnected right hemisphere can recognize Kanji and respond appropriately in non-vocal matching tasks whilst it cannot recognize Kana. The right hemisphere, then, can apparently process an ideographic system when it is not inhibited from so doing by the left.

Perhaps the right hemisphere can learn a new ideographic system when left hemisphere damage is sufficiently extensive to remove its inhibitory influence; perhaps the re-routing of an already acquired alphabetic system from left to right hemisphere control is a far more difficult task. We simply do not know. Nonetheless, there is evidence from English-reading subjects which suggests that inhibitory factors play some role in the RVF superiority effect. Left cortical damage not only depresses word recognition scores in the contralateral (right) field, but also increases scores in the ipsilateral (left) field, relative to the performance of non-brain-damaged control subjects (Shai, Goodglass and Barton, 1972; Moore and Weidner, 1974).

What next?

Although our knowledge of the neurological substrate for reading skills is in a fairly primitive state, there appears to be, at the moment, no experimental or clinical evidence which contravenes the general outlines of the dual-coding hypothesis. This fact may, however, be more of a liability than a virtue, for, in part, it reflects the very loose constraints that the model imposes upon the types of 'theoretically-possible' data.

(The virtue of the 'phonological encoding is obligatory' position was that it was easy to falsify.) The dual-coding hypothesis would hold considerably greater interest if we could
specify in detail the precise nature of the code involved.
(Black-box models are typically opaque on this kind of issue.)

For example, it has usually been assumed that "semantic
coding" refers to some kind of componential analysis into semantic primes (Marshall, Newcombe and Marshall, 1970; Weigl and
Bierwisch, 1970). Errors in this code are then held to underlie
the types of response shown in Figure 2. But Beringer and Stein
suggested that such responses might rather be mediated by visual
imagery, the errors thus being analogous to object-or-picture-
naming errors. The word evokes an internal picture which the
patient then attempts to 'name'. Beringer and Stein thought
that the introspections of their patient supported this position.
For example, the response Reichstag → "Berlin" was followed by
the subject reporting "I had an impression of somewhere I had
been, where there was so much to see and to look at, you had to
sit down on a park bench and then look at it all, the whole
picture." The 'internal picture' hypothesis has recently enjoyed a resurgence on the basis of reports that the rated
'imagery value' of words correlates positively with the probability that the subject with acquired dyslexia will correctly
read individual words (Richardson, 1975; Vermeulen, 1975). The
cogency of the view has yet to be evaluated.

The more general point that I have been trying to argue
for is simply that information-processing models of reading
must take account of the diversity of orthographic principles.
It is possible that different scripts are read in much the same
way according to the same kinds of strategy and drawing upon the
same brain-mechanisms. But it may be that scripts (and methods
of teaching scripts) create strategies and even determine (in
the sense of functionally validate) certain aspects of brain-
organization. (Even within a uni-scriptal community the range
of individual variation in right hemisphere capacity is very
striking, Zaidel, 1973.)

The suggestion of 'biological Whorfianism' for reading may
appear ludicrous. But it has been mooted that the process of
learning to read may influence the pattern of hemispheric specialization characteristic of the adult (see Gorlitzer von Mundy,
1957; Cameron et. al, 1971). And more recently, Albert (1975)
has reported data which suggest that the functional patterns of
interhemispheric integration may differ as a consequence of
whether one's native language is read from left to right or
right to left. It would be a brave man who felt that our understanding of reading and the brain was sufficiently advanced to
rule out such possibilities.

References

Albert, M.L. (1975) Cerebral dominance and reading habits. Nature, 256, 403-404.

Allport, D.A. (1976) On knowing the meaning of words we are unable to report: The effects of visual masking. In S. Dornic (Ed.) Attention and Performance VI, London and New York: Academic Press.

Andreewsky, E. (1974) Un modele semantique - application a la pathologie du langage: Alexie aphasique. T.A. Informations, 2, 3-27.

Asayama, T. (1914) Über die Aphasie bei Japanern. Deutsches Archiv für klinische Medizin, 113, 523-529.

Baker, E., Berry, T., Gardner, H., Zurif, E., David, L. and Veroff, A. (1975) Can linguistic competence be dissociated from natural language functions? Nature, 254, 509-510.

Baron, J. (1973) Phonemic stage not necessary for reading. Quarterly Journal of Experimental Psychology, 25, 241-246.

Baron, J. and McKillop, B.J. (1975) Individual differences in speed of phonemic analysis, visual analysis, and reading. Acta Psychologica, 39, 91-96.

Beringer, K. and Stein, J. (1930) Analyse eines Falles von "Reiner" Alexie. Zeitschrift für die Gesamte Neurologie und Psychiatrie, 123, 473-478.

Böttcher, R. (1974) Zur Rolle von graphischen und semantisch-syntaktischen Faktoren beim Wortlesen. Zeitschrift für Psychologie, 182, 40-67.

Cameron, R.F., Currier, R.D. and Haerer, A.F. (1971) Aphasia and literacy. British Journal of Disorders of Communication, 6, 161-163.

Chao, Y.R. (1968) Language and Symbolic Systems. London: Cambridge University Press.

Chomsky, C. (1970) Reading, writing and phonology. Harvard Educational Review, 40, 287-309.

Chomsky, N. (1964) Current Issues in Linguistic Theory. The Hague: Mouton.

Chomsky, N. and Halle, M. (1968) The Sound Pattern of English. New York: Harper and Row.

Clark, H. (1973) The language-as-fixed-effect fallacy. Journal of Verbal Learning and Verbal Behavior, 12, 335-359.

Conrad, R. (1972) Speech and reading. In J.F. Kavanagh and I.G. Mattingly (Eds.) Language by Ear and Eye. Cambridge, Mass.: MIT Press.

Dale, P. (1972) Language Development: Structure and Function. Hinsdale, Illinois: Dryden Press.

Dixon, N.F. (1956) Symbolic associations following subliminal stimulation. International Journal of Psycho-Analysis, 37, 1-12.

Dubois-Charlier, F. (1971) Approche neurolinguistique du

probleme de l'alexie pur. Journal de Psychologie, 68, 39-67.

Edgerton, W.F. (1941) Ideograms in English writing. Language, 17, 148-150.

Erickson, D., Mattingly, I.G. and Turvey, M.T. (1973) Phonetic activity in reading: An experiment with Kanji. Haskins Laboratories Status Report on Speech Research, SR-33, 137-156.

Gardner, H. and Zurif, E. (1975) BEE but not BE. Oral reading of single words in aphasia and alexia. Neuropsychologia, 13, 181-190.

Geschwind, N., Quadfasel, F.A. and Segarra, J.M. (1968) Isolation of the speech area. Neuropsychologia, 13, 181-190.

Goldstein, K. (1948) Language and Language Disturbances. New York: Grune and Stratton.

Gorlitzer von Mundy, V. (1957) Zur Frage der paarig veranlagten Sprachzentren. Der Nervenarzt, 218, 212-216.

Halle, M. (1969) Some thoughts on spelling. In K.S. Goodman and J.T. Fleming (Eds.) Psycholinguistics and the teaching of reading. Newark, Delaware: International Reading Association.

Hansen, D. and Rodgers, T.S. (1968) An exploration of psycholinguistic units in initial reading. In K.S. Goodman (Ed.) The Psycholinguistic Nature of the Reading Process. Detroit: Wayne State University Press, 1968.

Holmes, J.M. (1973) Dyslexia: a neurolinguistic study of traumatic and developmental disorders of reading. Unpublished Ph.D. thesis: University of Edinburgh.

Holmes, J.M. (1976) Regression and reading breakdown. In A. Caramazza and E. Zurif (Eds.) The Acquisition and Breakdown of Language: Parallels and Divergencies. Baltimore: Johns Hopkins University Press.

Imura, R. (1943) Aphasia: characteristic symptoms in Japanese. Psychiatrica et Neurologia Japonica, 47, 196-218.

Jeffrey, D.C. and Longuet-Higgins, H.C. (1975) A real-time speech intonation spectrometer. Department of Linguistics, Edinburgh University, Work in Progress, 8, 145-148.

Kershner, J.R. and Gwan-Rong Jeng, A. (1972) Dual functional hemispheric asymmetry in visual perception: Effects of ocular dominance and post exposural processes. Neuropsychologia, 10, 437-445.

Klima, E.S. (1972) How alphabets might reflect language. In J.F. Kavanagh and I.G. Mattingly (Eds.) Language by Ear and Eye. Cambridge, Mass.: MIT Press.

Klima, E.S. (1975) Sound and its absence in the linguistic symbol. In J.F. Kavanagh and J.E. Cutting (Eds.) The Role of Speech in Language. Cambridge, Mass.: MIT Press

Kotani, S. (1935) A case of alexia with agraphia. Japanese Journal of Experimental Psychology, 2, 333-348.

LaBerge, D. (1972) Beyond auditory coding. In J.F. Kavanagh
    and I.G. Mattingly (Eds.) Language by Ear and Eye.
    Cambridge, Mass.: MIT Press.

Lhermitte, J., Lecours, A.R., and Ouvry, B. (1967) Essai d'
    analyse structurale des paralexies et des paragraphies.
    Acta Neurologica et Psychiatrica Belgica, 67, 1021-1044.

Low, A.A. (1931) A case of agrammatism in the English language.
    Archives of Neurology and Psychiatry, 25, 556-597.

Lyman, R.S., Kwan, S.T. and Chao, W.H. (1938) Left Occipito-
    parietal Brain Tumor with observations on alexia and
    agraphia in Chinese and in English. The Chinese Medical
    Journal, 54, 491-516.

McKeever, W.F. (1974) Does post-exposural directional scanning
    offer a sufficient explanation for lateral differences in
    tachistoscopic recognition? Perceptual and Motor Skills,
    38, 43-50.

Makita, K. (1968) The rarity of reading disability in Japanese
    children. American Journal of Orthopsychiatry, 38, 599-
    614.

Marshall, J.C. and Newcombe, F. (1966) Syntactic and semantic
    errors in paralexia. Neuropsychologia, 4, 169-176.

Marshall, J.C. and Newcombe, F. (1973) Patterns of Paralexia.
    Journal of Psycholinguistic Research, 2, 175-199.

Marshall, M., Newcombe, F. and Marshall, J.C. (1970) The
    microstructure of word-finding difficulties in a dysphasic
    subject. In G.B. Flores d'Arcais and W.J.M. Levelt (Eds.)
    Advances in Psycholinguistics. Amsterdam: North-Holland.

Meyer, D.E., Schvaneveldt, R.W. and Ruddy, J.A. (1974) Func-
    tions of graphemic and phonemic codes in visual word
    recognition. Memory and Cognition, 2, 309-323.

Moore, W.H. and Weidner, W.E. (1974) Bilateral tachistoscopic
    word perception in aphasic and normal subjects. Percep-
    tual and Motor Skills, 39, 1003-1011.

Morton, J. (1964) A model for continuous language behaviour.
    Language and Speech, 7, 40-70.

Morton, J. (1970) A functional model for memory. In D.A.
    Norman (Ed.) Models of Human Memory. New York: Academic
    Press.

Ohashi, H. (1965) A case of alexia with agraphia. In Clinical
    Cerebral Pathology. Tokyo: Igaku Shoin.

Patterson, K.E. and Marcel, A.J. (1976) Some observations on
    aphasia and dyslexia: Impairment in the phonological re-
    presentation of written words. Quarterly Journal of
    Experimental Psychology (In press).

Richardson, J. (1975) The effect of word imageability in ac-
    quired dyslexia. Neuropsychologia, 13, 281-288.

Rozin, P., Poritsky, S. and Sotsky, R. (1971) American children
    with reading problems can easily learn to read English
    represented by Chinese characters. Science, 171, 1264-1267.

Rubenstein, H., Lewis, S.S. and Rubenstein, M. (1971) Evidence
    for phonemic recoding in visual word recognition. Journal
    of Verbal Learning and Verbal Behavior, 10, 645-657.
Saffran, E.M. and Marin, O.S.M. (1976) Reading without phonolo-
    gy: Evidence from aphasia. Quarterly Journal of Experimen-
    tal Psychology (In press).
Sasanuma, S. (1974) Kanji versus Kana processing in alexia with
    transient agraphia: a case report. Cortex, 10, 89-97
Sasanuma, S. and Fujimura, O. (1971) Selective impairment of
    phonetic and non-phonetic transcription of words in
    Japanese aphasic patients: Kana vs. Kanji in visual recog-
    nition and writing. Cortex, 7, 1-18.
Sasanuma, S. and Monoi, H. (1975) The syndrome of Gogi (word-
    meaning) aphasia: selective impairment of Kanji processing.
    Neurology, 25, 627-632.
Shai, A., Goodglass, H. and Barton, M. (1972) Recognition of
    tachistoscopically presented verbal and non-verbal material
    after unilateral cerebral damage. Neuropsychologia, 10,
    185-191.
Shallice, T. and Warrington, E.K. (1975) Word recognition in a
    phonemic dyslexic patient. Quarterly Journal of Experi-
    mental Psychology, 27, 187-199.
Sturtevant, E.H. (1917) Linguistic Change. Chicago: University
    of Chicago Press.
Sugishita, M., Iwata, M., Toyokura, Y., Yoshioka, M., and
    Yamada, R. (1976) Long term observation of visual discon-
    nection syndrome in partially split brain patients: Kanji
    versus Kana (In preparation).
Velletri-Glass, A., Gazzaniga, M. and Premack, D. (1973)
    Artificial language training in global aphasics. Neuro-
    psychologia, 11, 95-104.
Vermeulen, J. (1975) The role of semantic variables in reading
    and writing: a case study. Subfaculteit Psychologie,
    Universiteit van Amsterdam, Report No. FL 12-8-75-169.
Wales, R.J. and Marshall, J.C. (1966) The organization of
    linguistic performance. In J. Lyons and R.J. Wales (Eds.)
    Psycholinguistics Papers. Edinburgh: Edinburgh University
    Press.
Weber, R. (1968) The study of oral reading errors: a survey of
    literature. Reading Research Quarterly, 4, 96-119.
Weigl, E. and Bierwisch, M. (1970) Neuropsychology and Linguis-
    tics: Topics of common research. Foundations of Language,
    6, 1-18.
Weir, R. and Venezky, R.L. (1968) Spelling-to-sound patterns.
    In K.S. Goodman (Ed.) The Psycholinguistic Nature of the
    Reading Process. Detroit: Wayne State University Press.
Yamadori, A. (1975) Ideogram reading in alexia. Brain, 98, 231-
    238.
Yamadori, A. and Ikumura, G. (1975) Central (or conduction)

aphasia in a Japanese patient. Cortex, 11, 73-82.

Zaidel, E. (1973) Linguistic competence and related functions
   in the right cerebral hemisphere of man following commis-
   surotomy and hemispherectomy. Unpublished Ph.D. thesis:
   California Institute of Technology.

BEYOND PARSING AND LEXICAL LOOK-UP: AN ENRICHED DESCRIPTION
OF AUDITORY SENTENCE COMPREHENSION

Anne Cutler

Massachusetts Institute of Technology

Introduction

Sentence comprehension is like riding a bicycle--a feat far
easier performed than described. Understandably, most psycholinguistic attempts to characterize the comprehension process
have resorted to simplification. If--the tacit approach seems
to be--we can isolate for experimental investigation the most
basic components of comprehension, then on the basis of what we
learn we can construct at least an outline model of the process;
after all, any model can always be enriched.

This paper is an attempt at enrichment of the basic model.
In fact, it is more than that, since it will argue that even the
most basic model of auditory sentence comprehension must incorporate more than the minimal elements to which many descriptions
have hitherto been confined. Take for example the following
enumeration of the components of a sentence comprehension model:

> The listener must recognize the appropriate set of words
> in the flow of speech directed at him. This will re-
> quire him to find a match between some internal repre-
> sentation of the way each word sounds and properties
> of the incoming information about the speech waveform.
> Once a word is recognized, its meanings must be re-
> trieved. If there are several such meanings, the one
> appropriate to the current context must be selected
> and combined with the meanings of other words in order
> to form an interpretation of the entire sentence.
> Wherever the appropriate manner of combination de-
> pends upon syntactic properties of the sentence, such
> as word order or the groupings of words into phrases,
> these syntactic properties must be determined and put
> to use. (Wanner, 1973, pp. 166-167)

Sentence comprehension consists according to this account of
three stages--identification of word boundaries, lexical look-up,
and perception of syntactic structure, or parsing. No argument
can be raised with the inclusion of these components in the
model. However, it will be suggested that these three stages do
not suffice to characterise completely the process of sentence
understanding. Take for example the sentence

  (1) Cassandra is a real genius.

This sentence may be spoken in a tone of reverence and admiration, in which case it expresses praise of Cassandra. But it may also be spoken in a quite different manner, with what is known as an ironic intonation contour (nasalized, with heavy stress on certain words). In this case it is far from expressing praise of Cassandra: quite the reverse. Ironic intonation has the effect of producing a conveyed meaning which is the converse of the literal meaning (Cutler, 1974); and there is no doubt that a listener would apprehend this conveyed meaning, not the literal meaning, of such an utterance; that is, he would comprehend that the speaker intended to say that Cassandra was anything but a genius. It is difficult to see how this fact about sentence comprehension can be encompassed by a model which includes only the operations of word identification, lexical look-up, and parsing.

Similarly, suppose (2) to be spoken in such a way that the primary stress of the sentence falls on "above":

(2)   The above sentence was ironically intended.

While the proposition expressed by the sentence can be retrieved by the three basic operations listed, an extra dimension has been added which they would not retrieve--the implication that some unspecified other sentence (or sentences) was not ironically intended. If, on the other hand, the word "intended" receives the primary stress, the implication changes: the reader will no doubt agree that (2) now suggests that the intention was not realized. Such variations are called changes in the focus of a sentence; it is surely the case that implications of the kind they express, like intonationally signalled irony, are computed when a sentence like (2) is heard.

The following pages contain some specific suggestions about the manner in which the basic parsing-plus-lexical-look-up model of sentence comprehension needs to be enriched. One suggestion will be the inclusion of a processing stage subsequent to the establishment of the literal meaning of a sentence in which this meaning may be revised. This stage will be called stage B; accordingly, "stage A comprehension" will refer to the construction of a sentence's literal interpretation. Most of stage A comprehension is accomplished before the utterance has been completed.

Making Use of Prosody

It will not have escaped the reader's notice that both ironic intent and focus information are intimately bound up with the prosodic, or suprasegmental, structure of a sentence: irony can be signalled by nasalization, exaggeratedly slow speaking rate, very heavy stress, or all of these, while the focus of a

sentence in general corresponds to the location of the main sentence stress. In order to examine how these phenomena might be
registered in sentence processing, then, let us consider the
suprasegmental aspects of speech.

These consist, it is generally agreed, of variations in
pitch, stress and timing relations. Pitch variation is usually
arbitrarily defined as variation in the fundamental frequency of
a signal; the other two dimenisons, however, are not so easily
circumscribed. Timing, for example, is certainly expressed in
the relative durations of the various segments of the speech
wave; but silent intervals that can occur between segments also
play a role in determining the rhythmic pattern that is an important aspect of a sentence's timing. Stress, again, is a perceptual feature which is manifested acoustically by an extremely
complex interaction between all suprasegmental aspects of the
utterance, not to mention segmental factors as well; vowel quali-
ty (formant structure) is a segmental phenomenon, but vowel reduction, namely a shift in formant frequency from the sounds
which fall in the outer portions of the vowel quadrant towards
those of the center (/ə/, schwa), is a phenomenon determined by
stress level in many languages. (For a comprehensive description of the nature of suprasegmental phenomena see Lehiste, 1970).

Some evidence that suprasegmental factors play an important
role in stage A comprehension of a spoken sentence has recently
been collected from studies using the phoneme-monitoring technique. This is a task in which subjects are asked to understand
a sentence and at the same time to listen within it for the
occurrence of a specified word-initial target sound, and to press
a button when they hear a word beginning with this sound. Reaction time (RT) to the target phoneme in this task, it is argued,
is directly related to the difficulty of processing the sentence
at the time when the target phoneme occurs--RTs are lengthened,
for example, by the occurrence immediately prior to the target-
bearing item of a low frequency word (Foss, 1969) or of an
ambiguous item (Foss, 1970).

It was noticed in certain phoneme-monitoring studies that
RTs were faster when the target-bearing item itself was an "open
class" item (noun or verb) than when it was a "closed class"
item (for example, a preposition or conjunction). It is generally the case that open class words carry a higher level of sentence stress than do closed class words. Accordingly, Cutler
and Foss (in press) measured RTs to targets on open and closed
class items while manipulating stress level of the target-
bearing item independently. They found that RTs were significantly faster to targets on stressed items, irrespective of
word class, whereas removal of the stress differences between
open and closed class items also removed the RT difference between them.

It might be argued that this result bears no great import,

since there are notable acoustic differences between stressed
and unstressed words. Stressed words are in the main longer in
duration and higher in pitch than unstressed words, and their
amplitude is somewhat greater; unstressed words, moreover,
generally undergo vowel reduction. Thus one might wish to explain the Cutler and Foss result in terms of acoustic advantages
of stressed items: heightened intelligibility facilitates identification of the phonemes, and location of a match for the
phonemic string in the mental lexicon, thus allowing faster
identification of the target phoneme in the required word-initial
position.

      That this is not the whole story, however, is demonstrated
by a further experiment (reported in Cutler, 1975). In this study
a number of sentences were recorded in two intonation versions,
with the target-bearing item of each sentence receiving high
stress in one version and low stress in the other. Thus in (3),
in which the target phoneme is /d/, the target-bearing item
"dirt" receives high stress in (3a) and reduced stress in (3b):

      (3) a.   She managed to remove the dirt from the rug,
               but not the berry stains.

          b.   She managed to remove the dirt from the rug,
               but not from their clothes.

The stress assigned to the target item was determined, as can be
seen from these examples, by varying the endings of the sentences to manipulate what is commonly called contrastive stress
(Bolinger, 1961). The point at which the two versions of each
sentence vary, however, occurs sufficiently later than the target for the response button to have been pressed by the time
that part of the sentence is heard by the subject.

      In addition to these two versions of each sentence, a third
version, spoken in as neutral a tone as possible, was recorded.
In this third version the stress level of the target item was
intermediate, falling between the high- and low-stress versions.
The actual target-bearing words were then removed from the high-
and low-stress versions of each sentence by tape-splicing, and
replaced by identical copies of the same target-bearing item
taken from the intermediate-stress version of the sentence. As
a result of this manipulation, the two experimental versions of
each sentence contained acoustically identical target-bearing
items. The two versions differed, however, in the intonation
contour which preceded them, one contour being consistent with
the occurrence of a high-stress item at the location of the
target-bearing word, the other being consistent with reduced
stress at that point.

      If acoustic advantages of stressed items were solely re-
sponsible for the RT advantage of stressed target words in the
Cutler and Foss study, no difference would be expected between
the high- and low-stress versions of each sentence, since the

target-bearing items themselves were acoustically identical. In fact, however, significantly faster RTs were recorded for the items which occurred in high-stress position; i.e., the stressed words maintained their RT advantage, despite the fact that they had lost the advantages of greater intelligibility.

The sole difference between the high- and low-stress versions of each sentence in this experiment lay in the intonation contour preceding the target-bearing item. It must therefore be assumed that the RT difference reflects an effect of this contour variation. We must assume, in other words, that the subjects were making use of the suprasegmental information in such a way that their processing of the sentence at the point of occurrence of the target-bearing item was affected by whether that item was expected, on the basis of the intonation contour which preceded it, to carry high or low stress.

Since the RTs were faster if the item was expected to bear high stress, processing at that point of the sentence was apparently facilitated in some way by the expectation of stress. A reasonable interpretation is that particular attention has been directed to locations of highly stressed items. Moreover, the effect was produced in this case solely by manipulation of the preceding intonation contour, indicating that an active search for the locations of high stress proceeds in the form of a tracking of the intonation contour. A model of sentence comprehension which incorporates a search for highly stressed items is obviously more complex than a basic parsing-plus-lexical-look-up model. However, the evidence of these phoneme-monitoring studies compels us to expand the model in this way.

Semantic Focus

In the introductory section of this paper the notion of semantic focus was introduced. Sentences (4) and (5), in which upper case letters represent highly stressed items, differ on this dimension, the focus of the former being "Felicity", of the latter "caviar".

    (4) FELICITY eats caviar for breakfast.

    (5) Felicity eats CAVIAR for breakfast.

Jackendoff (1972) defines focus as the information in a sentence which is assumed by the speaker not to be shared by him and his audience. Halliday (1967) draws a distinction between "new" and "given" information, where "what is focal is 'new' information; not in the sense that it cannot have been previously mentioned, although it is often the case that it has not been, but in the sense that the speaker presents it as not being recoverable from the preceding discourse" (p. 204).

Our current problem is the extent to which this notion

is relevant to the description of sentence processing. Can it
be said, for example, that in order to understand a sentence it
is necessary to have identified its semantic focus? If a hearer
understands (4) and (5) as identical, can he be said to have
understood them?

   The position taken here will be that he cannot. That is, it
will be argued that focus information constitutes an integral
part of the semantic representation constructed by the sentence
comprehension device. Successful comprehension necessarily includes the knowledge that (4) and (5) are different; further,
comprehension of (6) will entail that the hearer realizes that

   (6) Felicity eats CAVIAR for breakfast?

acceptable responses include (7) and (8), but not (9) or (10):

   (7) Yes, she like to indulge herself.

   (8) She's on a fish-only diet.

   (9) Did you think it was Samantha who did?

   (10) No, for dinner.

   There is evidence from at least one psycholinguistic study
that focussed items in a sentence are differentially represented
from non-focussed items shortly after the completion of comprehension. Hornby (1974) presented subjects with cleft and pseudo-
cleft sentences and required them to judge whether a picture presented for a brief interval beginning one second after presentation of the sentence accurately reflected the sentence's content.
He found that subjects were more likely to make errors with respect to the noun phrase in the non-focussed part of the sentence
than with respect to the focussed noun phrase. For example, a
subject who had heard (11) would be more likely to respond

   (11) It is the girl who is petting the dog.

"true" to a picture of a girl petting a cat than to a picture
of a boy petting a dog.

   Suppose, however, that it could be shown that whether or
not an item is focussed affects the way it is processed during
Stage A comprehension. As we have seen, the focus of a sentence
and the location of that sentence's main stress coincide; would
it therefore be beyond reason to suggest that the active search
for the main sentence stress during sentence comprehension is in
fact a search for the sentence's focus?

   If this is indeed the proper explanation for the stress effect, we would expect an effect of focussing an item in a sentence analogous to the effect of assigning an item high stress.
That is, we should be able to demonstrate that phoneme-monitoring
RTs are accelerated if the target word is focussed.

   The main problem with such an approach lies in the fact that
sentence focus and primary sentence stress coincide; stress

produces an effect on phoneme-monitoring RTs, therefore to demonstrate that focus produces an analogous effect it is necessary
to remove the confounding with stress, to keep item stress constant whether or not the item is focussed. Thus, focus cannot
in this case be defined as the location of the main sentence
stress; instead, an alternative means of focussing a particular
item must be used. Among possible solutions is the use of the
cleft (e.g., 12) and pseudo-cleft (e.g., 13) constructions, which
are also considered to have a focussing effect (Jackendoff,
1972; Akmajian, 1970).

    (12)   It was cleft sentences that Portia refused
            to utter.

    (13)   The construction that Doris used most was the
            pseudo-cleft.

    Two investigations provide evidence for an effect of focus
in phoneme-monitoring analogous to the effect of stress. In
the first (reported in Cutler, 1975), focus was manipulated by
the use of cleft and pseudo-cleft sentences describing simple
agent-action-object situations; RT to a target-bearing item
which was clefted was compared to RT to the same item in non-
clefted position. Since cleft and pseudo-cleft sentences cannot be spoken naturally without assigning high stress to the
clefted item, the sentences were not spoken, but instead were
generated on a speech synthesizer, with which it was possible to
hold the fundamental frequency and amplitude inputs for a sentence constant, and to use identical durational specifications
for each occurrence, clefted or non-clefted, of any individual
item. Thus acoustic invariance of the target-bearing item
across its various appearances was ensured. The results indicated that focussed (clefted) target-bearing items indeed
elicited faster RTs than the same items when not focussed.
    However, it is unfortunately also the case that varying the
focus of an item by means of clefting makes it no longer possible
to hold the item's position in the sentence constant. In the
sentences used in this experiment focussed items occurred at the
end of a clause more often than did non-focussed items. Phoneme-
monitoring latency is known to decrease towards the end of a
sentence or clause (Foss, 1969; Shields, McHugh & Martin, 1974;
this effect will be discussed in greater detail below). In two
pairs of items which differed in focus of the target but not in
the position of the target with relation to a clause boundary,
tests showed that the focussed member of the pair still elicited
faster RTs; nonetheless, these results are suggestive rather
than convincing.
    A recent investigation by Jerry Fodor and myself, however,
attacked the problem differently. In this study the means by
which focus was manipulated was extra-sentential; a question was
asked, immediately prior to the sentence, which directed the

listener's attention to one or another part of the sentence.
Thus the problem of confounding focus with position of the target item within a clause was avoided, in that the syntax of the
sentence remained constant regardless of whether or not the
target-bearing item was focussed. It was also unnecessary to
control stress by using synthesized speech; the experimental
sentences were recorded exactly once, and each was spoken without
applying particularly high stress to any item.

In each sentence two words were designated as target-bearing
items, and two questions were formulated for each sentence, one
of which directed the attention of the listener to that part of
the sentence in which the first target-bearing item was located,
while the other focussed attention on the part of the sentence
containing the second target-bearing item. Thus, (14) could be
preceded by the target specifications /b/ or /d/, and by the

(14)   The woman with the bag went into the dentist's
       office.

(15)   Which woman was it that went into the office?

(16)   Which office was it that the woman went into?

questions (15) and (16), which focus attention on the two target-
bearing items "bag" and "dentist's", respectively.

By means of tape-splicing, four materials sets were constructed; each experimental sentence occurred with a different
combination of target specification and preceding question in
each set. The splicing technique enabled the same recording of
the base sentences to be used in each set, so that each subject
heard an acoustically identical version of each sentence, regardless of which target-question combination preceded it.

If non-suprasegmental cues to the semantically most central
portions of the sentence can be used in the same manner as suprasegmental cues, then we would expect that focussing a word within
a sentence, by means of asking a question to which it provides
an answer, would facilitate RT to that word's initial phoneme.
For the example sentence (14), that is, we would predict that
RTs to the first target, /b/, would be faster if the subject had
heard (15) than if he had heard (16), whereas RT to the second
target, /d/, would be faster if the subject had heard (16) than
if he had heard (15). Since each subject heard the same recording of all experimental sentences, acoustic factors of course
cannot be invoked to explain RT differences.

Exactly the predicted interaction was found. Thus we have
shown that semantic focus can exercise an effect (on phoneme-
monitoring RT) prior to the completion of Stage A processing.
Moreover, by demonstrating an effect of focussing an item
analogous to the effect of assigning high stress, we have provided support for the notion that the strategic value to the
sentence processor of an active search for the locations of high

sentential stress is that the processor is thereby enabled to
direct attention to the location of the sentence focus, to the
semantically most central portion of the utterance. The greater
attention paid to the stressed and/or focussed elements is reflected in shorter phoneme-monitoring latencies.

Does it seem far-fetched to envisage the sentence processing
mechanism monitoring the intonation contour of an incoming sentence as part of an active search for the sentence focus? Some
recent work (Allen & O'Shaughnessy, to appear) demonstrates that
the acoustic prerequisites for this view are certainly fulfilled.
Allen and O'Shaughnessy recorded a large number of sentences in
which various devices were used to indicate the sentence's focus,
including clefting, pseudo-clefting and preposed questions, and
then measured the fundamental frequency contours of these sentences. They found that all methods of focussing produced reliable and similar effects on the pitch contour, with fundamental frequency accent falling in each case on the element which
was focussed. In other words, speakers produce fundamental
frequency cues to the semantically central elements of an utter-
ance--is it surprising that the listener seeks to make use of
these cues?

Presuppositions, Context and the Interpretation of Irony

The notion of focus is held to be accompanied by a corresponding notion of presupposition (Jackendoff, 1972), the presuppositions expressed by (4) and (5) being that somebody eats
caviar for breakfast, and that Felicity eats something for breakfast, respectively. Jackendoff defines presupposition as the
information which the speaker assumes his audience to share with
him. Does the conclusion that the identification of sentence
focus comprises part of Stage A comprehension imply that the presuppositions carried by a sentence are likewise identified during
this stage?

As with focus, there is evidence that the presuppositions of
a sentence are available to the hearer at least shortly after
comprehension has been completed. Offir (1973) tested subjects'
recognition memory of a sentence which they had heard embedded
in a short paragraph. She found that changes which had been made
in the sentence were more likely to be recognized if they affected the presuppositions carried by the sentence than if they did
not--even though the sentence was often more greatly changed in
the latter case. Hornby (1971) found that subjects asked to recall cleft and pseudo-cleft sentences may make mistakes in surface structure, but are unlikely to make mistakes about what the
sentence presupposes and what it asserts.

There exists no evidence, however, that presuppositions of
a sentence are computed during Stage A comprehension. Note that

the suggestion of an active search for, and the direction of particular attention to, the location of the focus implies that attention is directed away from the semantically less central parts of the utterance. It will be argued that the computation of presuppositions borne by these parts belongs, despite the intimate relation of presupposition with sentence focus, more properly with the interpretation of certain extra-sentential factors.

Although there exists no experimental evidence to buttress this argument, some circumstantial evidence can be called upon. A great many sentences do not carry presuppositions at all, whereas, in the broad sense of focus that has been used in this discussion, every sentence has a focus; in every spoken sentence there is a point at which the relative stress level is higher than in the rest of the sentence, and this point will always correspond with a semantically central portion of the message. Thus although each utterance will contain parts which are less central, these elements will not necessarily involve a presupposition, and the apprehension that a particular part of a sentence is less important does not entail that the sentence is thereby understood to involve a presupposition.

Note that this discussion has been in at least one respect greatly oversimplified. As Morgan (1969) has pointed out, there are two distinct types of presupposition, sentential and lexical. It is the former type that can be determined by the suprasegmental contour assigned to the sentence. The latter type is carried by a lexical item, for instance the word "stop", as in (17):

(17) Have you stopped beating your husband?

None of the points raised above apply to the lexical presupposition; there is surely a case to be made for inclusion of this type of presuppositional import in the entry allotted the particular item in the mental lexicon. The present discussion will continue to confine itself to sentential presupposition.

The computation of presuppositions of a sentence will be held to be similar to the computation of contextual effects on the interpretation of a sentence. It is surely true that many sentences cannot be said to be understood until they are understood in context. The host of a noisy party, interpreting a neighbor's utterance of

(18) I'm trying to sleep.

as a statement of fact rather than as a request to be quiet has not successfully comprehended it. Similarly, the ironically spoken (1) is misunderstood if it is taken as praise.

However the effects of irony and context on the interpretation of a sentence take place at a level which is certainly beyond Stage A. Ironic intonation, as we have seen, produces a conveyed meaning which is the converse of the literal meaning,

i.e., it negates the proposition expressed by the literal reading of the sentence. But the negation of a proposition cannot
be understood without the proposition itself being understood--
in other words, successful comprehension of the ironically intended message is contingent upon successful comprehension of
the literal meaning of the sentence. Likewise, the context alone
does not lead to apprehension of the request expressed by (18),
despite the fact that, under the circumstances, the appearance
of a neighbor in pyjamas amounts to a message in itself; after
all, the hearer's reaction would be quite different if the utterance were (19) or (20). That is to say, the literal meaning of

(19) May I join the party?

(20) Do you realize the house is on fire?

the utterance must again be retrieved before the contextual interpretation can be applied to yield the final interpretation.

The interpretation of irony, context and presuppositional
structure does not seem to comprise part of Stage A, the establishment of a sentence's literal meaning. To account for the
obvious effects of these factors on the understanding of utterances, it is therefore necessary to enrich the sentence comprehension model by the inclusion of a stage, subsequent to the
establishment of the literal meaning of an utterance, in which
the literal meaning is embellished or revised in the light of
extra-sentential considerations--i.e., Stage B.

It is likely that Stage B consists of a number of different
operations. The effect of ironic intonation in reversing the
literal meaning of a sentence is presumably the result of a different sequence of operations from those producing the effect of
context on the interpretation of (20). (However, note that
ironic effect can also be achieved by context: when two people
walk into an empty bar, the utterance (21) will be understood as

(21) Sure is lively here tonight.

ironic regardless of the intonation used.) The identification
of the presuppositions carried by the sentence, and the checking
of these against the hearer's knowledge and beliefs, result no
doubt from a different set of procedures again. It is therefore
quite possible that Stage B is not a unitary stage, but that
there are multiple independent serial stages which a basic semantic representation passes through before the sentence comprehension device is completely finished with it. However, the point
of these brief remarks is just that comprehension cannot be considered to be complete once the literal meaning of the sentence
has been established. Revisions of this representation do take
place as a result of such factors as ironic intonation and the
influence of context, although it is not necessarily the case
that every sentence undergoes such revisions. (It is worthy of
note that one of the few instances in which such effects would

be almost if not entirely absent is the processing of isolated
sentences during a typical sentence comprehension experiment.)
The stage at which these revisions take place is subsequent to
lexical look-up and the establishment of syntactic structure,
but it must nevertheless be considered an integral part of the
model of the comprehension process.

Implications of the serial position effect

One of the most reliable findings in sentence comprehension
tasks using RT methodology is that stimuli in the later portions
of a sentence produce shorter response latencies than do stimuli
in the earlier portions. Thus, Foss (1969) reported longer
phoneme-monitoring RTs to targets occurring earlier in the sentence than to targets occurring later, a result also found by
Shields, McHugh and Martin (1974). Holmes and Forster (1970)
found that clicks in the second half of a sentence were detected
faster than clicks in the first half. All of these writers discussed the serial position effect in terms of facilitated processing towards the end of the sentence; Foss successfully dis-
posed of three possible objections: that the effect merely
reflects the subjects' lower criterion for response later in the
sentence; that it reflects differential occurrence of target
items with relation to surface structure phrase boundaries; and
that it results from a reduction in the number of possible
structural continuations following target items in the later
part of the sentence.

A further possible explanation for the serial position effect arises from the phenomena discussed earlier in this paper.
In a sentence in which no particularly heavy stress is applied
to any element, the point at which the stress level will be
highest will lie at or near the end of the sentence. The expected semantic effects accompany the suprasegmental: in the unmarked case, given information in a sentence precedes new information (Halliday, 1967). An experimental result which supports
this explanation is that of Hornby (1972); in a task involving
subjects' judgements of various surface structure expressions of
simple agent-action-object sequences, Hornby found that active
sentences in which the agent was heavily stressed produced results similar to those produced by cleft-agent sentences, whereas active sentences in which no heavy stress was applied were
treated similarly to cleft-object sentences.

It is reasonable to assume that the serial position effect
in part reflects the fact that the point of highest stress, the
semantic focus, to which the sentence processor seeks to direct
attention, lies unless otherwise determined in the last part of
the sentence. Where sentential stress was not specifically
manipulated, experiments in which the serial position effect was

reported can be presumed to have used sentences in which the
focus occurred at the end of the sentence.

It is unlikely, however, that a focus explanation can account entirely for the serial position effect. The phoneme-
monitoring experiment reported earlier, in which focus was
manipulated by means of preposed questions, exhibited a strong
serial position effect despite explicit extra-sentential cues
to the semantic focus. While focus exerted the predicted effect, RTs to the later-occurring target were overall faster than
to the earlier-occurring target. It would appear that there is
some further component of the serial position effect besides
the search for the semantic focus.

In what way might completed processing of earlier parts of
a sentence facilitate processing of later parts? There exists
a considerable body of evidence that just such facilitation does
not happen when one might on common-sense grounds expect it to
be particularly useful, namely in the resolution of lexical ambiguity. Phoneme-monitoring RT is lengthened immediately following the occurrence of an ambiguous lexical item (Foss, 1970),
and a preceding context which renders only one reading of the
ambiguous item acceptable does not remove the ambiguity effect
(Foss & Jenkins, 1973; Cutler & Foss, 1974).

This effect presumably reflects retrieval from the mental
lexicon of all the readings listed for the particular item.
Although it may be impossible to use biasing context to limit
retrieval to only the relevant reading, another kind of facilitation from preceding context is conceivable. Imagine, for
example, that one of the operations of the sentence processor is
the construction of hypotheses about the content of the incoming utterance (cf. Forster, 1975). The strategic value of such
hypotheses might lie merely in reducing uncertainty about the
incoming message, given the degraded nature of the signal upon
which the speech processor operates. After all, the most sali-
ent and at the same time most amazing fact about speech comprehension is its speed, even though in real speech situations
sounds, syllables, even words are missing from the spoken realization of the message, the sounds that are present may be distorted or compressed, and the whole signal is, on top of this,
received often through considerable extraneous noise. The determination of word boundaries in this degraded input, and hence
of the strings which are to be sought in the mental lexicon,
might reasonably be considered a highly tentative operation;
the retrieval of a reading which matched the semantic hypothesis
constructed for that part of the sentence would presumably en-
courage the processor to accept that interpretation and to re-
frain from trying alternative patterns of segmentation.

Further, the semantic hypotheses could be more specifically
useful in expediting the choice between alternative readings
retrieved from the lexicon for ambiguous items. In the

phoneme-monitoring experiments on ambiguity, biasing context
exercised a facilitating effect on RT to targets in both ambiguous and unambiguous control sentences. The context effect did
not remove the RT lengthening due to ambiguity, which we take to
be a lexical effect, but it did slightly reduce it. On the view
proposed here, this reduction would be due to an effect at the
point of choice between the alternate readings.

The serial position effect can be considered to reflect the
operation of semantic hypotheses in the following way: in the
early part of the sentence the constructed hypotheses may often
prove wrong and need to be revised, thus adding to the momentary
processing load and leading to slower RTs in phoneme-monitoring
and click detection tasks. As the sentence is decoded, however,
the hypotheses are more likely to be correct and to need less
revision, so that less of the available processing capacity is
taken up with hypothesis formulation and testing, and the detection of phoneme or click targets can be accomplished more rapidly.

Strong support is provided for this view in the work of
Forster on the effects of plausibility (reported elsewhere in
this volume). Subjects asked to judge whether or not a string
of words is an acceptable sentence of English produce longer
RTs to sentences which are implausible in content--though completely grammatical and meaningful--than to sentences which are
plausible. An implausible input will on the average generate
more hypotheses before the correct one is hit upon than will a
plausible input.

That phoneme-monitoring is sensitive to the effects of
plausibility has recently been demonstrated by Morton and Long
(1976), who found that target-bearing items which had a lower
probability of occurrence in a particular context elicited longer
RTs than items with a higher probability of occurrence in that
context. If the above view of the serial position effect is
correct, it might be expected that RT to phoneme (or click) targets in implausible sentences would show a lesser reduction
towards the end of the sentence than RT to targets in plausible
sentences. This hypothesis awaits experimental investigation.

The testing of semantic hypotheses during Stage A comprehension is independent of the similar notion of testing of syntactic hypotheses suggested for example by Bever (1970), although the two suggestions are of course compatible. Forster
and Olbrei (1973) have shown that semantic variables do not simplify syntactic processing; but it is conceivable that the
reverse may be the case.

Finally, a conception of the sentence comprehension process
which involves the formulation and testing of hypotheses about
the content of the input is highly compatible with the notion
put forward above: that an active search is undertaken for the
semantically most central parts of the sentence. These elements

would be of more use than any other in the construction of the
correct hypothesis; thus it makes eminent sense for a hypothesi-
zing processor to search for them.

Conclusion

It is a truism to state that sentence comprehension is an
extremely complex process. Nonetheless, psycholinguists are all
too prone to lose sight of this complexity. A simplified conception of the components of a comprehension model may seem to
be desirable as a basis upon which research hypotheses may be
formulated. But an adequate model of parsing and lexical look-
up simply does not constitute an adequate model of auditory
sentence comprehension.

The research reviewed here has shown that the model needs
also to take into account the processing of the prosodic structure of an utterance, which takes at least in part the form of
an active search for the location of the main sentence stress.
We have seen that this effect appears to reflect the coincidence of main sentence stress and sentence focus; i.e., that the
search for the primary stress is in fact a search for the semantic focus. It has been suggested that the comprehension of
spoken sentences involves the construction and testing of hypotheses about the content of the input, and that the location of
a sentence's semantically most central portion is actively sought
in order to facilitate the construction of the correct hypothesis. These phenomena properly belong in even the most basic
model of auditory sentence comprehension.

Further, it has been noted that the proper understanding of
certain sentences must be based on a semantic representation
which is not identical with the literal meaning of the sentence,
and that some sentences bear presuppositions which are demon-
strably available to the listener once the sentence has been
comprehended. It was suggested that the sentence comprehension
model be enriched by the addition of one or more stages subsequent to the identification of the literal meaning in which
transformations of this meaning on the basis of various factors,
some of them extra-sentential, may be accomplished. It should
be noted that this latter type of enrichment of the model is not
confined to the comprehension of speech, but applies also to
reading.

A description of auditory sentence comprehension enriched
in the directions suggested in this paper may still be a far
from complete one, deficient in countless aspects. But it will
certainly be closer to the truth than the unimproved model
which preceded it.

References

Akamjian, A. (1970) On deriving cleft sentences from pseudo-cleft sentences. Linguistic Inquiry, 1, 149-168.

Allen, J. and O'Shaughnessy, D. (To appear) The effect of focus-shifting transformations on fundamental frequency contours.

Bever, T.G. (1970) The cognitive basis for linguistic structures. In Hayes, J.R. (Ed.), Cognition and the Development of Language, New York: Wiley.

Bolinger, D.L. (1961) Contrastive accent and contrastive stress. Language, 37, 83-96.

Cutler, A. (1974) On saying what you mean without meaning what you say. Papers from the Tenth Regional Meeting, Chicago Linguistic Society, 117-127.

Cutler, A. (1975) Sentence Stress and Sentence Comprehension. Unpublished Ph.D. dissertation, University of Texas.

Cutler, A. and Foss, D.J. (1974) Comprehension of ambiguous sentences: the locus of context effects. Paper presented to the 46th annual meeting, Midwestern Psychological Association, Chicago.

Cutler, A. and Foss, D.J. (In press) On the role of sentence stress in sentence processing. Language and Speech.

Forster, K.I. (1975) The role of semantic hypotheses in sentence processing. In Bresson, F. and Mehler, J. (Eds.), Current Approaches to Problems in Psycholinguistics, Paris, CNRS.

Forster, K.I. and Olbrei, I. (1973) Semantic heuristics and syntactic analysis. Cognition, 2, 319-347.

Foss, D.J. (1969) Decision processes during sentence comprehension: effects of lexical item difficulty and position upon decision times. Journal of Verbal Learning and Verbal Behavior, 8, 457-462.

Foss, D.J. (1970) Some effects of ambiguity upon sentence comprehension. Journal of Verbal Learning and Verbal Behavior, 9, 699-706.

Foss, D.J. and Jenkins, C.M. (1973) Some effects of context on the comprehension of ambiguous sentences. Journal of Verbal Learning and Verbal Behavior, 12, 577-589.

Halliday, M.A.K. (1967) Notes on transitivity and theme in English, Part 2. Journal of Linguistics, 3, 199-244.

Holmes, V.M. and Forster, K.I. (1970) Detection of extraneous signals during sentence recognition. Perception & Psychophysics, 7, 297-301.

Hornby, P.A. (1971) The role of topic-comment in the recall of cleft and pseudo-cleft sentences. Papers from the Seventh Regional Meeting, Chicago Linguistic Society, 445-453.

Hornby, P.A. (1972) The psychological subject and predicate. Cognitive Psychology, 3, 632-642.

Hornby, P.A. (1974) Surface structure and presupposition. Journal of Verbal Learning and Verbal Behavior, 13, 530-538.

Jackendoff, R.S. (1972) Semantic Interpretation in Generative Grammar. Cambridge, Ma.: MIT Press.

Lehiste, I. (1970) Suprasegmentals. Cambridge, Ma.: MIT Press.

Morgan, J.L. (1969) On the treatment of presupposition in transformational grammar. Papers from the Fifth Regional Meeting, Chicago Linguistic Society, 167-177.

Morton, J. and Long, J. (1976) The effect of word transitional probability on phoneme identification. Journal of Verbal Learning and Verbal Behavior, 15, 43-51.

Offir, C. (1973) Recognition memory for presuppositions of relative clause sentences. Journal of Verbal Learning and Verbal Behavior, 12, 636-643.

Shields, J.L., McHugh, A. and Martin, J.G. (1974) Reaction time to phoneme targets as a function of rhythmic cues in continuous speech. Journal of Experimental Psychology, 102, 250-255.

Wanner, E. (1973) Do we understand sentences from the outside-in or from the inside-out? In Haugen, E. and Bloomfield, M. (Eds.), Language as a Human Problem, New York: Norton, 165-185.

SYNTAX AND SENTENCE INTERPRETATION

John Limber
University of New Hampshire

Linguistic communciation is a process whereby two or more individuals may send and receive messages encoded in a human language. A structural unit of these languages is the sentence. A theory of sentence interpretation seeks to explain how skilled listeners routinely interpret a wide variety of utterances encountered in their everyday linguistic activities.

The nature of understanding. An issue that immediately confronts any effort to develop a theory of sentence interpretation is that there are degrees or levels of understanding. My not understanding a request to close the door when spoken in Finnish is quite a different matter than my failure to understand a statement in English concerning some principle of quantum mechanics. Understanding is an open ended dimension; at one end it is fixed firmly upon specific linguistic information and skill, but it unfolds rapidly into a complex web of virtually unknown conceptual abilities and personal experiences.

In casual conversation we normally assume the listener is understanding us unless he questions us or makes an unexpected reply. However, we also know that merely participating in a conversation does not ensure that all participants understand one another--or even care to. In more important discussions or research contexts, one wants evidence that the listener understands the message. Repetition generally will not do. One expects something more, something that indicates some analysis or comprehension on the part of the listener. Of increasing reassurance might be evidence that the listener is able to answer simple questions, formulate reasonable paraphrases, and make plausible inferences on the basis of the utterance. Hearing that Sally is heavier than Sue, a listener who understands knows that Sue is lighter than Sally. After mentioning that I had to return a birthday gift because it was too tall for my livingroom, I can expect listeners to guess that the gift might have been a lamp, a plant, a grandfather clock or even a pet giraffe. Certainly, as readers may verify for themselves, the guesses are not made at random but are based instead on presuppositions on the use of the adjective tall (Limber, 1969) among other things. Indeed, it is the listener's ability to reliably make such inferences that provides an extremely important empirical constraint upon any theory of sentence interpretation.

The focus here is upon the role of syntax in the interpretive process. Hence, it is necessary to restrict the inquiry to
those aspects of the message that are carried by the linguistic
code itself. This is a substantial and artifical restriction,
for it is clear that the interpretation accorded a sentence on
any given occasion may vary according to a variety of extralinguistic parameters. Such things as prior communications,
winks, grimaces, gestures, tone of voice, metaphorical extension,
and, of course, the pragmatics of reference (Limber, 1976) all
contribute to the meaning of an utterance in conjunction with
its intrinsic semantic content. We know that the subject of
I am sick must refer to the speaker; yet the actual referent of
I obviously depends on who the speaker is. An utterance of
I'm not very hungry tonight may on one occasion be taken as a
reflection of the speaker's hunger; yet on another, as a polite
rejection of a second helping of sauerkraut with ginger. It is,
therefore, common practice to distinguish between the meaning
associated with a sentence on the basis of its linguistic form
and an interpretation given to that sentence on any particular
occasion of its use. To reinforce this distinction, it is useful to say that every sentence in the language has a semantic
representation assigned to it by the grammar and a semantic
interpretation constructed by the listener on the occasion of
every utterance of that sentence.

Sentence interpretation is, thus, a function of the semantic representation of the sentence and the relevant context
variables. The semantic representation in turn is computed from
the phonological, syntactic, and lexical information available
to the listener as a consequence of knowing a language. A
theory of sentence interpretation, therefore, must be more than
a grammar of a language in the sense of Chomsky (1957, 1965).
Rather than just a characterization of the structures of language, it must deal with the psychological processes involved in
using that grammatical information. As Chomsky has remarked
more than once, a grammar is a model of neither a speaker nor a
listener.

Programmatically it is useful to distinguish several
stages in the development of a theory dealing with these processes of sentence interpretation: (1) determining the nature
of the information a listener must extract from the sentences of
a discourse, (2) formulating explicit hypotheses as to how that
information might be obtained, and (3) evaluating those hypotheses with the available evidence to ascertain which of potentially many equivalent processes are in fact employed by
listeners. Relevant evidence would include the listener's in-
ferential performance as mentioned above, data relevant to the
actual on-line processing of sentences, studies of language
development, and even results of neurological investigations.
Few would deny that at some far off time psychological theories

must ultimately be reconciled with physiology. Studies of
language development are likely to prove of more immediate bene-
fit, because any prospective sentence processing model must be
learnable. Moreover, it is not unreasonable to suppose that
features of the interpretation process which are obscured in
the skilled listener may be more transparent during their development. I shall come back to this point at the close of this
discussion.

   On the neglect of syntax. Until quite recently, psychology
had ignored syntax even more than it did other aspects of language. From the time of Descartes through the behaviorism of
the 1950's, few psychologists actively treated human language
as a serious problem for psychology. There are a number of
reasons for this neglect. While Descartes viewed language as
one of the most important human behaviors, he saw it merely as
a reflection of human thought or reason, and on many occasions
he remarked to the effect that it would take very little effort
for anyone to invent language and indeed if animals had any
reasoning capacity at all, they too would use language. Influencing Descartes was the fact, egocentric to humans, that one's
first language is learned and generally used without conscious
effort by all humans, including the dumb, stupid, and insane.
For Descartes, as for William James and many other psychologists,
conscious activities were of foremost interest. James, for
example wonders, in the opening of his Principles (1890) whether
machine-like activities such as piano-playing, buttoning, or
talking belonged within psychology. Of course, one of the basic
features of language processes is its automatic nature, its in-
accessibility to introspection. The behaviorists, on the other
hand, saw no reason to treat human language any differently from
other behavior. Why study something as messy and complex as
language, when the same underlying principles of behavior can be
obtained from simpler creatures in controlled situations?

   Those few who did deal explicitly with human language seldom went beyond what Fodor, Bever and Garrett (1974) have termed
the "naming paradigm" of language, the view that the learning
and using of a language is the learning and using of names for
things. When anyone did venture into language structure beyond
associative or probabilistic structure, typically it was in
connection with the analysis of a narrow class of constructions
such as yellow wall, sincere prostitute, Tom is a thief, or
colorful ball. Not surprisingly, it was primarily among those
individuals with an applied interest--professional linguists,
language instructors, missionaries, and students learning a
second language--that a respect for the complex structure of
human language developed.

   The discovery of syntax. The recognition of the theoretical importance of syntax in human language arose from two
sources during the 1950's; namely, the rapid development of

digital computers and the work of Noam Chomsky (e.g. 1955,
1957). Computers had a dual influence. On one hand, the development of high level programming languages entailed increasingly complex syntactic processors; on the other, the availability of these machines fueled the hope of devising an
automatic language translator that could translate from one
language into another; for example, from Russian into English.
    These developments were not unrelated. Chomsky's work
(1959a, 1959b) on formal grammar was recognized as an important
contribution to the growing field of computational linguistics
while Chomsky himself was connected for a time with a machine
translation project directed by Victor Yngve at M.I.T. Both
computer applications and Chomsky continue to have a powerful
impact on the psychological study of language processes, and
syntax in particular. Chomsky not only constructed a formal
theory of human language structure, he argued persuasively that
linguistics actually was part of psychology. In addition he
effectively challenged the relevance to the study of human language of the then dominant behaviorist paradigm.[1]

Syntax and Psychological Processes

    In Syntactic Structures Chomsky suggested that the process
of sentence understanding might be reduced to the problem of
explaining how the underlying component sentences (then kernels)
were understood, these basic sentences of everyday usage were
formed. At the same time, he was careful to point out that his
model of human language had no direct implications for the processes of either producing or understanding sentences, beyond
characterizing the nature of linguistic structure. He has re-
iterated this admonition against considering a generative grammar as either a model of the speaker or listener in almost every
later publication. A particularly detailed consideration of
this matter may be found in Chomsky (1961), wherein he distin-
guishes clearly between the grammar G_i of some language and a
function g, such that g (i,n) is the description of a finite
automaton that takes certain of the sentences of the language as
input and gives structural descriptions assigned to these

---

[1] Chomsky's (1959) criticisms of B.F. Skinner's speculations in
Verbal Behavior were not only directed to Skinner's radical behaviorism, but also to any behaviorist or empiricist account of
the nature of higher mental processes. As he remarks in a re-
print of that review, Skinner's work was selected only because
it was the most carefully thought out presentation of the empiricist position available (Jakobovits and Miron, 1967).

sentences by G_i as output, and where n is a parameter determining the capacity of the automaton. That the automaton accepts only some sentences and not others is no more surprising than the fact that an individual who has mastered the rules of multiplication may be unable to calculate 3,872 x 18,694 in his head. Naturally one would expect that as n increases, the automaton will be capable of understanding, in the appropriate sense, more and more of the sentences of generated by G_i. Thus, while psychologists may well be puzzled as to the psychological relevance of the grammar, G_i, it is without question not a performance or process model like the automaton g_i, of which Chomsky has little more to say.

It is well known psycholinguistic history that Chomsky was not taken very seriously on this matter. The earliest influence of Chomsky's work that I know of is found in a paper by Goodglass and Hunt (1958). There the derivational history of a sentence is utilized as a metric for the complexity of certain psycholinguistic processes. Within a few years, psychologists looking for alternatives to associative or probabilistic structure had turned to syntactic structure. G.A. Miller's (1962) paper was perhaps the most enthusiastic and influential in this regard. A number of very similar psychological models incorporating a generative grammar came under experimental investigation. Common to all of these models was the hypothesis that grammatical complexity--some formal index of linguistic structure--should predict processing difficulty. In one version, it was suggested that for every operation in the grammatical derivation of a sentence, there must be some corresponding mental operation involved in actually understanding that sentence. This came to be known as the derivational theory of complexity (DTC).

Despite some initial success, experimental efforts to demonstrate the psychological reality of grammar grew less convincing as a wider range of sentence types were examined. By 1966, Fodor and Garrett, in a review of the research up to that time, suggested an alternative proposal which they believed more compatible with the evidence than DTC. They proposed, in essence, that it was the "structural description of a sentence (including the specification of its base structure) but not the grammatical operations generating it, that was psychologically real."

That proposal was developed further in Fodor and Garrett (1967) and Fodor, Garrett, and Bever (1968). They suggested that listeners use a variety of surface structure cues to segment the sentence into clauses and to identify the main verb, which serves as the primary clue to the deep structure underlying the input. In other words, the grammatical organization of the input is dependent on heuristic procedures that assimilate the remaining surface structure elements to the appropriate deep structure "frame" associated with the verb of the clause.

I shall not take the time here to review the empirical evidence for and against either DTC or the Fodor, et al. proposals. Recent reviews are to be found in Greene (1972), and Fodor, Bever, and Garrett (1974). Instead it is worthwhile to take a closer look at the logic, such as it is, of these conceptions of the automaton, g, and their relation to the grammar, G.

The derivational theory of complexity has its most explicit realization in the context of an analysis by synthesis (A by S) model of speech perception (e.g. Chomsky, 1961; Matthews, 1962; Katz and Postal, 1964; and in particular, Halle and Stevens, 1964). In this model a sentence is recognized or understood when an acceptable match is obtained between some representation of the input signal and a synthesized, internally generated comparison signal. The grammar is explicitly employed as a source of these internally generated signals or structures. The representation of a recognized input sentence is determined as a joint function of the analysis done on the input and the structural description of the internal comparison signal at the time of a successful match.

One can imagine the A by S model operating along a continuum from extreme synthesis to extreme analysis, with a comparison possible at any point on that continuum. Extreme synthesis would involve generating a complete signal from the top down; that is, synthesizing the grammatical structure before selecting words and finally matching a completely synthesized sentence against a relatively unanalyzed representation of the input string. Extreme analysis, in contrast, would involve analyzing the input representation from the bottom up; that is, selecting words before grammatical categories and structures.

Extreme synthesis is surely a preposterous model of sentence recognition since no external constraints are placed on the recognition process until the synthesis is completed. In other words, no information about the input signal is utilized in the process of generating the comparison signal. Matthews (1962) estimated that a random synthesis of a given English sentence could take up to 10^{12} seconds, even with an a priori constraint that no sentence could be more than 20 words in length. Extreme analysis, on the other hand, immediately takes the input signal into account and involves creating an increasingly abstract description of that input, applying the grammatical rules in reverse, as it were. It was recognized even in the first papers discussing the A by S model that powerful heuristics must be available to make rapid use of the input signal in order to constrain the synthetic component.

The question is, with respect to DTC, what possible A by S model or models could lead to the expectation that sentence complexity is a function of grammatical derivation? The extreme synthesis, top down model, might lead to this expectation just on those occasions when it came up with a successful match.

between its synthesized comparison signal and the input. But, of course, for every successful comparison there will be a number of unsuccessful ones. Thus, the expected value of any dependent variable, say processing time, must include a component for those syntheses that do not match but nevertheless contribute to overall complexity. Going into the dependent measure, whatever it is, will be the contributions of all grammatical operations conducted, whether in the derivation of the successful comparison signal or in those of the multitude of unsuccessful ones. This interpretation of DTC can scarcely be taken seriously.

The analytic, bottom up version of DTC does not fare much better. It is true that one could expect grammatical derivations to predict complexity if all that were involved were running the derivation backwards; that is, applying the grammar inversely, beginning with the input signal and concluding with the base structure. But remember that even in a grammatical derivation of any sentence, more is involved than simply applying a sequence of rules; some determination must be made of which rules to apply. Every phrase-structure rule option, every transformation--optional or obligatory--must be consulted in some manner in the derivation of every sentence. The same must be true for any inverse application of the grammar in DTC. The structural index of conditions on application for every rule must be consulted and the current input structure examined with regard to each rule, regardless of whether that rule ultimately is applicable. There is absolutely no justification to suppose that the computations determining the application of a rule are negligible with respect to some dependent variable and that only those rules which actually do apply contribute to complexity. Indeed it is likely that, in any existent real time computational system, determining applicability of a rule would frequently be far more difficult than applying that rule.

One is led to conclude that the entire DTC episode in psycholinguistics was an ill thought-out affair. Anyone can verify for himself the lack of explcit justification for the conclusions drawn from the various experimental studies of that era, i.e. that grammatical operations, rather than a host of other factors (see Fodor et al., 1974), were responsible for the obtained results. Nevertheless, most DTC studies that were published after Yngve (1960) and Chomsky (1961) had explicitly raised the very plausible hypothesis that certain grammatical rules served to reduce psychological complexity just ignored that possibility.

The Fodor and Garrett (1966) empirical critique of DTC, along with their alternative proposal, pretty much marked the end of DTC, which was already the subject of considerable skepticism, particularly in light of recent revisions within linguistic theory (Chomsky, 1965). One important consequence of all this was to resurrect the question of the relationship between a grammar formulated according to linguistic guidelines

and the process models required by psychological theories. The
Fodor and Garrett (1966) proposal on the reality of structural
descriptions hardly clarified matters, as it was open to several interpretations. One of these is incomprehensible in that,
strictly speaking, structural descriptions cannot be divorced
from the rules that generate them. In all likelihood what they
were suggesting is that only certain of the structural descriptions generated by a grammar were of psychological interest; in
particular, features of the base and surface structures. But
this is to suggest that much of a grammar, G, is irrelevant for
a psychological model of sentence processing and that any notation capturing the appropriate relationship between the phonetic
representations of a sentence and its interpretation will suffice to provide the necessary empirical constraints upon a process model of interpretation. A similar conclusion was reached
earlier by Katz and Postal (1964) in their evaluation of analysis by synthesis models of recognition.

It would be inaccurate to conclude that the early studies
involving syntactic variables had no positive results. Of im-
mense importance is the fact that psychology no longer could
treat language as a collection of words or names for things.
Structure among words now meant more than associative overlap,
and syntax was more than an autoclitic response. Sentences were
recognized as a major unit in language behavior, having complex
rule-governed hierarchical structure.

Process models of syntactic analysis. In his discussion of
sentence comprehension, Garrett (1974) points out that there are
two major lines of attack on the question of how listeners assign structural analyses to sentences. One approach has been to
investigate sentence comprehension experimentally, in the hope
of establishing a set of constraints on the character of information processing routines that accomplish the task. The other
has been to attempt to specify in detail computational routines
or process models that will take as input the information represented in a string of lexical items and yield a syntactic
description of the string.

Algorithms that appropriately interpret a string of symbols
in accord with the syntax of the language are, by definition, a
necessary component of any computer programming language. The
early work in machine translation quickly revealed extraordinary
differences between artificial computer languages and natural
human languages.

These efforts at machine translation foundered in large
part upon the omnipresent ambiguity of natural languages, not to
mention the semantic problems (Bar Hillel, 1964; Yngve, 1964).
It comes as no surprise then that lexical, structural, and coreferential ambiguities, which abound in every day speech
(Garrett, 1974), also plague models of human sentence processing.
As listeners we only occasionally become aware of an ambiguous

utterance; yet any algorithm for the syntactic analysis of sentences (i.e. any parsing procedure or recognition grammar) must
contend with alternative analyses at many points within each
sentence. For example, in the DTC era, much was made of the
fact that in a number of experimental paradigms, passive sentences proved more difficult than their active counterpart.
This was taken as evidence for DTC since passive sentences had
additional steps in their grammatical derivations. Yet from
the perspective of any processing model of English, passive sentences have a local ambiguity or choice point at the by NP
phrase. The algorithm must be able to decide whether that
phrase indicates a passive agent or one of the other vexing prepositional phrases in English. In many cases these local ambiguities may be disambiguated by nearby context. But in many
others the local ambiguity translates into a global ambiguity;
that is, each alternative will result in a valid analysis for
the input string, as in (1). Notice that this

(1) The stolen gems were found by the fence.

particular complexity of passive sentences is simply a coincidence, as far as any grammatical rules are concerned. The complexity of (1) indexed, say, by response latency to a question
about it, is a function of the ambiguous structures permitted
by the by NP (passive vs. locative) and by the close associations among the words gems, steal, and one sense of the ambiguous fence.

The passive example reiterates a general point made above
with regard to DTC. Complexities attendant to the syntactic
processing of a sentence may be wholly unpredictable from the
grammar, G. Instead complexities are a function of the particular decision procedures and priorities implemented in the
syntactic processor.[2] A processor that awaits all input from a
sentence before beginning analysis will behave quite differently
from a processor that begins an immediate left to right analysis. A depth-first processor that follows only one path at a
choice point will behave differently from a breadth-first one
that attempts to compute all paths encountered simultaneously.

It is evident that certain of the many possible

---

[2]There is much more to it than this. Computational complexity
depends ultimately on the actual method and mechanism by which
the computations are effected. Any inference from a logical
analysis of a computation to the values of physical indices of
complexity must not overlook this fact. Consider estimates
about the relative complexity of common arithmetic computations,
e.g. addition vs. division, without knowledge of whether an
abacus, electronic calculator, or slide rule is employed.

realizations of a grammar will be more in line with a psychological model of the listener than others. The early developers
of syntactic analyzers for natural language had little concern
for the psychological implications of their programs: they
were concerned with efficiency in such endeavors as machine
translation, testing grammars, or man-machine communication
within very restricted subsets of language. A program devised
by Thorne, Bratley, and Dewar (1968) was perhaps the first program specifically intended to model the syntactic analyses required of a listener.[3] Their program analyzes an input sentence word by word, left to right, in a single pass. One of the
more interesting features of that program is that it does not
require accesses to a complete dictionary of English. Instead
it successfully analyzes the structure of a wide variety of
English sentences on the basis of a representation of a grammar
in the form of a directed graph and a closed class dictionary
of several thousand grammatical formatives, including inflections, along with a small number of verb classes. Obviously
this is not offered as a complete model of sentence interpretation, but only as a model for syntactic analysis of a surface
string into its base structure (Chomsky, 1965).

Thorne et al. (1968) reject a dictionary lookup for every
word for pragmatic and theoretical reasons. It is their argument that looking up each word individually complicates the
analytic process rather than simplifying it since nearly all
content words are ambiguous as to form class, not to mention
their multiple senses within a class. One implication of their
proposal is that listeners use syntactic information in order to
obtain the appropriate sense of a content word such as run, iron,
or play.   In other words, a listener does not retrieve the appropriate information for a given phonological form as an isolated unit, but under a specific syntactic description computed
from the syntactic context. A further implication of this proposal is that an individual learning a language can use the
syntactic analysis to derive meaningful information about a previously unknown word form from its syntactic context. This is
consonant with the fact that there is frequently a non-
negligible correlation between syntactic distribution and meaning (Limber, 1969) and also with the observation that children
have difficulty interpreting sentences with words such as easy,

---

[3]It is clear that Yngve had given the matter considerable
thought in connection with his machine translation work.
Hockett (1961) proposed writing a grammar from a listener's
perspective. The countless syntactic analysis programs written
in the 1960's were to my knowledge, not explicitly devised as
psychological models.

promise, or ask, which in certain constructions go against well
established syntactic generalizations regarding grammatical relationships (Limber, 1973).

Their analysis procedure constructs a diverging tree structure with nodes labelled in terms of "syntactic relations", e.g.
subject, passive verb, complement, and important high level
grammatical categories, e.g. statement, question, infinitive
clause, etc.. This construction process is predictive in that
all options possible at any point are investigated. A completed
path through this tree is essentially the recognition and analysis of a given sentence in terms of its base structures and
associated lexical items. At an ambiguous choice point all
paths are computed simultaneously. The relationship between the
transformational grammar on which Thorne et al. based their
analyzer and the analyzer program itself is not an obvious one.
For instance, grammatical relations are not defined in terms of
constituent structure but as labels on nodes associated with
certain surface formatives. Similarly the effects of certain
transformations in the grammar appear to be represented by
labelled nodes; directly entailed by specific surface configurations (e.g., passive verb). What is preserved from the grammar is primarily the base structure information associated with
particular surface structures. The intermediate structures,
even much of phrase structure within major constituents, are not
expressed.[4]

For the most part, the Thorne et al. program is an explicit
realization of the Fodor and Garrett (1966) proposal. Only base
structure information from a grammar is psychologically relevant. It is only a superficial difference that Fodor and
Garrett (1966) emphasized the importance of lexical information
associated with verbs since the Thorne, et al. program also includes complement-taking verbs in its dictionary.

Hence, it is somewhat surprising that the Thorne, et al.
syntactic analyzer did not receive more attention with psycholinguistics. Recent texts for example, Fodor, Bever, and
Garrett, 1975; Glucksberg and Danks, 1975; make no mention of
that work. Their basic notions have been kept alive, however,
within the artificial intelligence community. Bobrow and Fraser
(1969) and later Kaplan (1972), in particular, presented a model
intended to capture a number of generalizations about human

---

[4]The significance of such structures, including surface constituent structure, is unclear. Linguists appear to assign structures within major constituents; e.g., S, NP, VP, on the basis
of their theories, rather than on a direct empirical basis.
Experiments purporting to demonstrate surface constituent structure are hardly unequivocal within clause boundaries.

syntactic analysis (cf. Bever, 1970). Kaplan's model, an augmented recursive transition network (ATN) based on that presented
in Woods (1970), has several objectives. Like the models discussed thus far, it seeks to analyze an input sentence in terms
of its base structure components. Kaplan also suggests that
an adequate model must process strings in an amount of time pro-
portional to that required by human speakers and that any model
should discover and process anomalies and ambiguities as listeners do. In its psychological implications, Kaplan's model
differs from the Thorne, Bratley, and Dewar model in that it
conducts depth-first analyses and, consequently, has different
predictions for the analysis of ambiguous sentences. It also
seems that the Kaplan model requires much more lexical subcate-
gory information than the Thorne et al. model. Unfortunately,
from their respective program descriptions, it is difficult to
determine the consequences of this different data base with
respect to either performance or psychological significance.

One of the most important features of ATN and related program models is that they provide a medium for representing and
explaining a wide variety of facts about the psychological
processes of sentence comprehension, particularly the consequences of the interaction of a number of factors. Many generalizations about performance can only be captured in a model
of performance in contrast to the objectives of a grammatical
description. For example, both the Thorne et al. and the
Kaplan programs provide an index of complexity in terms of the
number of nodes constructed (arcs attempted, in ATN jargon).
Recently Wanner, Kaplan, and Shiner (1976) reported several experiments reasonably in accord with complexity predictions from
Kaplan's ATN program. Those predictions derive basically from
the path choice made at certain local ambiguities in a depth-
first, backup analysis. Clearly the number of arcs attempted--
and consequent predicted complexity--will be greater for those
sentences where the first choice was a deadend garden path.

There are other computer models frequently mentioned in
connection with psychological models of comprehension, particularly those of Winograd (1972) and Schank (1972). Most of
these appear to be of little interest here. The Schank model
explicitly denies the importance of syntax and need detain us
no longer. The Winograd model, on the other hand, is explicitly
concerned with syntax, yet makes no discernible psychologically
relevant claims beyond the well taken point that ultimately
syntax must be linked to a semantic and cognitive system. Yet
the simple block world to which Winograd's system is coupled,
along with its corresponding simple syntax has few implications
for human sentence processing (cf. Petrick, 1974).

Interpreting Complex Sentences

One can achieve considerable insight into the various problems surrounding a theory of sentence interpretation by going directly to the complex sentences of a language. These multi-clause structures, typically having two or more verbs in their surface structure, provide most of the hurdles for current linguistic and psycholinguistic theories. There are a number of very good reasons for focusing on complex sentences rather than simple sentences. First off, the projective or creative aspect of human language is reflected in our ability to formulate new and appropriate linguistic expressions for concepts that we previously may have never experienced. This is accomplished in English primarily through the use of complex nominalizations (Lees, 1960), particularly complement clauses and relative clauses. Complex sentences of all varieties, complement, relative, and assorted conjunctions, are common features of everyday speech. Even in the most informal interpersonal communication situations, where the need for referential power is at a minimum, 20 to 30% of all sentences may be complex. Similarly between 5 to 15% of all sentences produced by children between 2 and 4 are likely to be complex (Limber, 1976). Many of the things we talk about daily cannot generally be referenced other than by using complex expressions.

Interpreting complex sentences is generally a routine affair, accomplished with no conscious effort. It is perhaps instructive to take a look at a nonroutine complex sentence. Consider the example (2) which, I submit, is a

(2) The player kicked the ball kicked him.

perfectly good English sentence. In fact (2) represents at least two sentences. Despite the fact that (2) is only a two clause sentence, fewer than 3 of a hundred fluent English speakers are likely to interpret it correctly.[5] Close to 40% or more will report--with puzzlement--upon hearing that sentence in isolation, that they heard something to the effect that "The player kicked the ball and the ball kicked him." Another 20% may report hearing "The player who kicked the ball, kicked him." The remainder of the one hundred will report a variety of related fragments or incomprehensible paraphrases. What is it about (2)

---

[5] These sentences were recorded at a slow to normal speaking rate and played to varying numbers of listeners seated in a classroom. Each listener heard only one sentence and was required to paraphrase it and rate his/her confidence in that paraphrase on a 13 point scale.

that precludes its correct interpretation, when its structurally identical and semantically similar counterparts (3)
and (4) are accurately

> (3) The player thrown the ball kicked him.

> (4) The player kicked the ball thrown him.

paraphrased by at least several times as many listeners? Furthermore, when the structure is explained to listeners, (3) and
(4) are comprehended immediately while (2) continues to puzzle
many of them.

On almost anyone's theory of sentence processing there are
reasons to expect (2) to be complex. The basic difficulty is
that much of the normal redundancy as to the grammatical organization of the sentence has been removed. Although the listener
can easily assign the correct grammatical categories to the input string as NP VP NP VP NP, segmenting those constituents into
the proper clauses and determining the relationship between the
clauses presents a problem. A primary source of the difficulty
of (2), in contrast to (3) and (4), is the ambiguity of the -ed
inflection, which may indicate either a passive verb or a past
active form. Notice that in (3) and (4) the verbs of the main
and subordinate clauses can be discriminated by the contrast
between the -en and -ed inflections. The perceptual consequence
of the ambiguous -ed is to eliminate a crucial discriminative
cue to the relationship among the clauses. The failure of many
listeners to get (3) and (4) correctly appears in part due to
a failure to perceive the nasal inflection.

Another source of difficulty in the perception of (2) stems
from the fact it contains a reduced relative clause. The usual
complexity (Fodor and Garrett, 1967) resulting from the loss of
the relative pronoun is amplified enormously in (2) since its
loss also prevents the discrimination of the subordinate clause
verb from the main verb. In contrast to (2), the unreduced
versions in (5) and (6) are perceived accurately by over half of
the listeners. But something more than the ambiguity of -ed and
loss of the relative pronoun also seems at work. Compare the

> (5) The player that was kicked the ball kicked him.

> (6) The player kicked the ball that was kicked him.

complexity of (2) with (7), which listeners find even easier
than (3) or (4). Note that (7) has both the ambiguous -ed and

> (7) The player kicked in the head kicked him.

missing relative pronoun. The phrase in the head apparently not only aids in segmentation of the clauses, but also does not present the segmentation problem that the ball presents in (2) where it may be locally interpreted as either an object NP to the first VP or subject NP to the second VP, and as both by some listeners! Additionally there may be a number of other factors including the type of passive sentence, and the repetition of the verb kicked may marginally contribute to the difficulty of (2).

The incorrect and often fragmented, ungrammatical paraphrases reveal the efforts of the listeners to cope with the uncertainty of (2). The most common paraphrase takes both instances of kicked as active verbs and fabricates a conjunction and extra NP linking two independent clauses (...kicked the ball and the ball kicked...) or a relative pronoun linking an independent and dependent clause (...player who kicked the ball...). A substantial number of incomplete paraphrases include portions of the passive the ball was hit by the player without being able to integrate that fragment with the other portions of the sentence. It would be of interest to know how the various syntactic analyzers, such as Kaplan's ATN model, deal with such sentences. It is not obvious how that model or any such model would block the interpretation of (2). The constraint on explanatory simulations that they must not exceed the ability of humans is easily overlooked amidst the problems of simulating even a fragment of human language behavior. Nonetheless, models cannot be perfect if they are to be models of human behavior.

On the use of prosodic, lexical, and structural information. The above example illustrates the fundamental syntactic tasks facing a listener: assign lexical items to constituents, assign the constituents to their clauses, and determine the relationships among the clauses. To accomplish these tasks, a skilled listener has three major sources of grammatical information concerning the syntactic organization of sentences: the lexical information associated with each word in the listener's vocabulary, structural or syntactic information concerning the permissible configurations of grammatical categories, and prosodic features or suprasegmental information (Lehiste, 1970), including intonation contour, juncture, and stress or accent. Prosodic phenomena are mostly inevitably neglected in considerations of syntactic analysis, simply because they are subtle and fleeting, not to mention difficult to incorporate into a syntactic analysis program. I cannot say much about prosodics other than to suggest that prosodic phenomena might facilitate the processing of sentences such as (2) by providing suprasegmental information about subsequent structures as yet unheard. Thus in the version of (2) corresponding to (3), it may be that speakers can signal the subordinate nature of the first clause by a rising intonation contour over ball and perhaps by using other cues. I must say however that my own efforts to

facilitate the interpretation of (2) using intonation have as
yet been unsuccessful.

It is apparent that the most important source of information, lexical and structural, bear an intimate relationship to
one another. While the structure of a sentence is defined in
terms of grammatical patterns of grammatical categories, the
listener encounters only strings of words. Yet suppose--if only
to reveal its defects and the nature of English--that every
skilled listener has developed a kind of canonical sentence template or expected syntactic structure against which all input
sentences are evaluated. Learning to understand English is to
learn the template, its use, and the necessary amendments to it,
signaled by specific lexical items and syntactic patterns. As
a beginning, assume that all English sentences follow the general format of alternating NP and VP; that is, ...NP VP NP VP NP
VP NP.... Declarative sentences typically are signalled by an
initial NP while questions and imperatives an initial VP. Among
the many structures deviating from this simple pattern are those
with relative clauses, verbs taking more than one object NP,
prepositional phrases, adverbials, and conjunctions. This is
hardly a trivial list of exceptions; nevertheless there are
English sentences which do fit this description; e.g. (8) however implausible those with more than three VPs may be. To use

(8) The lady believed the man thought she knew the liar...

the template we assume the first NP encountered is the subject
of the sentence and the main verb is the last VP "paired" with
it, where "pairing" is a procedure described below in the discussion of relative clauses. For the moment, consider "pairing"
as simply taking the first VP following a subject NP as the
main verb. The object NP of the sentence is the following NP
and any VP NP... that goes with it. Thus the object NP of (8)
is taken as the man thought she knew....

Notice what happens if these rules are used to interpret a
sentence like (2). We get the utter nonsense that kicked is the
main verb with a complex object NP, the ball kicked him. If,
however, we interpret (9) similarly, we get just what the great

(9) The player believed the ball kicked him.

majority of listeners report. This sentence is reported with
greater confidence and accuracy than (3) and (4) and even (5)
and (6). This suggests there is yet another reason for the difficulty of (2), namely that its initial structural description
fits the format of an object complement sentence, a sentence
type having priority over a relative clause, independently of

lexical content.[6] Of course, it is just to filter out such
interpretations that Fodor and Garrett (1967) emphasized the
importance of the lexical information associated with the verbs,
and Thorne, Bratley, and Dewar (1968) put complement taking
verbs in their closed class dictionary. By the syntactic rules
suggested here both (2) and (9) will receive the same structural
description; only the semantic homunculus can reject (2) as
nonsense.

Space limitations fortunately prevent me from having to
discuss all of the exceptions to the model. It is necessary
however, to consider at least the first two, double object verbs
and relative clauses. One implication of the template is that
all verbs have one object NP, though it may be a complex sentential object. While verbs with no objects do not pose a
serious problem, those with the potential for double objects,
e.g. kick, give, believe, require special treatment. The
Thorne, Bratley, and Dewar analyzer operates on the breadth
first assumption that zero, one or two objects may follow any
verb and constructs potential nodes for all three. Kaplan does
not mention the matter explicitly, but in any depth-first analysis one path of three must be selected first. A compromise
third alternative might just utilize verb category information
to alert the listener to the possibility of a subsequent double
object, but make no decisions about assigning the first NP encountered to either indirect or direct object position until
all the data are available. A similar issue arises in the analysis of relative clauses discussed below. Verbs like believe,
which may take both a simple abstract NP such as fact or claim
and a sentencial complex object as in (10), also must be considered as exceptions. Predictably there are sentences, like

(10) The professor believed the claim the earth was flat.

(11) The professor told the woman the tale that the
      earth was flat.

(11), that combine the worst of (9) and (10) and have essentially a triple object NP.

Massive disruptions of the standard template occur in the

---

[6]Wanner, Kaplan, and Shiner, in their as yet unpublished work,
test very much the same proposal in their studies of sentences
like They told the girl that Bill liked the story. Over a
variety of lexical material, their listeners everwhelmingly interpret that structure as double object VP with a simple NP
(the girl) and a sentential NP (Bill liked the story). This is
in contrast to a nested relative clause interpretation (that
Bill liked (the girl)).

analysis of restrictive relative clauses, which may occur in any
NP position of the sentence. In order to interpret a relative
clause the listener must recognize the linguistic environments
signaling a relative clause, postulate a secondary sentence template, be able to assign the constituents of the entire string
to their respective clause templates, and in the process reconstruct any implicit or transformed constituents. It is
worthwhile to consider several examples in detail. First let
me briefly describe, quite informally, a typical linguistic
analysis of relative clauses.

The structure of a relative clause. A common relative
clause like (12) is constructed from two clauses, the main, or
matrix, and the subordinate, or constituent, clauses. In (12)
these correspond to the dog bit Bill and Bill bought the dog,
respectively. One might think of relative clause formation as
a process of attaching the constituent clause to the head NP in
the matrix clause, in this example the dog. A condition on that

(12)   The dog that Bill bought bit him.

attachment is that an NP in the constituent clause must be coreferent with the head NP to which it is attached. Coreference
is a grammatical relationship among NPs indicating they refer
to the same entity. The attachment process involves forming an
appropriate relative pronoun—that, who, which, whom, whose—
marking the coreferent NP in the constituent, and then moving
the pronoun to the front of the constituent clause, e.g. that
Bill bought the dog. Finally the constituent clause is attached
immediately following the lead NP in the main clause, and the
coreferent NP in the constituent clause is deleted, leaving no
trace. The complete structure is indicated in (13).

(13)   The dog that Bill bought (the dog) bit him.

A primary function of relative clauses in communication is
to describe a referent such that the listener will be able to
identify that referent, a kind of indirect reference whereby the
speaker uses information already presumed available to the listener in order to single out some individual—a dog in (12)—
about which the speaker is making some additional comment.
There are undoubtedly many other uses of such clauses. The
important point here is that all of them require that the listener reconstruct the grammatical relationship, e.g. subject,
object, indirect object, subject of object complement, object
of a preposition, etc., of the now deleted NP within the relative clause. The task of a listener finding herself in a
relative clause environment may be functionally outlined as
seeking to replace the NP corresponding to the relative pronoun
as she proceeds through the string of words coming to her from

left to right. While the listener does know that the NP must
be coreferential to the head NP, she cannot know without analysis of the sentence, what grammatical relationship that NP
played in the constituent clause.

Some common relative clause environments. The characteristic indicator of a relative clause is one of the several relative pronouns. Just in case the relative pronoun is coreferent
to an object NP in the constituent sentence, the relative pronoun itself may be omitted. Thus the that in (12) may be
deleted giving (14). In the resulting surface structure

(14)   The dog Bill bought bit him.

typically remaining the occurrence of two consecutive NPs itself
serves as a cue of high validity that the listener is entering
a relative clause. Notice that the back to back NPs violate the
NP-VP alternations of our canonical sentence format. Almost
never does this imply that a deleted VP must be recovered, as in
I ordered ham and eggs and Kita beans and weenies. When the
object relative pronoun is deleted but contiguous NPs do not
result, we may predict trouble for the listener. Of course they
have it cases like (2) and even (3) and (4), where the constituent clause was a passive, with subject and object NPs inter-
changed. Now when the object NP of the constituent clause is
deleted in normal relative clause formation, and if the relative pronoun is deleted (along with the auxiliary), the passi-
vized verb in the constituent clause immediately follows the
head NP and is liable to be taken as the main verb of the matrix
sentence. Thus the interpretive process breaks down.

A schematic outline of the more frequent relative clause
environments is presented in Figure 1 on the following page.
A listener encountering a noun phrase, NP_n, may find himself
in a relative clause if any of the constituents indicated in
that outline follow the NP. Also exemplified in Figure 1 are
some of the constructions in which those constituents may not
indicate a relative clause environment. I have indicated in
the third and fifth branch examples of certain postnominal modifiers which seem to overlap the traditional relative clause in
function; yet have a differing syntactic form, even though a
number of the generalizations about the analysis of relative
clauses are valid for those constructions. It may or may not
be coincidental that the same morphemes marking complement
clauses (Rosenbaum, 1967), that, -ing, and to turn up indicating
postnominal modification, e.g. (16) and (21) below, along with
-ing adjuncts as Anyone losing Humphrey gets a reward. Consider,
for example, a listener encountering (15). He hears an initial

(15)   The fact which Otto knew surprised everyone.

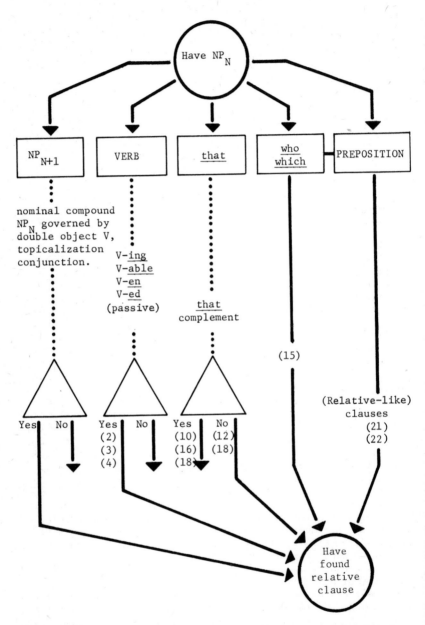

Fig. 1.   Some common relative clause environments and related
constructions.   Numbers in parentheses indicate examples in
text.   Paths through the test points are locally ambiguous.

NP followed by a relative pronoun, which, and he can be assured
that he is into a relative clause. On the other hand if he
heard (16) which differs only in choice of pronoun, he could not

> (16) The fact that Otto knew the answer surprised
>   everyone.

be so sure since the noun fact is one of the many abstract NPs
which may take an adjunct complement clause (cf. examples (10)
and (11)). Thus The fact that is locally ambiguous in a way
that The fact which is not. In the former, the listener requires further information to eliminate the relative interpretation and, not surprisingly, in some cases (e.g. (17)), the
sentence will be globally ambiguous between the relative and

> (17) The fact that Otto knew was surprising.

the complement interpretation.... It should be clear to the
reader why (17) but not (16) is ambiguous; if not, it soon will
be.
      Reconstructing the relative clause. Upon encountering a
potential relative clause environment a listener knows he is
now dealing with at least two clauses and that he must sort out
the constituents and reconstruct both the matrix and constituent clauses. Following the above account of relative clause
formation, this entails replacing an NP which is coreferential
to the head NP somewhere down inside the relative clause.
Essentially the listener is looking for a gap in the structure
of the clause caused by the previously described deletion process. In this way the listener may ascertain the grammatical
relationship of the deleted NP corresponding to the relative
pronoun.
      Recalling example (12), one can imagine a listener, upon
the valid hypothesis that that marks a relative clause, beginning to search for a potential source for the relative pronoun.
He knows, inversing my description of relative clause formation,
that the relative is coreferent with its left adjacent NP, the
dog, and that this NP is one of the constellation of NPs around
the verb bought in the constituent clause. He takes out another
sentence template for the constituent clause and begins to fill
it out from left to right. The first NP in the constituent
clause is Bill, which he interprets correctly as the subject of
the clause. Next he expects and finds a VP bought, which he
correctly assumes is the main verb of the clause. Now he predicts but does not find an object NP but instead finds another
VP, bit. Just as two consecutive NPs signal an embedding, so
two consecutive VPs signal a change from one clause to another.
The listener has a number of alternatives. The simplest is to
assume the unfilled object NP of bought is the source of the

deleted NP coreferent with the dog, i.e. that the relative pronoun is coreferent with the direct object of bought. At this
point the relative clause is reconstructed but the listener has
an "unpaired" VP, bit to assign somewhere. Again the simplest
solution is to pop back to the first sentence template which
only has its initial NP filled (with The dog) and still needs a
VP paired with it as main verb of the matrix clause. The listener correctly assigns bit as that main VP and the following
NP, him, as object NP to bit. The sentence is thus syntactically analyzed, to the extent of sorting out the clauses, re-
constructing deleted constituents, and assigning the several
constituents into their proper grammatical relationships.

These general interpretative principles can be extended to
reconstruct relative clauses of extraordinary complexity. For
those who did not figure it out at the time, we can now explain
why (17) but not (16) is ambiguous. In (16) there is just no
NP in the putative constituent template to be the source of the
deleted NP coreferent to that and, subsequently, to the fact.
The object position is already taken by the answer, and nothing
about the verb knew lets us postulate a secondary object NP,
in contrast to (18), where a secondary object NP, governed by

> (18) The fact that Otto told the teacher surprised
>   everyone.

the verb told is possible. Example (18) is, of course, ambiguous precisely for the same reason as (17).

An even more complex relative is (19). Initially the

> (19) The professor that the students believed was
>   arrested died.

analysis follows exactly along the path for the analysis given
above for (12). Upon encountering the VP was arrested our listener might well do as before and assign the relative pronoun
that as the coreferent object NP to believed, as if the constituent clause were the students believed the professor. He now
pops back to the main clause template and pairs off was arrested
with the initial NP, the professor as if it were the main VP in
the matrix sentence. To his dismay, the next constituent is
also a VP, namely died. He has another unpaired VP and no
higher clause to pop up to. It should be apparent where that
line of analysis went astray. It was back in the constituent
template, when the relative pronoun was taken as a direct object
NP to believed and was arrested was taken as the matrix VP. Our
listener had another choice at that point, which was to assign
was arrested as a secondary verb in the constituent template,
i.e. as the verb in complex sentential object to believe.
There is now a gap at the subject NP position within that

complex object NP. That is the true source of the deleted NP
coreferent with <u>that</u> and <u>the professor</u>. Now when <u>died</u> is encountered, the listener can appropriately pop back into the
main clause and pair off <u>died</u> with <u>the professor</u> in the main
clause. Thus the main clause is <u>The professor died</u> and the constituent clause is <u>the students believed (the professor) was
arrested</u>.

    Sentences such as (19) raise a number of familiar questions
about the actual process of interpretation. I described the
analysis of (19) as a depth first back up analysis. That was
primarily for expository reasons and to parallel its analysis
with that given earlier for (12). Yet many listeners have no
difficulty with (19) and do not report any conscious back up
process. If listeners always tried to complete the analysis of
a clause or phrase and immediately move to a higher level of
analysis as Chapin, Smith, and Abrahamson (1972) proposed, some
of them should report it. Perhaps some in fact do; but there
are other alternatives that deserve careful experimental inquiry. Can listeners use prosodic information to avoid making
a decision of premature closure? Do they compute more than one
alternative path as Thorne, Bratley, and Dewar's (1968) analyzer does, or as Garrett (1974) has suggested? Or is there simply some sort of time delay or buffer between input and analysis
that operates to prevent incorrect constituent assignment when
immediately following constituents will eliminate one or another
alternative path?

    I would like to consider one final example relative clause
type that illustrates how the relative clause analysis interacts
with the interpretation of infinitival complement sentences like
those in (20). Those examples illustrate a quite general rule
in English; namely, that for most verbs in their infinitive form,

(20) a. I want to leave.
     b. I want the taxman to leave.
     c. The farmer expected the cow to eat old hay.
     d. The farmer expected the cow to eat.

the leftmost antecedent NP should be interpreted as the "subject"
NP of the infinitive. Although linguists may debate whether in-
finitives can have subject NPs, it is clear that in (20a), it is
the speaker of sentence that will leave, just as it is clear in
(20b) that it is the taxman who will leave. The same is true
for those relative clause-like infinitival modifiers as in (21),
although here the interpretation is complicated when the subject

(21) The doctor for you to see is Mucus Welby.

(22) The doctor to see is Mucus Welby.

of <u>see</u> is implicit as in (22). Suppose one forms a relative clause using (20c) as the constituent and (23) as the matrix.

    (23)   The cow was purple with rage.

The resultant sentence is that shown in (24). But now substitute (20d) as the constituent sentence in place of (20c). The

    (24)   The cow that the farmer expected (   ) to eat
           old hay was purple with rage.

resulting complex sentence is (25), which is ambiguous precisely because of the interaction of the relative clause reconstruction

    (25)   The cow that the farmer expected (   ) to eat
           was purple with rage.

process and the rule of interpreting a subject of an infinitive. One interpretation has the sense of the farmer expecting to eat a cow that is purple with rage, while the other has the sense of the farmer expecting the purple cow to eat something. The reason for the ambiguity should be evident. The verb eat is a transitive verb that does not always require an explicit object NP. The difference between (20c) and (20d) is just that in (20c) there is an explicit object NP whereas in (20d) there is not. Yet in (20d) surely the farmer expected the cow to eat something, hence an implicit object NP. Now in the reconstruction of the relative clause in (25) there are two possible sources for the deleted NP. One is the cow from the constituent clause the farmer expected the cow to eat but the other is the cow from a constituent clause we have not yet considered, the farmer expected to eat the cow. Thus in contrast to the structures in (24), we have the structures in (26), both of which result in the identical surface structure. Thus, as the listener goes along at the level of his second sentence template,

    (26)   The cow that the farmer expected to eat (   )
           was purple with rage.

seeking the source of the deleted NP in the relative clause, he finds two potential sources, one after the other. That is, he might decide that the cow is coreferent with the subject of eat as in (25) or with the object of eat as in (26), with the infinitive interpretation rule supplying the farmer as the subject of eat. Notice that if I am correct about the syntactic ambiguity of (25) and (26), it considerably weakens the proposal that listeners take the first opportunity they come to in order to decide the coreferent of the head NP of a relative clause. In order for those sentences to have two interpretations, the listener must not yet have made a final decision when the second

gap becomes known to him. There are, of course, a number of
different interpretative schemes that would give this result.
Perhaps the NP (pronoun) NP configuration biases the listener
for an object NP interpretation regardless of options occurring
before the object NP position in the constituent clause is
reached. Perhaps the subject NP interpretation rule for infini-
tives "protects" that position from interpretation as coreferent
to the head NP except as a last resort. These and other alternatives require empirical evaluation.

The primarily heuristic analysis of relative clause reconstruction I have presented here can be summarized as a process
of expecting English sentences to follow an alternating pattern
of NPs and VPs, along with procedures for dealing with exceptions signalled structurally and lexically. Relative clauses
are identified by such cues, and another sentence template is
put into play. The analysis continues on a left to right basis
with every NP position being interpreted according to a complex
of coreference rules governed to some extent by specific verbs.
Consecutive verbs, as in (19), (27), and (28), signal an important choice point for the clausal recognition process. Does the

(27)   The workers that appeared tired after 5 days.

(28)   The workers that appeared tired quit after 5 days.

first verb dominate the second as a complement in the constituent clause, e.g. believed was arrested in (19) and appeared
tired in (28) or is the second in fact a verb from a higher sentence, e.g. tired in (27)? These matters are discussed further
in Limber (1970). Readers will profit greatly from working out
some examples for themselves. To that end, some interesting
examples are given in (29).

(29) a.   The boy students believed the professor
          expected to win lost.
     b.   The dog that bit the boy who knew the man who
          bought it died.
     c.   The dog that the girl knew the man bought barked
          continually.
     d.   The man who everyone knew hired the workers that
          just arrived tired.
     e.   The lion who saw the gorilla chased it.
     f.   The lion who saw the gorilla chased laughed.
     g.   The lion who saw the gorilla chase it laughed.

Some Neglected Issues

Here I should like to no more than mention several of the important issues facing further developments in the area of sentence interpretation. Each of these deserves far more discussion and analysis than I can offer here; nevertheless it is important not to overlook them.

Beyond syntax. Surely there is more to interpreting a sentence than organizing its constituents into the proper clauses. The content words of a sentence do far more than serve as filters to exclude meaningless structures, which is the function to which most syntactic analyzers put them. If the meaning of a word is viewed as the contribution which that word makes to the interpretation of its sentences, it is also clear that word meaning is more than a static set of semantic mediators, markers, or features that are put together by simple combinatorial rules. In many cases it would appear that word meanings must be construed as not only carriers of semantic material but much like active functions or subroutines that take linguistic and context parameters as inputs and whose outputs are the inferences typically made by listeners. Consider the sentences in (30). Now look at the corresponding interpretations in (31) that might

(30) a. This water is warm enough to swim in.
     b. Bob is fast.
     c. Chess is easy.
     d. Merrill suggested a goose for the secretary.

have been extracted by a listener from a specific conversation in which the examples in (30) were used. It takes no more than the examination of the protocols from a few listeners asked to

(31) a. According to state law, the water in the outdoor
        pool is suitable for swimming in.
     b. Bob is fast at solving two move chess problems.
     c. Chess is easy to learn.
     d. Merrill suggested that we might purchase a plump
        Christmas goose as a gift for the secretary.

interpret such sentences as in (30) to see that something beyond syntactic analysis is necessary to explain those interpretations.

Why syntax? This is a question that certainly deserves far more attention than it has ever received. As I suggested above, syntax has in large part been treated as a kind of nuisance variable by many psychologists; something that gets in the way of the business of studying meaning. Yet why should something as complex as the syntax of human language have evolved? Several speculative answers come to mind. The corresponding examples in (30) and (31) suggest one of them. Syntax serves to

economically package thoughts in a fashion suitable for vocal
transmission and subsequent interpretation. It is hardly a coincidence that in transformational grammars the surface structure is generally considerably reduced in structure from the
base structure, not to mention from any attempt at representing
semantic structure. Probably not unrelated to the notion of
economical packaging is the fact that a simple sentence or single clause is typically no more than seven syllables in length
and of one to two seconds duration. That figure is perfectly
in accord with the requirements of short term auditory memory
on one hand, and the requirements of the production system on
the other.

It may be more accurate to consider syntax as directing,
controlling, or structuring thought rather than packaging.
Thus in (30d) the surface structure follows a simple NP VP NP
format yet the meaning of suggest entails a propositional object rather than the simple object NP goose. It remains for the
listener to construct a proposition compatible both with the
linguistic context, goose in particular, and the extralinguistic
context. Much the same phenomenon can be observed in the language of two and three year olds where a single morpheme represents an entire proposition yet in context is sufficient to
convey the intention.

Syntax and language development. There are several perspectives one may take here. In terms of the function of syntax, it
serves to structure the perceptual inputs for the child much as
it does for the mature individual. As I have suggested elsewhere (Limber, 1973), given the kinds of verbs that young children first acquire, syntax is of even more value to the child
since there is a much more direct correspondence in their structures between surface structure format and the grammatical-
semantic relationship of the initial and final NPs. For the
mature listener, however, relatively few syntactic formats are
pressed into service to carry a much larger variety of grammati-
cal-semantic relationships. It is no surprise at all, therefore,
that when children encounter those exceptional lexical forms
such as easy, ask, promise, and a comparatively few others, they
interpret those sentences incorrectly. They simply are using
well-established syntactic interpretation rules concerning grammatical relationships and the assignment of coreference. Why
should those syntactic overgeneralizations be thought any different from the inevitable morphological overgeneralizations
involving verb inflections? It is not unlikely that the comparative regularity of the young child's syntax greatly facilitates
its acquisition of new structures and, in particular, vocabulary
items.

From quite another perspective it is important to keep in
mind that whatever procedures the mature listener uses in sentence processing, those procedures must be learnable. Hence it

is sensible to look toward the earliest syntactic structures
for potential evidence concerning the mature processing routines. The overgeneralizations of _easy_ and other similar forms
indicates that indeed syntactic patterns do play an important
role in the interpretive process, contrary to occasional suggestions that semantic processes are primary in young children.
An examination of the speech patterns of children during their
third year suggests that important features of the interpretive
process already underlie speech production at that age. For
example, alternating NP VP sequences are common; e.g. Watch me
hit ball. Similarly, young children perhaps never overtly express an NP in an object complement clause if that NP would be
coreferent with the last NP of the main clause; e.g., Me want
mommy read book but not me want me read book. Far more likely
is Me want read book. To a considerable extent the productive
structures of children apparent between two and six years make
a good beginning toward establishing the interpretive strategies discussed here.

References

Bar Hillel, Y. (1964) Language and information. Reading,
Massachusetts: Addison-Wesley.

Bever, T. (1970) The cognitive basis for linguistic structures.
In J. Hayes (Ed) Cognition and the development of language.
New York: Wiley & Sons, 1970, 229-353.

Bobrow, D. and Fraser, B. (1969) An augmented state transition
network analysis procedure in D. Walker and L. Norton (Eds)
Proceedings of the International Joint Conference on Artificial Intelligence. Washington, D.C., 557-568.

Chapin, P., Smith, T., and Abrahamson, A. (1972) Two factors
in perceptual segmentation of speech. Journal of verbal
learning and verbal behavior, 11, 164-173.

Chomsky, N. (1955) The logical structure of linguistic theory.
Mimeograph, MIT Library.

Chomsky, N. (1957) Syntactic structures. The Hague: Mouton
and Co.

Chomsky, N. (1959a) On certain formal properties of grammars.
Information and control, 2, 133-167.

Chomsky, N. (1959b) A note on phrase structure grammars.
Information and control, 2, 393-395.

Chomsky, N. (1959c) Review of B.F. Skinner, Verbal Behavior,
Language, 35, 25-58.

Chomsky, N. (1961) On the notion rule of grammar. In R.
Jakobson (Ed) Proceedings of the symposium on the struc-
ture of language and its mathematical aspects. American
Mathematical Society, 12, 6-24. (reprinted in Katz, J.
and Fodor, J. (Eds) Structure of Language. Englewood
Cliffs: Prentice Hall,(1964).

Chomsky, N. (1965) Aspects of the theory of syntax. Cambridge:
MIT Press.

Fodor, J.A., Bever, T. and Garrett, M. (1972) The psychology
of language. New York: McGraw Hill.

Fodor, J. and Garrett, M. (1966) Some reflections on competence
and performance, in J. Lyons and R.J. Wales (Eds) Psycholinguistic Papers, Edinburgh: Edinburgh Univ. Press,
135-179.

Fodor, J. and Garrett, M. (1967) Some syntactic determinants
of sentential complexity. Perception and Psychophysics, 2
289-296.

Fodor, J., Garrett, M. and Bever, T. (1968) Some syntactic
determinants of sentential complexity, II: verb structure.
Perception and Psychophysics, 3, 453-461.

Garrett, M. (1974) Experimental issues in sentence comprehen-
sion: complexity and segmentation. In C. Cherry (Ed)
Pragmatic Aspects of Human Communication. Dordrecht-
Holland: Reidel Publishing Co., 97-114.

Glucksberg, S. and Danks, J. (1975) Experimental psycholinguistics. Hillsdale, New Jersey: Erlbaum Associates.

Goodglass, H. and Hunt, J. (1958) Grammatical complexity and
     aphasic speech. Word, 14, 197–207.
Greene, Judith (1972) Psycholinguistics: Chomsky and psycho-
     logy. Harmondsworth: Penguin.
Halle, M. and Stevens, K. (1964) Speech recognition: A model
     and a program for research. In Katz, J. and Fodor, J.
     The Structure of Language. Englewood Cliffs: Prentice
     Hall.
Hockett, C. (1961) Grammar for the hearer in R. Jakobson (Ed)
     Structure of Language and its Mathematical Aspects; Pro-
     ceedings of the Twelfth Symposium in Applied Mathematics,
     12, American Mathematical Society.
Jakobovitz, L. and Miron, M.S. (1967) Readings in the psycho-
     logy of language. Englewood Cliffs: Prentice Hall.
James, W. (1890) The principles of psychology. New York:
     Dover Publications edition.
Kaplan, R. (1972) Models of sentence comprehension. Artifi-
     cial Intelligence, 3, 77–100.
Katz, J. and Postal, P. (1964) An integrated theory of lin-
     guistic descriptions. Cambridge: MIT Press.
Lees, R.B. (1960) Grammar of English Nominalizations.
     Bloomington, Indiana: University of Indiana Press.
Lehiste, I. (1970) Suprasegmentals. Cambridge, Mass.: MIT
     Press.
Limber, J. (1969) Semantic characteristics of English adjec-
     tives determined by their usage. Unpublished doctoral
     dissertation. University of Illinois, Urbana.
Limber, J. (1970) Toward a theory of sentence interpretation.
     Quarterly Progress Report of the Research Laboratory
     of Electronics, MIT, January, No. 96.
Limber, J. (1973) The genesis of complex sentences. In Moore,
     T.E. (Ed), Cognitive development and the acquisition of
     language. New York: Academic Press, 169–182.
Limber, J. (1976) Unravelling competence, performance, and
     pragmatics in the speech of young children. Journal of
     Child Language, 3, in press.
Matthews, G.H. (1962) Analysis by synthesis in natural
     languages. In Proceedings of International Congress on
     Machine Translation and Applied Language Analysis.
     London: H.M.S.O.
Miller, G.A. (1962) Some psychological studies of grammar.
     American Psychologist, 17, 748–762.
Petrick, S.R. (1974) Review of T. Winograd's Understanding
     Natural Language. Computing Reviews, August, 272.
Rosenbaum, F. (1967) Grammar of English complement construc-
     tions. Cambridge, Massachusetts: MIT Press.
Shank, R. (1972) Conceptual dependency: a theory of natural
     language understanding. Cognitive Psychology, 3, 552–631.

Thorne, J., Bratley, F. and Dewar, H. (1968) The syntactic analysis of English by machine. In Michie, D. (Ed), Machine Intelligence, New York: American Elsevier.

Wanner, E., Kaplan, R., and Shiner, S. (1976) Garden paths in relative clauses. Unpublished manuscript, Harvard Univ.

Winograd, T. (1972) Understanding Natural Language, New York: Academic Press, 1972.

Woods, W. (1970) Transition network grammars for natural language analysis. Communications of the ACM, 13, 591-602.

Yngve, V.H. (1960) A model and a hypothesis for language structure. Proceedings of American philosophical Society, 104, 444-466.

Yngve, V. (1964) Implications of mechanical translation research. Proceedings of the American Fhilosophical Society, 108, 275-281.

SOME GRAMMATICAL RELATIONS AMONG WORDS

Edward Walker

Massachusetts Institute of Technology

Introduction

By now the psychological reality of such basic generalizations about language as the segmentation of strings into
clauses, the necessity for both underlying and surface descriptions of clause structure, and the existence of ambiguity and
synonymity has been demonstrated satisfactorily. The "discovery"
that these phenomena affect the obscure forms of behavior recorded in psychological laboratories was reassuring, but it was
not remarkable. The linguistic generalizations involved are so
sweeping that demonstrating their effect on some behavior or
other depends as much on finding a responsive paradigm as on
certifying their credibility. Perhaps it is because the phenomena manifest such obvious observations about language that they
have sometimes been attributed to a "response bias." In fact,
even a biased response would serve to demonstrate the psychological reality of such fundamental generalizations to those for
whom the generalizing itself does not suffice.

Unfortunately, experiments which have attempted to move beyond basic generalizations about language to examine more subtle
or tendentious claims often have failed or have produced nettle-
somely contrary results. It is one thing to demonstrate that
the clause boundary marked by the comma in (1) is psychologically real (Garrett, et al., 1966); it is another to show that the
differences in the structures of (2) and (3) have a measurable
effect on psychological processes (Fodor, Garrett, and Walker,
forthcoming; Cooper, 1976).

(1) In her hope of marrying, Anna is surely impractical.

(2) John expected Mary to come before breakfast.

(3) John persuaded Mary to come before breakfast.

The experiments discussed below set out to demonstrate that
the existence of a subject or object relation between a noun and
a verb influences how fast that noun and verb can be recognized
immediately after the sentence in which they occurred. After
showing that a grammatical relation facilitates immediate recognition, the discussion proceeds to examine whether that facilitation depends on underlying, rather than superficial, relations
and observes a dominance hierarchy. In conclusion it is argued
that a 'first position' effect, which influences recognition

latencies regardless of underlying relations, constitutes evidence that sentences have psychological structure as well as grammatical structure.

Characterizing Grammatical Relations

In the diagram below, the noun-phrase immediately dominated by the sentence node dominating the main verb (NP_1) is in subject relation to that verb, and the noun-phrase immediately dominated by the verb-phrase node containing the main verb (NP_2) is in direct object relation to that verb. Another way of defining such relationships is to say that the subject is the instigator of the action identified by the verb; and the direct object is the person or thing affected by that action. Other relations between a noun and a verb than those shown in (4) are possible, but this discussion will concern itself only with subject and direct object relations, for which these vague definitions are adequate for the time being. For a more complete discussion of possible relations between nouns and the main verb of a sentence, see Fillmore (1968).

(4)

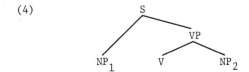

The swallow chased the sparrow.

It would be wise to remember that in defining grammatical relations either over structural descriptions or by noun functions, we have said nothing about how the structural descriptions or functions for a particular sentence come into existence. While structural descriptions and functions characterize what native speakers know about the relationships among the words in a sentence, they do not imply how speakers came to know who did what to whom, when and how the deed was done, with what, and so forth. A distinction must be made between a description of the relationships among words and the processes by which those relationships are perceived, remembered, produced, or otherwise manifest themselves in the behavior of a listener or a linguist.

It is sometimes argued that one could understand who did what to whom in a sentence by using strategies that are not entirely dependent on analyzing the structure of that sentence. For example, one might contend that grammatical relations can be determined from the order in which words occur in a string. Thus, the swallow could be taken as the subject of chased in (4) because it occurs first, immediately before the verb, after a

pause in speech, or in some other consistent and specific position. Corresponding positions might define the relation of
chased and the sparrow as well. Unfortunately, position alone
is sometimes an unreliable clue to function: the swallow occurs
in the same position in (4) and in (5), but it is not the underlying subject of chased in (5). Of course, comparing (4) and
(5) raises questions about how to define relations in different
types of sentences or in the surface and underlying descriptions
of sentences. But to point out that (4) and (5) are different
types of sentences is to concede that position, by itself, cannot always be depended on to determine grammatical function.

  (4) The swallow chased the sparrow.

  (5) The swallow was chased by the sparrow.

  Knowing which relationships are customary among the words
in a sentence can be a similarly unreliable clue to function.
Certainly a listener might assume that the cat and the sparrow
are the subject and object, respectively, of chased in such sentences as (6), because cats may be more likely to chase sparrows
than vice versa. But the specification of function cannot depend entirely on constructing likely relationships. Otherwise
we would boggle at (4), which alludes to no customary relationship, and we would invariably misunderstand (7), in which cus-
tom is violated. It is important to notice that (4) and (7) are
not bizarre sentences, however unusual the events they describe.
The point is that knowing which relationships are usual is often
useless in understanding a given sentence.

  (6) The cat chased the sparrow.

  (7) The sparrow chased the cat.

  Because the positions of words and their extra-sentential
meaning are not sufficiently reliable clues to the grammatical
relations among them, those relations are defined by referring
to the structure of the sentences which contain them. Indeed
structural descriptions are just formal notations of the relationships which hold and (by implication) do not hold among the
sub-components of a sentence. Because sentence structure,
rather than word order or semantic constraint, can be used reliably to characterize the composition of a sentence, structural
descriptions have often been used as a metric for predicting or
explaining the performance of listeners in a variety of experimental tasks.
  For example, in sentences (8) and (9), the positions marked
with an "a" differ structurally, even though their immediate
word environments are identical. A clause boundary separates
large and corporations in (8) but not in (9), because the

adverbial clause, <u>When profits are large</u>, is structurally distinct from the main clause, <u>corporations pay few taxes</u>. Furthermore, <u>large</u> and <u>corporations</u> are members of the same noun-phrase
in (9) because <u>large</u> modifies <u>corporations</u>. These differences
are illustrated in the structural descriptions shown in (10) and
(11).

(8) When profits are large, corporations pay few taxes.
                            a   b

(9) The presidents of large corporations pay few taxes.
                                a   b

(10)

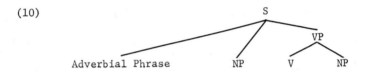

When profits are large, corporations pay few taxes.

(11)

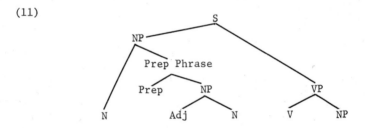

The presidents of large corporations pay few taxes.

It is generally presumed that a listener will find any task
which requires reference to both <u>large</u> and <u>corporations</u> more difficult to perform when based on (8), because one must refer to
more than one unit of description--either clause or constituent--
in order to accomplish the task. For example, it takes longer
to report that <u>corporations</u> was the next word after <u>large</u> after
listening to (8) than after listening to (9) (James and Gough,
1968); similarly, it takes longer to verify the presence of
<u>large corporations</u> after listening to (8) (Stewart and Gough,
1968).

On the basis of the assumption that referring to more than
one unit of description (constituent) is more difficult than
referring to a single unit, such results could be explained
either by the difficulty of providing an answer which requires
"crossing" a clause boundary in (8), or by the ease with which
a single constituent can be recognized or remembered in (9).

However, a different explanation would be required to encompass
the results involving <u>corporations</u> and <u>pay</u> in the same experiments. These two words produced correspondingly shorter latencies after (8); that is, <u>corporations pay</u> was recognized more
quickly after (8). But since the subject noun-phrase ends with
<u>corporations</u>, and the verb phrase begins with <u>pay</u>, in both sen-
tences; the boundaries between the two words (marked "b") must
be similar. Furthermore, the two words are members of only one
common constituent, the matrix sentence, in both sentences.

Certainly, it could be maintained that the structural relationship of <u>corporations</u> and <u>pay</u> is more "distant" in (9) because
more nodes intervene between <u>corporations</u> and the sentence node,
as the diagrams in (10) and (11) illustrate. Indeed, early
metrics of sentence complexity (Johnson, 1968; Blumenthal, 1967)
were distance metrics of one kind or another. However, distance
metrics are notoriously easy to violate by introducing elements
which add nodes to structure, but do not add difficulty. Furthermore, the hypothesis overlooks a difference between (8) and
(9) which is probably obvious to non-psycholinguists; namely,
<u>corporations</u> is the subject of <u>pay</u> in (8), but not in (9). In
other words, the effective difference between the two sentences
may not result from the mechanics of describing their constituency (<u>number</u> of intervening nodes, branching type, degree of embedding, etc.), but from the kinds of structures characterized
by that constituency. That is, the relations characterized by
the structural description, rather than features of the description, <u>per se</u>, affect recognition latency. If that is the case,
then shorter latencies should result even from recognizing a
noun and verb whose grammatical relation is defined across an
intervening context, in particular one containing clause boundaries like those shown in (12).

(12)

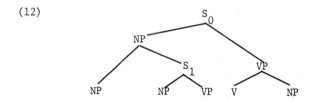

The scouts the indians saw killed a buffalo.

General Form of the Experiments

The results discussed below were produced by asking listeners to press a key indicating whether a noun and verb were "IN"
a sentence they had just heard. The two words, or probe, were
shown to the listeners simultaneously at the end of the sentence,

and the elapsed time, from the presentation of the probe (the
end of the sentence) to the listener's response, was recorded
as a measure of the facility with which the noun and verb were
recognized as being in the sentence.

Of course, the nouns and verbs in the probes and the kinds
of sentences containing them were chosen to test the influence
of various grammatical relations on recognition latency. For
example, if a subject relation in (12) facilitates recognition,
we should expect scouts killed and indians saw to be recognized
more quickly than scouts saw and indians killed,[1] because the
nouns and verbs in the first two probes are related in (12),
while those in the second two probes are not.

Scouts and Indians Experiment

An experiment on sentences like (12) was carried out, and
just the expected effect was demonstrated, along with a tendency
for faster recognition of scouts killed and scouts saw, compared
to indians saw and indians killed (Walker, Gough, and Wall,
1968; Bailey, 1976). The recognition latencies (in seconds)
are shown below:

scouts killed	scouts saw
1.02	1.06
indians saw	indians killed
1.06	1.12

[1] The definition of subject given earlier (adapted from Chomsky,
1965) would specify the entire noun-phrase, The scouts the
indians saw, as the subject of the verb. It is assumed here and
in the following experiments that only one word is the subject
of the verb. The same assumption is made about direct object relations. The scouts, alone, is an intuitively satisfactory answer to the question, "Who killed a buffalo?", and in languages
which decline nouns (such as German and Russian), only the head
noun of such constructions contains an affix indicating the
grammatical relation of the entire noun phrase to the verb. The
relative pronoun and any nouns within the subordinate clause are
declined according to their function within the subordinate
clause itself. However, the only justification for the assumption offered here is the outcome of the experiments, which fortunately place the burden of proof on those who would claim that
scouts is not the subject of killed.

The first result demonstrates that a subject relation facilitates recognizing a noun and a verb from main and embedded
clauses, both within and across internal clause boundaries.

In (12) scouts is both the logical (underlying) and superficial (surface) subject of killed, and indians is the logical
and superficial subject of saw. As (5) illustrates, the logical
and superficial relation of a noun and verb may differ, depending on the form of the sentence in which they occur. Having
demonstrated that discontinuous relations facilitate recognition,
it is natural to ask next whether underlying or surface relations
govern that facilitation. In this respect, it is interesting to
speculate why the probes containing scouts were recognized faster than those containing indians.

Looking at the structural description of (12), a number of
explanations of this tendency suggest themselves. First, the
sentence the indians saw... is embedded within the main sentence,
the scouts...killed a buffalo. If a dominance hierarchy among
the component sentences of (12), as well as the relations among
the words themselves, influences recognition, then probes containing scouts would have been recognized faster than those
containing indians, all other things being equal.

Second, scouts actually is related to saw, although this
relation is somewhat obscured in the surface form of the sentence by the deletion of scouts from the embedded sentence, the
indians saw (the scouts), and by the absence of a relative pronoun introducing the relative clause. Such object relations do
facilitate recognition (Walker, 1969); and, thus, the probe containing scouts saw might have been recognized more quickly than
the genuinely unrelated indians killed.

Third, by virtue of being both the object of saw and the
subject of killed, scouts occurs in two of the component sentences of (12), while indians occurs in only one. Multiple
occurrence (double function) of a noun has been shown to influence performance on a variety of tasks (Wanner, 1969; Rowe,
1968; Bever, 1970). As a consequence of the double function of
scouts, probes containing that noun might have been recognized
more rapidly than those containing indians.

These first three explanations of the tendency to recognize
probes containing scouts faster all derive from the structural
role of scouts in (12), and they are, in a sense, simply different ways of saying the same thing, that scouts, in addition to
being the subject of killed, is the head noun of a relative
clause containing saw. Another class of explanations derives
from what is perhaps a more ingenuous observation; scouts is the
first content word of the sentence. Although a number of explanations of first position effects simply restate the phenomenon (see Young, 1968, for a discussion), to the extent that it
is possible to attach some function to the use and definition of
'first position', not all do. An examination of 'first position'

effects on recognition latency will occupy much of the later
discussion, but let us turn for the time being to the question
of underlying versus superficial relations.

Eager/Likely/Easy Experiment

Some of the structural features of (12) are contrasted in
sentences (13)-(15). In all three, bachelors is the surface
subject of are, but it assumes a different underlying function
in each. In (13) it is bachelors who are eager, and bachelors
who entertain someone else. In (14) it is again the bachelors
who entertain, but what is likely is that the entertaining will
occur at home. Similarly, what is easy in (15) is entertaining
at home, but in this case, someone else entertains bachelors,
and not vice versa. The relevant differences are illustrated in
the structural descriptions shown in (16)-(18).

(13) According to single women, bachelors are eager
to entertain at home.

(14) According to single women, bachelors are likely
to entertain at home.

(15) According to single women, bachelors are easy
to entertain at home.

(16)

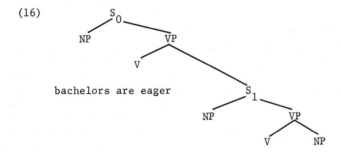

(17)

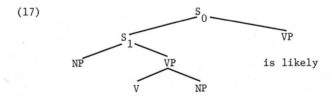

(18)

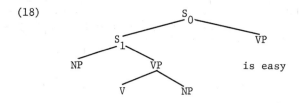

someone entertain bachelors

As a consequence of the relations described for (13), bachelors is the subject of two sentences, one of which, the eager sentence, dominates the other, the entertain sentence. In (14) bachelors is the subject of only the entertain sentence, which is subordinate to the likely sentence. And in (15) bachelors is the object of the entertain sentence, which is dominated by the easy sentence. In other words, bachelors is a subject in (13) and (14), but an object in (15); it is a member of a dominant sentence relation in (13), but occurs in only subordinate relations in (14) and (15); therefore, it occurs in multiple relations in only (13).

Assuming that probes of subject and object relations are recognized more rapidly when presented in noun-verb and verb-noun order, respectively, (Walker, 1969; 1972), the following predictions can be made. If surface relations alone determine which order of words will be recognized more rapidly, then all three sentences should elicit the same preference for probe word orders. On the other hand, if underlying relationships influence latency, then (13) and (14) should elicit a preference for bachelors entertain, relative to (15), which should elicit a corresponding preference for entertain bachelors. Similarly, if either dominance or multiple function facilitates recognition, then the latencies for probes of (13) should differ from those of (14) and (15), in overall latency, in degree of preference for one probe word order, or in both.

Of course, it is possible that some aspect of surface structure interacts with underlying functions to influence recognition; therefore, one probe word order may be preferred absolutely. Consequently, the difference in latencies for noun-verb and verb-noun probes produced by each sentence type must be compared. The latencies and differences of interest (in seconds) are shown below. The eager and easy sentences obviously differ in the predicted way. But the apparent differences involving the likely sentence, although in the predicted directions, are not reliable.

The result of the eager/easy comparison demonstrates that some aspect of underlying function (rather than surface function) interacts with probe word order to influence recognition latency, but the lack of significant differences involving the likely comparisons militates against deciding whether it is the kind of relation (subject vs. object) or the dominance-multiple function hierarchy which was operative: the easy sentence differs from the eager sentence in both aspects.

Sentence	Probe		
	bachelors entertain	entertain bachelors	difference
eager	1.20	1.19	.01
likely	1.22	1.12	.10
easy	1.34	1.08	.26

A similar attempt to demonstrate effects of underlying relations (Levelt and Bonarius, 1973) also failed to produce clear-cut results. No convincing differences could be found in the effectiveness of nouns or verbs as prompts for the recall of (19) and (20). In Dutch translation, these sentences can occur without the parenthesized words, and in that form they are ambiguous with respect to whether the professor is the perpetrator or the beneficiary of the seduction. In Finnish translation, affixes indicate the underlying function of professor in the seduce sentence.

(19) The professor is too ugly (for anyone) to seduce.

(20) The professor is too ugly to seduce (anyone).

Such sentences contrast the grammatical relation of professor and seduce in the embedded sentence, as do (14) and (15). However, (19) and (20) differ from (14) and (15) in that professor also has a role in the ugly sentence and, thus, they resemble (13) as well. The lack of results suggests (negatively) that dominance or multiple function, and not the kind of relation in question, produced the eager/easy differences, but what is needed is a direct contrast of surface and underlying relations which is not confounded with dominance and multiple function.

Active/Passive Experiment I

Presumably, the number and hierarchy of relations is the same in (21) and (22). In both, the Englishman does the boiling, and the vegetables get boiled, even though the surface structure role of the nouns changes as the voice of the sentence itself changes. The theory that underlying grammatical relations interact with probe word order predicts that Englishman boiled and boiled vegetables will be recognized faster than their reverses, regardless of sentence voice. On the other hand, if it is

surface function which interacts with probe word order, then
Englishman boiled and _boiled vegetables_ will be preferred after
the active sentence (21), and _vegetables boiled_ and _boiled
Englishman_ will be preferred after the passive sentence (22).
Presumably, no prediction can be made on the basis of a dominance
hierarchy or multiple function.

(21) The Englishman boiled the vegetables.

(22) The vegetables were boiled by the Englishman.

The latencies (in seconds) for probes containing the subject and object are summarized below.[2]

	Probe	
Sentence voice	Englishman boiled	boiled Englishman
Active	1.06	1.27
Passive	1.21	1.18

	boiled vegetables	vegetables boiled
Active	1.09	1.17
Passive	1.24	1.05

The surface structure order is preferred after both sentence voices, a result which suggests that the _eager/easy_ difference should be attributed either to dominance or to multiple
function, but not to the underlying relations involved. In that
case, however, it remains puzzling that the _eager_ and _likely_ sentences do not differ: the same dominance and multiple function
predictions would be made for that pair as for the _eager/easy_
pair.
In considering whether sentences (21) and (22) constitute
a valid contrast of underlying and surface relations, it must be
pointed out that they differ in one respect from the other sentences discussed: given what we know about Englishmen, boiling,
and vegetables, only one functional relationship of the nouns
and verb is possible. Jokes about cannibalism and drunkeness
aside, Englishmen do not get boiled, they do boiling; and vegetables get boiled. Such sentences are said to be irreversible
(Slobin, 1966), in that there is a strong semantic constraint

---

[2] These data were made available by R.E. Wall (1970).

on which relationships of a noun and verb are possible.

By design, this was not true of the sentences used in the other experiments discussed here. In those sentences the crucial grammatical comparison could be applied to all possible noun-verb combinations. In the hope that the plausibility or implausibility of a particular relationship would neither produce nor vitiate the desired results 'accidentally', in the scouts and indians experiment, every sentence was tested in four versions so that each of the two nouns was paired with each verb in each structural position. In the eager/likely/easy experiment, the same surface subject and infinitive verb occurred in all three sentences and thus in all three possible relations. And in the large corporations pay experiments, the same words served all the functions tested.

The kind of irreversibility illustrated by (21) and (22), whether absolute or pragmatic, as in (23), does influence the speed with which pictures of actions can be compared with the meaning of sentences about those actions (Slobin, 1966) and the latency with which the underlying subject and object can be produced following the presentation of such sentences (Herriot, 1969).

(23)   The doctor treated the patient.

Active/Passive Experiment II

In contrast to (21) - (23), the relationships in sentences (24) and (25) are reversible: either noun can assume subject or object function.

(24)   The politician insulted the heckler.

(25)   The heckler was insulted by the politician.

The recognition latencies (in seconds) from an active/passive experiment[3] using such sentences are shown below. In this case, each noun was tested in each relation in both sentence voices in order to guard against the possibility that, although by definition either noun can do, or have done to it, the action denoted by the verb, one may be more likely to do so than the other.

The results are paradoxical. Obviously the probe containing the underlying subject (politician insulted or insulted politician) is recognized more quickly in noun-verb order,

---

[3]These data were also provided by R. E. Wall.

<u>Probe</u>

	politician insulted	insulted politician
Sentence voice		
Active	1.02	1.36
Passive	1.05	1.37
	insulted heckler	heckler insulted
Active	1.09	1.17
Passive	1.32	1.16

regardless of sentence voice. From this result one might conclude that an underlying subject relation interacts with probe
word order to influence recognition latency. However, for
probes containing the underlying object, it is apparently the
surface function which interacts with probe word order, because
the verb-noun probe (<u>insulted heckler</u>) is recognized more quickly after the active sentence; and the noun-verb probe (<u>heckler
insulted</u>), after the passive sentence. In other words, the
results are half a loaf, and the question is, "Which loaf?"

It has been suggested that the effect of reversibility on
sentence verification and on the extraction of subject and object from sentences demonstrates that reversible and irreversible sentences are perceived differently. An interaction of
meaning-based (semantic) and form-based (syntactic) processes
has been proposed in which the semantic processes are used to
advantage on irreversible sentences, while processing reversible
sentences is more difficult in that it relies on syntactic routines alone. Forster and Olbrei (1973), argue against such an
interaction of semantic and syntactic processing, claiming instead that syntactic processing is an autonomous component of
sentence understanding, even though overall effects of semantic
support (constraint) can be observed.

Certainly, there are some differences between reversible and
irreversible sentences in the results presented here, but there
are several reasons why it is difficult to argue from these differences that syntactic and semantic processing either interact
or proceed autonomously.

In the first place, the response required by the experiments
implicates many psychological processes, any of which could have
produced differences in recognition latency. The latencies were
recorded for a manual response produced by presenting the probes
visually, immediately after a tape-recorded sentence. In order
to perform this kind of cross-modal task, some central representations of the sentence and the probe must have been compared

both the appropriate non-verbal response made. In other words, both the sentence and the probe must already have been "perceived"; the sentence (at least) must have been stored and retrieved; and the results of a comparison between it and the probe must have been used to produce a manual response. There is no direct way of knowing whether the latencies represent perceptual, storage, retrieval, comparison or production phenomena, either separately or in combination. More importantly, there is no way of knowing whether the differences in latency should be attributed to processing the sentence, the probe, or both.

Even if one assumes that they represent one process, the evidence is a mixed bag. When only the fastest recognized probes are considered, there appears to be no overall reversibility effect. Although it might be argued on an ad hoc basis that reversibility affects only non-preferred order probes or probes containing the subject or object nouns, considered separately, apparently no general explanation can be based on relation, voice, or sentence position. In other words, there is little evidence in these results of a consistent difference between reversible and irreversible sentences. By the same arguments, there is little evidence of a consistent difference between active and passive sentences. From one point of view the fundamental inconsistent datum in this case is the shorter latency produced by surface order probes containing the underlying object of passive sentences (heckler insulted or vegetables boiled).

First Position Effects

But the underlying object of a passive sentence occurs in first position, and there was evidence of a 'first position' effect in the scouts and indians experiment. In that experiment, probes containing the first noun (scouts) were recognized faster, whether or not the words in the probe were related. There is additional evidence of a first position effect in the eager/likely/easy experiment. A phrase containing a noun always preceded the experimental comparison in order to remove the latter from initial position. Sentences (13) - (15) illustrate one such phrase. Recognition latencies for probes containing those nouns (e.g., women entertain and entertain women) were collected as controls for any overall differences due to sentence versions. The resulting latencies (in seconds) are shown below. Although the control noun assumed various functions in the phrases containing it, there was no significant difference in the preference for noun-verb order, either across sentence versions (controlling successfully for the experimental difference) or across sentences. The apparently increased preference for noun-verb order in the easy version may result from a change to

subject function--in sentence (15) <u>women</u> <u>entertain</u> <u>bachelors</u>--
but by no means all of the appended phrases were of the type
illustrated in (13) - (15).

In other words, there is evidence from the experiments discussed here which implies that probes containing the first noun
of a sentence are special. In the <u>scouts</u> and <u>indians</u> experiment, probes containing the first noun tended to be recognized
faster, even though those nouns were involved in different relations depending on the verb with which they were paired. In
the active/passive experiments, noun-verb order was preferred
for probes containing the first noun of the surface sentence,
regardless of its (single) underlying function. And in the
<u>eager</u>/<u>likely</u>/<u>easy</u> experiment the first noun was again recognized
faster in noun-verb order, regardless of the kind or number of
functions involving it. It can even be argued that Levelt and
Bonarius' failure to find convincing differences in prompted recall for nouns of different functions should be attributed to
using the first noun as a prompt.

If the consistently faster recognition of active/passive
object probes in surface order is attributed to a 'first position' effect, then the "difference" between the two experiments
becomes the degree of preference for noun-verb order in subject
probes. The difference (in seconds) between noun-verb and verb-
noun latencies from the two experiments is shown below.

	Noun in Probe	
Irreversible Sentence	Englishman	vegetables
active	.21	.08
passive	.03	.19
Reversible Sentence	politician	heckler
active	.34	.08
passive	.32	.16

Various explanations based on the possibility that listeners have, or develop, processes which use the semantic constraints in irreversible sentences or probes of them can be
offered, but the other experiments presented here were designed
to exclude semantic constraint. Therefore, any further inquiry
into the interaction of semantic constraint and grammatical
relations must await additional research.

Since the results presented earlier constitute such strong
evidence that underlying grammatical relations, perhaps in conjunction with dominance or multiple function, influence

recognition latency, the obvious hypothesis is that some other
aspect of sentence structure influences recognizing probes containing the first noun of the sentence.

The surface structure relations of a noun and verb must be
distinguished from the underlying relation of that noun and
verb because different linguistic generalizations are based on
each relation. For example, the suffix of a verb indicating
person and number agrees with the subject, but the underlying
structural description characterizes their logical relation, in
which the noun may assume one of several functions. In (26)
and (27), it is the number of dogs which decides which form of
to be will occur, regardless of whether the animals in (27) received innoculation from more than one innoculatrix. On the
other hand, dogs may not occur as the underlying subject of
innoculate (except by some extension of the meaning of innoculate or dog) because that verb cannot occur with a non-human
subject. Furthermore, nouns with various underlying logical
relationships to the verb may assume surface subject status, as
(29) - (32) illustrate. The linguistic aspects of this practice
are discussed in Fillmore, (1968).

(26) My dog was innoculated against rabies.

(27) My dogs were innoculated against rabies.

(28) John is easy to please.

(29) Handguns kill people.

(30) Dixie is where I wanta be.

(31) What time of year is best for visiting Melbourne?

To place a noun in initial position is to imply, all things
being equal, that it is the psychological subject of the sentence,
whatever its logical or surface structure relation to the main
verb (Bloomfield, 1916). The word or phrase in initial position
is what the sentence is about; the rest of the sentence constitutes what is being said about that initial word or phrase.
Various terms have been employed to make this distinction;
psychological subject and predicate, theme and rheme, topic
and comment, what is new and what is old, etc. (see Lyons, 1969;
334 ff. for an extensive discussion).

By this argument then, the 'first position' effect should
be attributed to a division of the sentence into a psychological
subject and predicate; a division into who or what the sentence
is about and what the sentence says about that subject. Obviously the psychological subject may assume a variety of underlying
functional relationships with the main verb of its sentence,

which may or may not be reflected directly in surface structure.
It should be pointed out immediately that psychological
subjects need not occur in initial position. Other linguistic
devices such as the placement of stress, the choice of speech
rate and intonation, the use of italics, or the manipulation
of definiteness may interact with word order. Thus, the psychological subject may or may not be the noun with which the verb
agrees in person and number in the surface form of the sentence,
and it may or may not be the first noun of the sentence.

In choosing the passive voice, a speaker chooses to make the
underlying object noun the psychological subject of the sentence.
It has been argued that the choice of voice implies a choice
of "importance" (Johnson-Laird, 1968) and influences the order
in which nouns occur in replies to questions (Grieve and Wales,
1973). But the definiteness of nouns is a better predictor of
the choice of topic in (32) and (33) than word order (Grieve,
1973). The obvious prediction yet to be tested, is that such
manipulations of topic and underlying relation would influence
recognition latency and qualify the 'first' in the 'first position' effect.

Conclusion

The experiments presented here provide evidence that the
psychological relationship among nouns and the main verb of a
sentence is not determined by a metric based on the distance
by which they are separated in a structural description, but
rather by the grammatical relationships which that description
characterizes (scouts and indians experiment). Furthermore,
the grammatical relationships which influence recognition latency are not those of surface structure, but the logical or functional relationships (and, perhaps, dominance/multiple function
hierarchy) characterized in underlying structural descriptions
(eager/likely/easy and active/passive II experiments).

Notwithstanding these logical relationships between a noun
and verb, the psychological subject (topic) of a sentence has a
unique relationship to the verb which contravenes the effects
of underlying relations on recognition latency.

Thus it appears that the psycholinguistic structure of a
sentence describes not only who did what to whom, but also who
(or what) the sentence is about and what happened.

References

Bach, E., and Harms, R. (1968) Universals in Linguistic Theory,
Holt, Rinehart and Winston.

Bailey, L. (1976) Personal communication.

Bever, T. (1970) The cognitive basis for linguistic structures.
In J.R. Hayes (Ed.), Cognition and the Development of
Language, New York: Wiley.

Bloomfield, L. (1970) Subject and predicate (1916). In Hockett,
C., A Leonard Bloomfield Anthology, Indiana University
Press.

Blumenthal, A. (1967) Prompted recall of sentences. Journal
of Verbal Learning and Verbal Behavior, 6, 203-206.

Caplan, D. (1972) Clause boundaries and recognition latencies
for words in sentences. Perception and Psychophysics, 12,
73-76.

Chafe, W. (1970) Meaning and the Structure of Language, University of Chicago Press.

Chomsky, N. (1965) Aspects of the Theory of Syntax, Cambridge,
Mass.: MIT Press.

Cooper, W. (in press) Syntactic control of speech timing: A
study of complement clauses. Journal of Phonetics.

Dixon, T., and Horton, D. (1968) Verbal Behavior and General
Behavior Theory, Englewood Cliffs, New Jersey: Prentice-
Hall.

Fillmore, C. (1968) The case for case. In Bach and Harms,
Universals in Linguistic Theory, Holt, Rinehart and Winston.

Forster, K.I. and Olbrei, I. (1973) Semantic heuristics and
syntactic analysis, Cognition, 2(3), 319-47.

Garrett, M., Bever, T., and Fodor, J. (1966) The active use of
grammar in speech perception. Perception and Psychophysics,
1, 30-32.

Grieve, R. (1973) Definiteness in discourse. Language and
Speech, 16.4, 365-72.

Grieve, R. (1976) Accuracy, latency and syntax of answers to
active and passive sentences. Forthcoming.

Grieve, R. and Wales, R. (1973) Passives and topicalization.
British Journal of Psychology, 64.2, 173-82.

Halliday, M. (1967) Notes on transitivity and theme in English.
Journal of Linguistics, 3.

Herriot, P. (1969) The comprehension of active and passive
sentences as a function of pragmatic expectations. Journal
of Verbal Learning and Verbal Behavior, 8, 166-69.

Hockett, C. (1958) A Course in Modern Linguistics, MacMillan.

Hornby, P. (1972) The psychological subject and predicate.
Cognitive Psychology, 3, 632-42.

James, C. and Gough, P. (1968) Constituent structure and the
recall of sentences. Midwestern Psychological Association.

Johnson, N. (1968) Sequential verbal behavior. In Dixon and
     Horton, Verbal Behavior and General Behavior Theory,
     Englewood Cliffs, New Jersey: Prentice-Hall.
Johnson-Laird, P. (1968) The choice of passive voice in a
     communicative task. British Journal of Psychology, 59, 1,
     7-15.
Levelt, W. and Bonarius, M. (1973) Suffixes as deep structure
     clues. Methodology and Science, 6, 7-37.
Lyons, J. (1968) Introduction to Theoretical Linguistics.
     London and New York: Cambridge University Press.
Rowe, P. (1968) The Comprehension of Syntactic Structures by
     Children, MIT Dissertation.
Slobin, D. (1966) Grammatical transformations and sentence
     comprehension in childhood and adulthood. Journal of
     Verbal Learning and Verbal Behavior, 5, 219-227.
Stewart, W. and Gough, P. (1968). Unpublished.
Wall, R. (1970) Personal communication.
Walker, E. (1969) Grammatical Relations and Sentence Memory.
     Indiana University Dissertation.
Walker, E. (1970) Structure in sentence memory. Quarterly
     Progress Report No. 96, Research Laboratory of Electronics,
     MIT.
Walker, E. (1972) The effect of structure on scanning strate-
     gies. Perception and Psychophysics, 12(5), 427-429.
Walker, E., Gough, P. and Wall, R. (1968) Grammatical relations
     and the search of sentences in immediate memory. Midwes-
     tern Psychological Association.
Wanner, E. (1969) On Remembering, Forgetting, and Understanding
     Sentences. Harvard University Dissertation.
Young, R. (1968) Serial learning. In Dixon and Horton, Verbal
     Behavior and General Behavior Theory, Englewood Cliffs,
     New Jersey: Prentice-Hall.

LINGUISTIC DESCRIPTIONS AND PSYCHOLOGICAL ASSUMPTIONS IN THE STUDY OF SENTENCE PERCEPTION

William Marslen-Wilson

Committee on Cognition and Communication
Department of Behavioral Science
The University of Chicago

Introduction

Perception is a process that inescapably involves knowledge, and in the perception of spoken language one kind of knowledge that must be involved is the listener's knowledge of the language in question. Thus any attempt to understand the process of sentence perception will at some point have to come to grips with the problem of how linguistic knowledge is represented in the mind of the listener. This is a problem both about the content of linguistic knowledge and about the form in which it is represented. I will concentrate in this paper on the latter problem, and I will discuss this question in terms of the consequences for psycholinguistic research into sentence perception of having taken transformational generative grammar (TGG) as a model for the form of the internal representation.

The initial discussion of these questions should be seen as quite independent of the long-standing disputes as to the proper relationship of transformational linguistic theories and psychological theories of specific aspects of linguistic performance. Whether or not linguists wish to reserve to themselves the option of withdrawing their theories from particular kinds of contact with psychological evidence, it is perfectly legitimate for the psycholinguist to propose a role for the linguistic theory in the explanation of sentence perception, so long as the success or failure of the linguistic theory in this role is not seen as bearing directly on its adequacy as a formal linguistic theory. Of course, if the linguist wishes to expand the explanatory domain of his or her theory to include such phenomena as the use of linguistic knowledge in sentence processing, then he or she will have to take account of its suitability in this regard. In fact, there are signs that linguists are willing to undertake such an expansion, and I will discuss the implications of this later in the paper.

There are a number of ways in which the form of a linguistic theory can influence psychological theorizing about sentence

perception. Most directly, one may take the operations specified by the grammar to correspond in a fairly literal sense to
the processing operations involved in actual sentence perception.
It was this hypothesis, first stated by Miller (1962a) and Miller
and Chomsky (1963), which motivated the experiments in the early
1960's on the so-called "Derivational Theory of Complexity" (cf.
Fodor, Bever, & Garrett, 1974). Namely, that "performance on
tasks requiring an appreciation of the structure of transformed
sentences is some function of the nature, number and complexity
of the grammatical transformations involved" (Miller & Chomsky,
1963, p. 481). This proposal was rapidly and convincingly dis-
credited, chiefly through the arguments of Fodor and Garrett
(1967), leading to a general abandonment of the notion that a
TGG was directly realized in the sentence processing system.

Despite this rejection of TGG as a psychological process
model, it has continued to have a fundamental, though less transparent, influence on psychological theorizing about the organization of sentence processing. Given the original pre-theoretic
assumption that the mental "competence grammar" is properly characterized by a transformational theory (see Levelt (1973) for a
discussion of the empirical basis for this belief), and given
that the linguistic theory does not specify how sentences are
actually processed, then let it instead specify the abstract
structures onto which the input is mapped, leaving cognitive and
perceptual theories to describe the processing procedures which
enable this mapping to take place. This in its time was a reasonable proposal, just as the Derivational Theory of Complexity
once was, but it is important to realize just how powerful are
the constraints that such an assumption places upon our research
into the processing system. For it means not only that the listener's internal representation of his linguistic knowledge has
a transformational format, but also that the goal of the processing system is to construct a linguistically defined object, the
deep structure of the input sentence. Thus our processing questions are determined by essentially linguistic considerations:
knowledge of the language is of such-and-such a form, and the
listener gains access to it by building deep structure representations of the sentences he hears (e.g., Fodor et al., 1974;
Clark, 1974).

In this sense, then, the conceptual framework for the psycholinguistic study of sentence perception remains a linguistic
one--in particular a transformationally oriented one. We need
to consider carefully whether this is a fruitful state of affairs.
I will argue that it is not, that there is little reason to expect it to be, and that the influence of TGG has led to a serious
gap in the kinds of questions we have been asking about sentence
perception and comprehension.

The reason for this is quite straightforward. Formal linguistic descriptions are constructed without reference to time.

Entry into the system, whether from top or bottom, and at whatever level of description, is assumed to be simultaneous across
the entire string. It is a basic principle of transformational
derivations that all the elements in a string be simultaneously
available for the manipulations and rearrangements necessary to
derive its abstract structure. This assumption of simultaneity
of access is a legitimate one where the description of language
as a formal object is concerned, but it is thoroughly alien in
spirit to the dynamic use of knowledge that inheres in any real
perceptual process. It was not, for example, simple perversity
that led researchers in computer-based natural language processing to abandon transformational descriptions as a way of representing linguistic knowledge in their systems; it was precisely
this opacity of the descriptions with respect to the dynamic use
of knowledge in making processing decisions (e.g., Woods, 1970;
Winograd, 1972). But if, as a foundational assumption, one does
take a transformational description as a model for the form of
the mental representation of linguistic knowledge--and thus as
the target of the listener's processing procedures--then one is
forced into a particular view of how the processing system could
operate.

Psycholinguists have in the past postulated processing
theories that are generally compatible with the assumption of
simultaneity of access. Namely, theories in which the listener
is seen as accumulating the input in a short-term memory at the
beginning of a clause, while at the end of a clause he is actively organizing an internal representation of what he has just
heard (for a recent statement of this view, see Bever & Hurtig,
1975). This allows the possibility, then, that the listener
does have the entire string at his disposal when he begins to
map it onto his internal representations of linguistic knowledge.
But the time-course of this process has never been clearly specified, so that there is no step-by-step information-processing
description precise enough to enable one to determine just where
and when the input interacts with the listener's linguistic
knowledge. These processing theories have never been stated nor,
indeed, investigated in such a way that they could explicitly
conflict with transformational descriptions of the form of the
mental representation.

This is not to say that psycholinguistic research has not
concerned itself at all with what happens before the listener
reaches the end of the clause or sentence. But it is fair to
say that the motivation for research into within-sentence processing procedures was primarily to find ways of explaining how
the listener assembled the incoming input into an appropriate
form for projection at the end of a clause onto the deep representation of the string--an approach similar in spirit, though
not in detail, to the original proposals of Miller and Chomsky
(1963), in which a perceptual model "M" contained two components:

a limited capacity immediate processor "M_1," whose task was to assign a surface structure analysis to incoming strings, and a component "M_2," whose task was to determine the deep structure of the input string, using as its input information the output transmitted to it by M_1. The major deviation from this general model in recent theorizing seems to have been the postulation of "perceptual strategies" (Bever, 1970; Fodor et al., 1974), which are heuristic assumptions about the likely relationship of the surface order of items in a string to their representation in deep structure. These strategies turn out to be too weak for effective use in an implemented processing system (cf. Kaplan, 1972), but they are of interest because they represent an attempt to restate information contained in a TGG competence model in a form usable by a left-to-right processing system. This in fact is a familiar theoretical move. In response to the argument that knowledge represented in a TGG format is unusable in processing, it is suggested there is a mental translation algorithm, whose function is to construct computationally usable recognition procedures from our mental "competence grammars" (cf. Fodor et al., 1974, pp. 371-372). I will discuss the explanatory value of this construct later in the paper.

A direct consequence of assuming a transformational model of linguistic representations has been a general lack of interest in sharpening up our picture of the temporal properties of sentence processing. This was partly because the failure of the Derivational Theory of Complexity led psycholinguists to lose faith in the value of relating linguistic structural complexity to questions about time, partly because a transformational representation provides no reference points for dealing with left-to-right temporal order, and partly for more subtle reasons. For if the point of contact between the input and the internal representation of linguistic knowledge is only properly dealt with by the linguistic theory when entire clauses and sentences have become available, then it is only natural to focus one's research attention on what happens at these points, and to use experimental techniques appropriate to this interest. Namely, post-sentence measures, such as sentence grammaticality judgements, sentence verification tasks, sentence anagram tasks, memory-probes, and the like, which reflect the subjects' internal representation of the input sentence as a whole, but which can be only weakly sensitive to whatever happens while the subject is listening to the sentence in the first place. The results of experiments using post-sentence measures do not give us the kind of information about on-line processing that an adequate processing theory requires. And unfortunately the one line of research (e.g., Foss, 1969) that did explore immediate processing has relied on a task, phoneme monitoring, whose relationship to linguistic processing variables is difficult to interpret (cf. Savin & Bever, 1970; McNeill & Lindig, 1973; Foss & Swinney,

1973), and whose use may have been based on incorrect assumptions
about the nature of the processing system (Morton & Long, 1976;
Tyler & Marslen-Wilson, forthcoming).

This general concentration on post-sentence variables also
leads to the danger of a slight circularity in the evidence for
the assumption that a TGG adequately describes the internal representation of linguistic knowledge. For one kind of psychological evidence that a TGG is designed to reflect, which constitutes a major empirical constraint on its adequacy as a linguistic theory, is the intuitions of the speaker-hearer about the
grammatical structure of sentences in the language. Thus whatever the psychological reality of the rest of the grammar, the
structural descriptions that a TGG assigns to sentences will
reflect some psychologically real phenomenon. To the extent
that the grammatical properties of entire sentences affect the
subject's performance in post-sentence response tasks, then the
results will be consistent with a linguistic description that
captures these properties. But this would be true of any such
description, and does not necessarily single out TGG as the psy-
cholinguistically correct formalism to use; and certainly it
need say nothing at all about the psychological reality of the
procedures that need to be postulated to achieve a TGG-based
representation in the first place.

The discussion so far can be interpreted in a number of
ways. One possibility is that although the points I have made
may be well taken, the TGG assumption is nonetheless correct,
and the processing system is in fact organized in the way that
this assumption requires. The alternative possibility, clearly,
is that the TGG assumption is not correct, and that the relationship of the input to the internal representation of linguistic
knowledge is of a quite different nature than such an assumption
seems to require. But the primary, and perhaps the most damag-
ing, effect of the TGG assumption, with its implicitly static
view of the processing functions of linguistic knowledge, is
that it has not led to the kind of research which would enable
us to discriminate properly between these two alternatives.

The experimental evidence that I will summarize in the next
two sections of the paper is intended to deal directly with some
of these neglected processing issues. The following rather
general framework has been adopted for considering these questions. Let us assume that the comprehension of a normal spoken
sentence involves the analysis of the input in terms of at least
four sources of stored knowledge, which can be labelled phonetic,
lexical, syntactic, and semantic. From the point of view of
these preliminary experiments, all that is meant by these labels
is that the listener normally needs to identify the speech-
sounds and the words that the speaker is uttering, the syntactic
relationships between these words, and the semantic representation derivable from this information. I have been investigating

the time-course of the interactions between these different
sources of knowledge, and the direction of information-flow between them. When during sentence processing does syntactic and
semantic information about the input become available to the listener, and how does this higher-order information interact with
his assignment of initial phonetic and lexical descriptions to
the succeeding words in the string?

The results, I will argue, indicate that the TGG assumption
is at best misleading, and at worst thoroughly incorrect. On
their weakest interpretation the results show that much more is
happening "on-line" than had been explicitly recognized or
demonstrated; on a stronger interpretation they show that the
listener is able to understand a sentence--to construct a syntactic and semantic representation of it--as he hears it. That,
in effect, the listener's linguistic knowledge is available to
him, and is used by him, in a way that is inconsistent with the
basic organizing principles of transformational linguistic descriptions.

Some Within-sentence Processing Phenomena

To investigate on-line processing procedures, it is necessary to use experimental techniques that are sensitive to the
subject's performance during sentence perception. To this end,
I initially relied on the speech shadowing task, in which the
subject repeats back speech as he hears it. Of particular interest here are the so-called "close" shadowers. These are
individuals who can shadow speech at extremely short response
delays--measuring the duration of the interval between the onset
of a word in the material they are hearing and the onset of the
same word in their repetition. Close shadowers can reliably and
accurately shadow normal connected prose at mean latencies of
around 250 msec, which is a lag of little more than a syllable.
These latency estimations represent the mean of 150 measurements
for each subject tested, derived from two 300-word passages.
Measurement points were assigned equally to the beginning, middle, and end of each sentence in the shadowed material, and are
accurate to within ± 10 msec (Marslen-Wilson, 1973a; 1973b).

This level of performance has an important methodological
consequence that also holds, though less strongly, for subjects
shadowing at longer delays--the shadowing distance for most
subjects falls in the range 400-750 msec. The very short delay
between the subject's hearing a particular word and starting to
repeat it means that we can specify rather precisely just what
he has heard up to that point in his response. The shadowing
task reflects what the subject knows about the sentence up to
the point of repetition, but not beyond that point. There is
therefore no question, in interpreting his performance, of

"backwards" effects on processing decisions of information that only becomes available later in the sentence or which is based upon the listener's knowledge of the sentence as a whole.

Within the framework of a TGG-influenced psycholinguistics, the most natural interpretation of very short latency shadowing --and one that I initially adopted--is that the shadowers could only be performing the most rudimentary phonetic or syllabic analyses on the input, and that their output could not be based on any kind of syntactic or semantic analysis. I have tested for this possibility in several experiments, and have yet to find any evidence that the shadowers do not perform a syntactic and semantic analysis of the material as they repeat it.

In an early experiment (Marslen-Wilson, 1973a; 1973b) I tested close and distant shadowers' memory for a passage they had shadowed without knowing they would be asked questions about it. If the shadower is not interpreting the material semantically, then he should not have available to him information that could only derive from these forms of analysis. The more distant shadowers, however, might show more normal levels of recall, since they shadow the material at distances that would allow more extensive processing to take place. But the results revealed no relationship between shadowing latency and memory for content. Both groups performed very well, and, in fact, at the same level as a control group of non-shadowing listeners.

The results of the memory test show that syntactic and semantic information is available to the shadower irrespective of latency, but they do not exclude the possibility that he only analyses the input in these terms after he has repeated it. The close shadowers could produce their output just on the basis of a preliminary analysis, and perform the rest of the analysis later. Such a procedure should be reflected in their errors. If the shadower's performance were based, for example, on only a phonetic analysis of the material, then his errors could be constrained by the phonological character of the material, but not by its syntactic or semantic properties. Furthermore, if the distant shadowers do perform a fuller on-line analysis, then there should be latency-dependent differences in the types of errors which the subjects make. The longer the shadowing latency, the more constrained the errors should be by their structural context. Notice the significance, in this connection, of using the shadowing task. For it not only measures the temporal properties of processing, but it also produces an output whose qualitative deviations from the original can be directly interpreted as reflecting the kinds of knowledge that the on-line processor has available at the point of deviation.

In the two passages of normal prose previously shadowed, there were 111 errors that could be analyzed according to their grammatical congruence with their prior context. Of these, only 3 were structurally inappropriate--for example, repeating "They

were wet to the skin..." as "They were <u>went</u> to the skin...".
All the other errors were both semantically and syntactically
congruent with their preceding context, and this held true for
subjects at all shadowing latencies. The implication of this,
that close and distant shadowers have the same kinds of information available to them to guide their word-by-word repetition,
is supported by the qualitative similarities between the errors
made at different latencies. In one case, for example, six subjects made errors at the same point. In the context "He had
heard at the Brigade...," five subjects (with latencies ranging
from 250 to 550 msec) repeated the sentence as "He had heard
<u>that</u> the Brigade...". Another close shadower repeated this sec-
tion as "he had heard <u>it</u>...". A particularly revealing error in
this situation was when the change from "at" to "that" led to a
further change downstream that was syntactically consistent with
the new version but not with the original. Thus one subject
(mean latency of 350 msec) repeated "He had heard at the Brigade
that the Austrians..." as "He had heard <u>that</u> the Brigade <u>had</u>...".
It is difficult to account for this kind of structural contin-
gency between errors without assuming some direct involvement of
syntactic knowledge in on-going processing.

I also asked whether the shadowers differed in the frequency
of occurrence of grammatical errors at different points within
clauses. It remained possible that structural information was
indeed only available towards the ends of clauses, and that the
reason ungrammatical errors were not found at short shadowing
latencies was because few errors of any kind were made at the beginnings of clauses. The 108 grammatical errors were sorted
according to whether they occurred at the beginning, middle, or
end of a clause. Close and distant shadowers did not differ in
the distribution of errors, and made just as many errors at the
beginnings of clauses as elsewhere. A remaining suggestion is
that the close shadowers' grammatical errors occurred only when
they were shadowing at longer latencies than average. To assess
this, the close shadowers' latencies for the word immediately
preceding each grammatical error was measured. The results
showed that these errors usually occurred when the subjects'
latencies were significantly shorter than average, as if they
were placing more reliance on the predictive properties of the
higher-order context.

Nor can the grammatical sensitivity of the close or distant
shadowers' errors be accounted for simply in terms of a general
constraint on the shadower to produce a well-formed output. Inspection of the individual errors showed that the shadowers'
performance, at whatever latency, was responsive to the specific
requirements of the sentence being shadowed. The appropriateness
of any given error was contingent upon an awareness of the semantic and syntactic properties of the items preceding the error.
Thus, in the example given above, the subjects would need to

have extracted the structural implications of "heard" to make
the appropriate error of saying "that" instead of "at".

Taking a different approach, one can demonstrate the close
shadower's on-line utilization of syntactic and semantic information by depriving him of such information. It turns out that
close shadowers perform more poorly on semantically anomalous
prose than on normal prose, and worse still on random word-order
material (Marslen-Wilson, 1973a). More delicately, one can
place single anomalous words in an otherwise normal sentence
that the subject is shadowing. These words can be syntactically
or semantically anomalous with respect to their context. Shadowing performance could only be disrupted by such anomalies if
the shadower is processing the material to a level at which the
anomaly can be detected. And, again, close shadowers are just
as affected by syntactic and semantic anomalies as are the more
distant shadowers. In fact, some recent work by a student here,
Karen Lindig, suggests that shadowers are sensitive even to
anomalies defined at the level of an entire discourse. Lindig
used situations of the type devised by Bransford and Johnson
(1973), in which a particular sentence, although internally perfectly normal, is incongruous with the rest of the passage when
a misleading topic has been given. The shadowing performance of
her subjects (all distant shadowers) began to deteriorate as
soon as the incongruity of the critical sentence started to become apparent.

In summary, the general implication of these various shadowing results is that when one has clear experimental access to
the kind of representation that is being generated on-line, one
finds that a syntactic and semantic analysis appears to be available much earlier in processing than previous research had led
us to assume. Thus to account for these shadowing phenomena I
have proposed an alternative approach to sentence perception,
which is described in the next section of the paper, together
with two experiments testing its major predictions.

An On-line Interactive Approach to Sentence Perception

The TGG-influenced approaches to sentence perception that
I described earlier did not see the temporal order of the informational relationships within the processing system as a major
experimental issue. Consequently it is difficult to find an
unambiguous statement of what these relationships were thought
to be like. The kind of model that seems to have been generally
assumed, and which makes the most sense in a TGG framework, was
a "staggered serial" model, in which the input to any higher
level of analysis consists of the outcome of analyses conducted
just at a lower level of analysis. Thus, for example, only after sufficient phonetic analysis has occurred to specify a word

does the lexical analysis begin. Similarly, the input to a syntactic analyser would be the output of sufficient words from the lexical analyser to constitute a syntactic unit, such as a phrase or a clause. Although the last explicit statement of such a model was in an early psycholinguistic paper by Miller (1962b), it is implicit in the more recent clausal processing hypotheses (Bever, Garrett, & Hurtig, 1973; Fodor et al., 1974), and, furthermore, allows the contact between the input and the internal representation of syntactic knowledge to take place in a way consistent with the TGG assumption.

The shadowing data, in contrast, demonstrate that the listener not only lexically and phonetically analyzes each word as he hears it, but also simultaneously extracts its syntactic and semantic implications, and uses these implications to guide his processing of subsequent words in the sentence. These phenomena suggest an "on-line interactive" view of sentence perception, in which each word, as it is heard in the context of normal discourse, enters into the processing system at all levels of description, and is interpreted at all these levels in the light of whatever information is available at that point in the processing of the sentence. And instead of the hierarchical and stratified relationship between different forms of analysis presupposed in the serial model, it is more natural to think of an on-line interactive system as being heterarchically organized, with no strict chain of informational command (Winograd, 1974; Winston, 1975).

It would be premature to think of this view of sentence processing as a fully developed model, but it does make a number of testable claims about sentence perception that firmly distinguish it from the serial model. Firstly, that the listener begins to develop a syntactic and semantic interpretation of the material from the first word of the sentence, and, secondly, that this higher-order information interacts directly with the immediate identification of the words in the incoming message. I have tested this second claim in a sentence shadowing experiment in which the phonetic cues for particular lexical identification decisions were co-varied with violations of syntactic and semantic constraints (Marslen-Wilson, 1975). The subjects heard sentences containing tri-syllabic words such as "president," "company," and "tomorrow." The first, second, or third syllables of these words were changed to make them into nonsense words (thus: "howident," "comsiny," and "tomorrane"). In addition, these critical words were themselves either normal with respect to their sentential contexts, or were syntactically and/or semantically incongruous.

I had noticed in previous experiments that shadowers tended to restore disrupted or mispronounced words to their original form. In this experiment I was investigating the frequency of such word restorations as a function of (a) which syllable was disrupted, (b) whether the word was congruent with its context, and (c) the shadowing latencies of the subjects. If the inter-actions between different levels of analysis take place only after the initial lexical identification of the word, then the frequency of word-restoration should be independent of context. The shadower would have no basis, in his initial repetition, for rejecting contextually anomalous restorations. If, however, immediate identification does interact on-line with the semantic and syntactic context, then it becomes possible for context var-iables to affect word-restoration frequency. The significance of using close shadowers in this task is that at shadowing la-tencies of 250 msec, their repetition of the critical words would be initiated when only the first syllable could have been heard. Thus the temporal location of any context effects ob-tained at these latencies would be restricted to the intiial processing of the incoming word.

The results were clear-cut, and exactly as predicted by an on-line interactive approach. Subjects only restored words (e.g., repeated "comsiny" as "company") with significant fre-quency in the conditions where the first one or two syllables of the critical word were consistent with some word that itself was congruent with the preceding higher-level context--as, for example, in the sentence "If the letter doesn't arrive today, then it's bound to arrive <u>tomorrane</u> unless something has really gone wrong". Restorations never occurred when the first syllable of the word was disrupted, and were very infrequent, no matter which syllable was changed, when the disrupted word appeared in an inappropriate syntactic and/or semantic context. And, most importantly, this pattern of word restorations held as strongly at latencies of 250 msec as at latencies ranging up to 1050 msec. The close shadowers' performance reveals a direct reciprocal interaction during processing between the lexical interpretation of the phonetic input and the developing syntactic and semantic representation of the sentence.

The other major claim of an on-line interactive approach is that syntactic and semantic interpretations begin with the first word of a sentence. In the shadowing study just described, the critical words were all located towards the end of a 10-20 words long test-sentence. A second experiment, therefore, carried out in collaboration with Lorraine Tyler, was intended to investi-gate similar interactive effects, but in a situation where the critical words varied in position throughout the test-sentences (Marslen-Wilson & Tyler, 1975; Tyler & Marslen-Wilson, forth-coming). To achieve these ends, we used three different moni-toring tasks, co-varied with three prose contexts, and crossed with nine target-word locations ranging from the second to the tenth word in the test-sentences.

In the monitoring task the subject listens to a sentence and makes a timed response when he hears the monitoring

target-word. In the task we called Identical monitoring, the
subject knows in advance exactly which word to listen for. In
Rhyme monitoring he listens for a word that rhymes with a cue-
word given in advance, and in Category monitoring for a word
that belongs to a taxonomic category specified in advance. Performance on Identical monitoring provides a baseline for assess-
ing performance in the Rhyme and Category tasks. These two
tasks both require that the subject hear the entire target-word
before he can respond. But in the Rhyme task the further requirement is simply that he match the sound of the target with
that of the cue-word, which need only require a phonetic analysis of the target-word. In Category monitoring, the subject
must identify the taxonomic category of the target-word. This
requires some semantic analysis of the target before a response
can be made. By placing the Rhyme and Category target-words at
different serial positions in the test-sentences, we can measure the time-course with which the necessary information for
making these decisions becomes available.

But perhaps the most important variable in this experiment
was the manipulation of types of prose material, such that each
monitoring target-word could appear in each of three types of
sentential context--Normal Prose, Syntactic Prose, and Random
Word-Order Prose. These differ in the kinds of information
that they make available to the listener. In Normal Prose, all
forms of analysis are potentially available. In Syntactic
Prose, the sentences are syntactically normal but have no semantic interpretation, while in Random Word-Order Prose syntactic
analyses are also not available. To the extent that the monitoring tasks depend for their execution on the types of sentential analysis absent in Syntactic and Random Word-Order Prose,
then the subjects' response times will increase relative to
Normal Prose. According to the on-line interactive approach,
these interactions between task and context should not only
occur in all monitoring tasks, but should also be detectable
early in the test-sentences. Note that in this first version
of the experiment the subject was presented with two sentences
on each trial, with the target always occurring in the second
sentence (for example: "The church was broken into last night.
Some thieves stole most of the lead off the roof").

In discussing the results I will concentrate on the word-
position effects, since the other aspects of the results only
serve to corroborate the conclusions drawn from the sentence
shadowing experiment described earlier (for these details, see
Marslen-Wilson & Tyler, 1975). However, it is worth noting
that in the Normal Prose context condition the mean latencies
for Rhyme and Category monitoring were the same. That is, in
Normal Prose it takes no longer to make a semantically based
decision than it does to make a phonetically based decision.
The listener is constructing a unified multi-level

representation of the material as he hears it, and the "higher"
and "lower" level attributes of this representation are equally
accessible for making the monitoring response. Whereas a serial
model has to predict longer latencies for Category as opposed
to Rhyme monitoring, since the defining characteristic of a
serial model is that higher-level decisions must, at least to
some measurable extent, await lower-level decisions. It is important for our purposes that Category monitoring in Syntactic
and Random Word-Order Prose was indeed much slower than Rhyme
monitoring, since this implies that the similarity between the
two in Normal Prose is dependent on the availability of an on-
going semantic analysis.

The effects of the word-position variables were very much
as the on-line interactive model would predict. Latencies decreased as a linear function of word-position in all three monitoring tasks in Normal Prose, and in Identical and Rhyme monitoring in Syntactic Prose. But no word-position effects were
found in the conditions in which hearing more of a sentence did
not give the subjects additional information at the sentential
levels of analysis that they were apparently using to guide
their responses. Thus in Syntactic Prose Category there were no
semantic analyses available to be developed as the sentence was
heard, while in the Random Word-Order conditions there was no
syntactic framework available either.

An important point about these position effects was that
the size of the differences between conditions remained constant
from the second to the tenth position. The slopes of the linear
regression lines were almost exactly parallel for all the major
effects, so that, for example, the advantage of Normal Prose
over Syntactic Prose in both Identical and Rhyme monitoring was
the same at all word-positions. This is consistent with an
approach to sentence perception which claims that analyses of
all types are initiated with the first word of a sentence. However, the consistent 50-75 millisecond advantage of Normal Prose
monitoring obtained for the first two or three words of a sentence is not fully accounted for by information internal to that
sentence alone. At least some of this early Normal Prose advantage was due to the presence of the lead-in sentence in each
trial, as we showed in a further experiment in which we ran the
same stimuli a second time, but with the first sentence omitted
(Tyler & Marslen-Wilson, forthcoming). What we found, for all
monitoring tasks, was that the linear regression lines now con-
verged at the beginning of the sentence, so that there were no
longer any differences between prose materials for the first
two or three word-positions. The specific shifts were just in
the Normal Prose curves; that is, in the prose conditions in
which the first sentence could provide a semantic context into
which the interpretation of the second could be immediately
embedded.

Although a serial model could be adjusted to predict the differential decreases in latency across word-positions for the different types of material in the one-sentence version of the task, it cannot explain the effects found when the lead-in sentence was present. A serial model makes no provision for the integration of semantic context information into the immediate processing of subsequent sentences; the only feasible point of contact would be when the semantic analysis of the sentence starts later in processing, after a sufficiently large segment of the input had been heard. To account for the observed effects of inter-sentential context on the processing of the first words of a sentence, it is necessary to postulate a process within that sentence which is itself initiated at the beginning of the sentence, and which involves levels of analysis in terms of which inter-sentential semantic constraints can be expressed.

It is likely that the processing relationships between sentences, touched upon in this last study, are a primary factor in ordinary sentence perception, and it is noteworthy that TGG-influenced psycholinguistic research has had very little to say about such issues. But this is not surprising, given a view of linguistic knowledge which is explicitly sentence based and nowhere allows for the influences of the informational and communicative context in which sentences are normally uttered. In any case, as I remarked above, a serial view of sentence processing is not well adapted to representing the processing effects of contextual variables.

In discussing the research summarized here, I have avoided using the term "model" to describe the view of sentence perception being proposed. The purpose of the experiments was to elucidate the general temporal characteristics of on-line sentence processing, and to measure, as it were, the qualitative transfer function of the system at different points in its operation. As such, the experiments provide a clear outline of the kinds of phenomena that any adequate model of sentence perception will have to be able to explain, but they do not of themselves discriminate between many different accounts of the internal structure of this system. However, the questions that I raised in the introduction to the paper are precisely questions about the general characteristics of sentence processing. It is at this level of description that TGG-based assumptions have had their most powerful influence on psycholinguistic theorizing, and in the next section of the paper I will discuss the implications of our results for the empirical adequacy of these assumptions.

The Uses of Linguistic Knowledge in Sentence Processing

The basic question I have been discussing concerns the role of knowledge in sentence perception. It is useful at this point to restate the issue in the following framework. An adequately descriptive theory of how people process and understand sentences will need to be built around an explicit analysis of the three-sided informational relationship that holds between the spoken input, the listener's processing representation of this input, and his stored representation of linguistic knowledge (cf., Bobrow & Brown, 1975). If it is assumed that the processing representation is akin to a transformational deep structure, and · that the internal representation of linguistic knowledge corresponds to a TGG, then this places a particular interpretation on the basic informational relationships in the system.

For we are assuming a definition of linguistic knowledge such that it cannot directly contact the representation of the input until it has been compiled into the appropriate deep structural format. This format, in turn, differs from the linear surface characteristics of the input in ways which require that relatively large segments become available before a deep structure analysis can be confidently assigned. Taking these factors together, we are forced into a situation where the informational relationships between the representation of the input and stored linguistic knowledge are only properly specifiable at a few points in the analysis--in particular at the ends of sentences and clauses. This leaves severely underdetermined one side of the basic informational structure of the system--namely, the original processing relationship between the input and whatever interim representations are computed in anticipation of major constituent boundaries.

These TGG assumptions, and the informational structures they require, are empirically justifiable only if the on-line sentence processor does not in fact have direct access to the kinds of structural information that would be represented in a mental competence grammar. But the shadowing data, and the experiments testing their implications, strongly suggest that knowledge about linguistic structures is directly involved in on-line processing; that the listener interprets the syntactic (and semantic) implications of each word as he hears it, and actively uses this knowledge to guide his processing of subsequent items in the string. If the basic informational relationships are of this type, then they place their own constraints on the mental representation of linguistic knowledge. And these constraints are not consistent with transformationally organized knowledge representations. For the processing system requires a representation that is organized for left-to-right access and codes the structural possibilities in the language in such a way that each word, as it is heard, is immediately interpretable

in terms of the possible continuations of the string with which
it is compatible.

The problem here for a TGG is not that it fails to capture
the left-to-right constraints that hold between items in a sentence. The problem is that nowhere in the grammar are these
kinds of interdependencies directly represented. It is the grammar as a whole that combines appropriately related words to form
sentences, as a function of the overall interactions of transformational operations with the organization of the underlying base
strings. The listener, however, cannot use information represented in this fashion. The on-line processing data show that he
cannot be searching up and down possible derivational sequences
in a TGG competence grammar to extract information about what
kinds of words can appear in which contexts.

A possible move at this point, that is apparently consistent with the assumption of a TGG competence grammar, would be
to assign the necessary left-to-right processing information to
the mental lexicon, so that each entry had appended to it a
listing of the structures in which it could participate (cf.,
Fodor, Garrett, & Bever, 1968). But this in itself would not be
adequate, because the listener needs to be able to keep track of
constraints that cannot be specified in a simple list--discon-
tinuous dependencies are a major example. Since such constraints
are represented elsewhere in the grammar in a form that is not
directly usable by the listener, this same information will need
to be incorporated into the lexicon as well. This in turn requires that the structural conditions associated with each word
be assigned considerable computational powers of their own. In
fact these additions would need to be equivalent to the kinds
of augmentation that are required to enable recursive finite
state grammars to cope with discontinuous serial dependencies
(Woods, 1970). This leaves us in the position of postulating a
lexicon that has computational powers formally equivalent to
those of the grammar as a whole.

Thus the attempt to expand the lexicon reduces, in this
case, to the postulate that in addition to a TGG-like mental competence grammar there is also a mental "performance grammar",
which is what we use in processing sentences. From the point of
view of the research described here, the postulate of a mental
performance grammar that meets the informational needs of the
processing system is a plausible one. In theory, it is not in-
compatible with the claim that there is also a TGG-based mental
competence grammar, but for this latter claim to have any
practical significance, it is necessary to define the relationship between the two grammars. Hence the proposal that the performance grammar is constructed from the competence grammar by
way of a mental "translation algorithm" (cf., Fodor et al.,
1974). But unfortunately this is, at present, a quite vacuous
proposal, since, as Fodor et al. (1974) rightly point out, we

have no way of knowing whether such an algorithm could be constructed, or what relationship its output would bear to the
original competence grammar. So until the feasibility of this
translation procedure can be demonstrated, to suggest it serves
no purpose, except to save the claim that the mental competence
grammar is of a normal transformational form. Stated in this
way the TGG assumption becomes extraordinarily weak, and does
not constrain in any practical way our theories about the mental
organization of linguistic knowledge and its use in sentence
perception.

These difficulties for a TGG-based model of mental competence also cast doubt on the further assumption that the initial
target of the processing system is a deep structure representation of the input. The informational relationships in an on-
line interactive system, with the representation of linguistic
knowledge that they apparently require, leave no clear processing function for this hypothesized deep structure to fulfil.
Contact between the input and stored linguistic knowledge is
apparently possible without the construction of an intermediate
deep syntactic representation. Nor, on an on-line interactive
approach, does it seem necessary to postulate a syntactic deep
structure to mediate the relationship between the syntactic
analysis of the input and its semantic interpretation--which is
what the TGG framework has seemed to require. For if the structural syntactic properties of the input can be extracted on-line,
then the temporal informational properties of the system offer
no obstacle to the immediate use of this syntactic information
in a semantic interpretation of the input. In fact, the experimental results summarized earlier are perfectly compatible with
this possibility.

The TGG assumptions, and the fundamentally serial informational relationships that they presuppose, predict a temporal
asymmetry in the availability of syntactic, as opposed to semantic, information about the incoming material. But in no case
was such an asymmetry detectable. In the analysis of the shadowing errors, for example, I found no examples of errors that
were syntactically normal but semantically inappropriate. The
insertion of semantic anomalies, which only exist as anomalies
for the processor in terms of the semantic structure of the entire preceding string, affected the immediate shadowing performance of even the closest shadowers. Similarly, in the experiment testing the effects of syntactic and semantic context on
frequency of word-restoration (Marslen-Wilson, 1975), subjects
at all latencies were no more likely to restore a word that
was syntactically normal, but semantically anomalous, than they
were to restore a word that was anomalous in both respects.
Finally, the effects across word-position of the presence of a
semantic level of analysis upon monitoring performance (Marslen-
Wilson & Tyler, 1975) ran exactly parallel to the effects of

syntactic variables. Whether or not these consistent effects
reflect the computation of a final or an intermediate representation of the input, they do show the listener to be actively
analyzing the syntactic and the semantic implications of the
material as he hears it, beginning with the first word of the
sentence.

This is not, of course, direct evidence that a deep syntactic representation is not, nonetheless, being computed. But the
postulation of such a representation was originally intended to
fulfill specific functions in the processing system. In the
informational system that our results indicate, these functions
have been rendered redundant, with the consequence that the deep
structure assumption no longer retains a clear explanatory value.
And this, in effect, is the basic problem with the cluster of
TGG assumptions I have been discussing. They form a coherent
and justifiable approach to sentence perception only if the processing structure of the system corresponds to their requirements. To the extent that the processing system in fact allows
for the kinds of interactions that I have described, then the
TGG assumptions become increasingly redundant and empirically
unmotivated.

The implications of these apparent inadequacies of the TGG
model are fairly straightforward for the psycholinguist, and I
will discuss them briefly in the final section of the paper.
But the question also arises at this point of the implications
for the linguistic theory itself. As I mentioned in the introduction, criticism of the psycholinguistic realizability of a
TGG need not be taken as reflecting upon its adequacy as a formal grammatical theory. But if a linguistic theory is to be
taken seriously as a general theory of human language, then its
applicability to a central aspect of normal language use--the
perception of spoken language--would seem to be a significant
issue for the linguist. And although there continues to be
legitimate dispute as to the desirability of treating transformational theory as a true branch of cognitive psychology (cf.,
Chomsky, 1972, p. 1), some recent developments within linguistics have made surprisingly strong claims for the psychological
relevance of a TGG. Since the version of TGG in question, the
"extended lexical" model proposed by Bresnan (1976), differs
in some critical respects from the "Aspects" TGG (Chomsky, 1965)
whose implications I have been discussing, it is worth considering in detail the value of this new proposal for psycholinguistic research into sentence perception.

Psychological Realism in Models of Transformational Grammar

In discussing the extended lexical model we should make
clear what kind of psychological reality is being claimed for

this grammar. Bresnan is not arguing just that a TGG charac-
terises the mental competence grammar, or even that it maps onto
a mental performance grammar, but that the structure of the grammar directly mirrors the structure of the processing system. To
quote directly: "A realistic model of grammar must be...'realizable.' That is, we should be able to define for it a realization mapping to a psychological model of language processing.
Such a realization should map distinct grammatical rules and
units into distinct processing operations and informational
units in such a way that the different rule types of the grammar
are associated with different processing functions" (Bresnan,
1976; [emphases omitted]). Bresnan's paper marks, then, the
return of transformational theory to a position similar in spirit to the original proposals of Miller (1962a) and Miller and
Chomsky (1963), in which the linguistic theory is intended to
function as a kind of psychological process model. Unfortunately, it is not clear that Bresnan understands what would constitute a proper test of the psychological viability of a perceptual processing theory.

Bresnan is well aware that the Aspects TGG is quite inappropriate for realization as a process model, and she locates
the cause of this in its dependence on transformational operations to carry the primary descriptive burden of the grammar.
Not, however, because of the informational properties of a
transformational system, but because the complexity of the
Aspects transformational component would make it hopelessly
inefficient--and technically unfeasible--as an actual information processing system. Accordingly, in her assessment of the
realizability of the extended lexical model, Bresnan's arguments
center around the increased processing efficiency of its syntactic component. This increased efficiency is accomplished
by a drastic reduction in the role of the transformational component of the grammar, and a corresponding expansion of the
lexicon and of the semantic component. All lexically-governed
transformations, such as Passive, Equi-NP Deletion, and the
like, are dispensed with, and their functions are taken over by
lexical or functional composition rules. The result of this is
that surface structures now more closely resemble deep structures, even when one of the remaining transformations needs to
be applied, and that the postulate of a transformation cycle,
with its many intermediate levels of analysis intervening between deep and surface structure, is no longer necessary.

Bresnan argues, probably correctly, that this reduced syntactic component, unlike the syntactic component of an Aspects
grammar, could be realized in a workable processing system.
Her evidence for this is phrased in terms of the system's map-
pability onto an Augmented Transition Network (ATN) syntactic
parser (Woods, 1970; Kaplan, 1972). The phrase structure rules
of the grammar, defining the basic structural patterns of the

language, can be directly realized in the nodes and arcs of an
ATN, while the remnants of the transformational component are
statable "as processing operations that relate the structure
being recognized to the structure being built up in working
memory" (Bresnan, 1976). This distinction in the ATN parser
between processing operations that do or do not reflect transformational functions, may be further mirrored, Bresnan suggests,
in corresponding processing differences in the human analysis of
sentences of different types.

But there are a number of problems in evaluating Bresnan's
arguments here. One major reason for caution is that it is
doubtful how much significance should be attached to the realizability of the extended lexical model in an ATN parsing system.
As Woods (1970) has shown, the ATN formalism is equivalent in
power to a transformational grammar, so that any version of such
a grammar could in principle be realized as an ATN. And we are,
it should be noted, only talking about realization in principle,
since none of the extant ATN parsers can cope with the full
range of syntactic possibilities in the language, nor has any
version of a TGG been fully realized in an ATN formalism. So
it says very little for the psychological reality of a particular TGG that it can be realized in principle in an ATN--unless,
of course, the psychological reality of an ATN syntactic parser
of a particular type has itself been demonstrated. Therefore
the psychological research on ATN's (Wanner & Maratsos, 1974;
Wanner, Kaplan, & Shiner, 1975; Wanner & Shiner, 1975) cited by
Bresnan can only be taken to support the psychological realizability of the extended lexical theory under two conditions.
Firstly, that Wanner's ATN model correspond in the appropriate
ways to the extended lexical model, and, secondly, that this
research be intended to demonstrate the same kind of psychological reality for their ATN that Bresnan's proposals require.
But neither of these conditions seem to hold.

Wanner and Maratsos (1974) in fact state that "An ATN re-
covers functional information directly from surface structure.
There is no intervening application of transformational rules
to determine the deep structure of the sentence.... Models
which apply such rules have proven to be both computationally
unmanageable...and empirically unsatisfactory" (p. 7). But
even if Wanner's and his colleagues' ATN parser is construed as
including direct analogues of transformational rules, they seem
to be careful to avoid making strong claims for the psychological reality of the processing procedures realized in the parser.
Their strongest statement is that their results "support the
feasibility of using the ATN notation to construct psychological
models of sentence comprehension" (Wanner & Maratsos, 1974;
Wanner & Shiner, 1975). This amounts to saying that it is
fruitful to think about sentence comprehension as a left-to-
right process. I would hardly disagree with this, but it is

not the kind of demonstration that Bresnan's arguments require.

In any case, even if the syntactic component of the extended lexical model is realizable in a technically reasonable
parsing system, this does not address the most important issues
in the assessment of the extended lexical model as a processing
theory. Undoubtedly, the feasilbility or the efficiency of a
candidate processing model is an important consideration, but it
is not a metric that by itself demonstrates the plausibility of
the model as a psychologically real system. The psychological
plausibility of the system depends primarily on whether it can
meet the overall informational requirements of actual perceptual
processing. But Bresnan does not directly discuss the viability
of the extended lexical model in these terms.

The informational characteristics of the Aspects TGG are
relatively straightforward, since the major descriptive power
of the grammar is carried by the transformational component.
And transformational manipulations, operating on the structural
descriptions of entire strings, are empirically inadequate in a
psychological model because of the strict serial relationships
that they require between different levels of linguistic description. Thus, independently of its processing efficiency or
inefficiency, an Aspects model can be ruled out because it cannot provide information to the processor in the manner that an
on-line interactive approach requires. But the informational
properties of the extended lexical model are rather more opaque.
Most of the erstwhile functions of the transformational component have been shifted elsewhere, so that the primary descriptive
work of the grammar is now specified in terms of lexical and
semantic interpretive rules.

In the case of a Passive sentence, for example, the underlying grammatical function of the surface subject as the logical
object is no longer captured by a process of transformational
rearrangement that places the surface subject in the appropriate location in the base structure. In the extended lexical
model, the deep structure order of the Passive sentence directly mirrors the surface order of the string. It is the functional composition rules, operating on lexical items with particular
lexical relations associated with them in the lexicon, that construct a further level of representation, the semantic "functional interpretation", in which the surface subjects and
objects are now assigned their proper grammatical functions as
logical objects and subjects.

This shift in the primary descriptive functions of the
grammar means that the important informational relationships in
the grammar now become those between the deep structure representations of sentences and their interpretation by the combined
lexical and semantic components of the grammar. The syntactic
component of the model, consisting of the phrase-structure
rules and the remaining transformations, would do little more,

in a processing system, than relabel the surface string in deep
structural terms, with some minor transformational rearrangement of the surface order of the elements being occasionally
necessary. So the real test of the psychological adequacy of
the system does not lie in the realizability of the syntactic
component, but in the mode of operation of the next level of
the grammar. Certainly, when transformational rearrangements
are not required, then a deep structure description can be built
up left-to-right, as the sentence is heard. But are the functional composition rules that combine each lexical item into a
functional interpretation themselves able to work from left to
right? Or is their operation, like that of the transformations
they replace, also specified only in terms of the characteristics of entire strings and the lexical items that they contain?
The importance of elucidating the informational characteristics
of these aspects of the grammar is underlined by the consistent
experimental finding, mentioned earlier, that at least a preliminary semantic interpretation of the input is available to
the listener on-line.

Considered in its normal form, as a generative production
system, it is clear enough that the extended lexical model does
not derive sentences from left to right, but from the top down,
level by complete level of linguistic analysis. Within this
framework, the functional composition rules naturally apply under conditions where the entire string is available, and, equally naturally and parsimoniously, are defined at this level in
terms of canonical arrays of variables. Since Bresnan gives no
indication to the contrary, we must assume that if these functional composition rules were to be realized in a processing
system, then they would require inputs of the forms in terms of
which their operation is normally defined. In other words,
they appear to require a strict serial informational relationship between different levels of linguistic analysis, just as
transformational operations do. This means, in turn, that the
extended lexical model--whether it is viewed as a kind of process model, or as a candidate for a mental performance or competence grammar--is inconsistent with the on-line interactive
data in very much the same ways as an Aspects-based model would
be. But such an outcome would not be very surprising. For the
development of the extended lexical model was not, after all,
originally motivated by a desire to improve the realizability of
a TGG in a psychological model. Any such improvement, Bresnan
stresses, is to be seen as an unlooked-for by-product of changes
that were themselves motivated entirely by linguistic evidence
internal to the grammatical theory. If this is the case, and
since the primary empirical input to the grammar has certainly
not been its success or failure as a processing model, then it
should be quite accidental that any new version of the grammar
turn out to be better fitted than its predecessors to

psycholinguistic performance requirements.

Bresnan is quite correct in saying that there is great
potential value for both linguistics and psycholinguistics in
making linguistic theories directly accountable to facts about
processing systems. But she has not set about specifying this
accountability in a way that would make the relationship a useful one. The realizability of a linguistic theory in a perceptual processing model is not just a question of general analogi-
zing between rule types in the grammar and processing functions
in the psychological model. Nor is it simply a matter of the
degree of processing efficiency of one component or another of
a grammar. Especially not if an increase in efficiency is obtained just by shifting the important processing functions out
of the component in question into other parts of the grammar.
This may make limited aspects of the system easier to consider
from a processing point of view, but it in no way means that the
system as a whole is thereby any more psychologically real than
its predecessors. The technical feasibility of realizing a
grammar as a processing system is just a preliminary step. The
important test of its realism as a psychological model is then
to determine whether the pattern of information flow within such
a system in fact corresponds with what we know about the real-
time processing structure of human sentence perception. And
this is just the kind of test that Bresnan fails to apply.

Conclusions

In any kind of scientific activity, it is a reasonable pre-
caution to look closely, now and again, at the paradigmatic presuppositions in terms of which the activity is normally conducted. In the psycholinguistic study of sentence perception,
these presuppositions have derived directly from the form of a
transformational linguistic theory. It is of the nature of such
presuppositions that they are not themselves readily testable.
But what I have tried to do here is to point out the ways in
which these presuppositions have shaped the study of sentence
perception, and have led to a certain restricted class of theories about the possible properties of the sentence processing
system. The experimental evidence I presented does not of itself disprove these background assumptions, but in so far as it
suggests a dynamic approach to sentence processing that is inconsistent with the range of models that these assumptions have
led psycholinguists to propose, then I would argue that these
presuppositions may themselves have outlived their usefulness.

The processing target of the perceptual system is unlikely
to be something as straightforwardly linguistic as a transformational deep structure; the informational relationships within
the system are not strictly serial; and, most importantly, the

mental representation of linguistic knowledge cannot be adequately characterized by a transformational linguistic theory.
In other words, it seems appropriate for psycholinguists to look
for ways of characterizing the structure of human linguistic
knowledge that are more in tune with active perceptual processes,
and less constrained by the requirements of descriptivist formal
linguistics.

These conclusions may seem rather disturbing ones to have
to draw. For the basic issue is, after all, the relationship
of stored knowledge to perceptual process, and if we do not have
a usable characterization of stored knowledge then we are limited in what we can say about the perceptual process. This problem becomes especially urgent if the informational relationships
assumed in the TGG model are incorrect. For on the on-line interactive view, sentence perception cannot be considered to be an
operation carried out essentially independently of linguistic
knowledge, and just calling upon this knowledge now and then.
Rather, understanding a sentence is more like plotting a path
through some space of possibilities, where these possibilities
are stated, in part, in terms of the structures that the language allows. Evidently, to make any kind of sense of this
metaphor, one has to have some way of defining this space, of
specifying the paths that particular utterances can take as they
are being processed. Otherwise we will not be able to progress
much beyond the generalities that I have stated here as the
on-line interactive approach.

But the appropriate response to these problems is not to
return, willy-nilly, to the cluster of TGG assumptions that I
have been arguing against. For however impressive a structure
transformational theory may present, it is not a theory of the
right kind of linguistic phenomena. Chomsky was indeed correct
in stating that "investigation of performance will proceed only
so far as understanding of underlying competence permits"
(Chomsky, 1965, p. 10), but he may not have been correct in the
sense which he intended. For in terms of the performance data
on which it is in practice based, a TGG can only be considered
to be a theory of a formalized static competence, of a time-free
linguistic knowledge extrapolated from the metalinguistic intuitions of the idealized speaker-hearer (cf., Levelt, 1973). So
however successful TGG may be in characterizing its chosen empirical domain, there is no a priori reason to expect it to be
applicable to the quite different domain of the use of linguistic knowledge in sentence perception. The primary constraints
here are nothing like the primary constraints on a TGG; we are
not concerned with whether the system produces ungrammatical
outputs, but with whether we can specify the dynamic informational relationships, between forms of knowledge available at
different levels of the representational system and at different points in real time, that underly on-line processing

performance.

For a description of linguistic knowledge that is constructed with these considerations in mind, we will have to look
elsewhere. A plausible place to start might be the recent computer-based research into natural language processing systems
(cf., Winograd, 1974; Bobrow & Collins, 1975). For this is one
area of research that has had to confront directly these dynamic
informational problems. A language processing system can only
be successfully programmed if one can correctly specify what the
system needs to know at which point in its analysis of the input. However, this is not to suggest that a future psycholinguistics should borrow wholesale from one branch or another of
artificial intelligence. Given the sadly unfruitful history of
metaphors imported to psychology from other disciplines, any
new metaphor should be treated with caution. A psychological
model of linguistic knowledge should primarily be generated from
a psychological experimental base.

But the advantage of thinking about how to program our
theories is that it helps to bring into sharp focus what a psychological theory of sentence perception needs to be able to do.
This, after all, is the most natural starting point for developing our background assumptions about the kind of explanatory
structure we are looking for. The normal listener is not a kind
of transformational linguist trying to map a sentence onto a
grammatical theory. He is a participant in a social event, trying to interpret the utterances he hears in terms of the communicative intentions of the speakers in question. Even if we cannot fully reproduce this situation under laboratory conditions,
we can still try to capture, in our investigations of sentence
perception, its essentially goal-oriented and dynamic properties.
The adequate characterization of sentence processing from these
perspectives seems to be the necessary first step. For these
are the kinds of empirical constraints that will enable us to
set about constructing a theory of the mental representation of
stored knowledge, linguistic or otherwise, that actually can
function in a psycholinguistic "performance" model. It may be
the perceptual functions of knowledge that will tell us what a
theory of this knowledge needs to look like.

Acknowledgements

I am indebted to Lorraine Tyler for drawing my attention
to many of the issues raised here and to David McNeill, Michael
Silverstein, and Edward Walker for their comments on previous
versions of the manuscript.

References

Bever, T.G. (1970) The cognitive basis for linguistic struc-
    tures. In J.R. Hayes (Ed.), Cognition and the Development
    of Language. New York: Wiley.
Bever, T.G., Garrett, M.F., & Hurtig, R. (1973) Ambiguity in-
    creases complexity of perceptually incomplete clauses.
    Memory and Cognition, 1, 279-286.
Bever, T.G., & Hurtig, R. (1975) Detection of a non-linguistic
    stimulus is poorest at the end of a clause. Journal of
    Psycholinguistic Research, 4, 1-7.
Bobrow, R.J., & Brown, J.S. (1975) Systematic understanding:
    Synthesis, analysis, and contingent knowledge in speci-
    alised understanding systems. In Bobrow & Collins.
Bobrow, D.G., & Collins, A. (Eds.) (1975) Representation and
    Understanding. New York: Academic Press.
Bresnan, J. (1976) Toward a Realistic Model of Transformational
    Grammar. Paper presented at MIT-AT&T Convocation on Com-
    munications, Sessions on Language and Cognition, Cambridge,
    Mass.
Bransford, J.D., & Johnson, M.K. (1973) Considerations of some
    problems of comprehension. In W.G. Chase (Ed.), Visual
    Information Processing. New York: Academic Press.
Chomsky, N. (1965) Aspects of the Theory of Syntax. Cambridge:
    MIT Press.
Chomsky, N. (1972) Language and Mind (enlarged edition). New
    York: Harcourt Brace Jovanovich.
Clark, H.H. (1974) Semantic and comprehension. In Sebeok, T.A.
    (Ed.), Current Trends in Linguistics, Vol. 12. The Hague:
    Mouton.
Fodor, J.A., Bever, T.G., & Garrett, M.F. (1974) The Psychology
    of Language. New York: McGraw-Hill.
Fodor, J.A., & Garrett, M.F. (1967) Some syntactic determinants
    of sentential complexity. Perception and Psychophysics,
    2, 289-296.
Fodor, J.A., Garrett, M.F., & Bever, T.G. (1968) Some syntactic
    determinants of sentential complexity, II: Verb structure.
    Perception and Psychophysics, 3, 453-461.
Foss, D.J. (1969) Decision processes during sentence compre-
    hension: Effects of lexical item difficulty and position
    upon decision times. Journal of Verbal Learning and
    Verbal Behavior, 8, 457-462.
Foss, D.J., & Swinney, D.A. (1973) On the psychological reality
    of the phoneme: Perception, identification, and conscious-
    ness. Journal of Verbal Learning and Verbal Behavior,
    12, 577-589.
Kaplan, R.M. (1972) Augmented transition networks as psycholo-
    gical models of sentence comprehension. Artificial Intel-
    ligence, 3, 77-100.

Levelt, W.J.M. (1973) Formal Grammars in Linguistics and Psy-
    cholinguistics, Vol. III. The Hague: Mouton.
Marslen-Wilson, W.D. (1973a) Speech Shadowing and Speech Per-
    ception. Unpublished Ph.D. Thesis. Department of Psycho-
    logy, MIT.
Marslen-Wilson, W.D. (1973b) Linguistic structure and speech
    shadowing at very short latencies. Nature (Lond.), 244,
    522-523.
Marslen-Wilson, W.D. (1975) Sentence perception as an interac-
    tive parallel process. Science, 189, 226-228.
Marslen-Wilson, W.D., & Tyler, L.K. (1975) Processing structure
    of sentence perception. Nature (Lond.), 257, 784-786.
McNeill, D., & Lindig, K. (1973) The perceptual reality of
    phonemes, syllables, words and sentences. Journal of
    of Verbal Learning and Verbal Behavior, 12, 419-430.
Miller, G.A. (1962a) Some psychological studies of grammar.
    American Psychologist, 17, 748-762.
Miller, G.A. (1962b) Decision units in the perception of speech.
    IRE Transactions on Information Theory, IT-8, 81-83.
Miller, G.A., & Chomsky, N. (1963) Finitary models of language
    users. In R.D. Luce, R.R. Bush, & E. Galanter (Eds.),
    Handbook of Mathematical Psychology, Vol. II. New York:
    Wiley.
Morton, J., & Long, J. (1976) Effect of word transitional
    probability on phoneme identification. Journal of Verbal
    Learning and Verbal Behavior, 15, 43-52.
Savin, H.B., & Bever, T.G. (1970) The non-perceptual reality of
    the phoneme. Journal of Verbal Learning and Verbal Behav-
    ior, 9, 295-302.
Tyler, L.K., & Marslen-Wilson, W.D. (In preparation) The time-
    course of sentence processing events.
Wanner, E., & Maratsos, M. (1974) An augmented transition net-
    work model of relative clause comprehension. Unpublished
    manuscript.
Wanner, E., Kaplan, R.M., & Shiner, S. (1975) Garden paths in
    relative clauses. Unpublished manuscript.
Wanner, E., & Shiner, S. (1975) Ambiguities in relative
    clauses. Unpublished manuscript.
Winograd, T. (1972) Understanding Natural Language. New York:
    Academic Press.
Winograd, T. (1974) Five Lectures on Artificial Intelligence.
    Stanford AI Laboratory Memo AIM-246, Stanford University.
Winston, P.H. (Ed.) (1975) The Psychology of Computer Vision.
    New York: McGraw-Hill.
Woods, W.A. (1970) Transition network grammars for natural
    language analysis. Communications of the ACM, 13, 591-606.

SYNTACTIC PROCESSES IN SENTENCE PRODUCTION

Merrill F. Garrett

Massachusetts Institute of Technology

Introduction

No one will be surprised at the claim that it is possible both to speak and to understand nonsense:

(1)   Tribbles veek nargently ank doosons

Spoken, read, or remembered, the form of (1) taps powerful processing mechanisms that are the agency of our comprehension and production of straightforwardly interpretable sequences like (2):

(2)   Camels belch loudly at daybreak

Whether the interpretability of (2) renders its processing for production or comprehension different from that of (1) is scarcely an issue; but "how" it does so is another matter. In particular, it is surely conceiveable that the processing of (1), to whatever degree it is done, bears little relation to that of interpretable sequences like (2)--precisely because the assignment of features of sentence form is directly or immediately contingent on the semantic burden of whatever words are included in the sequence to be processed. In fact, proposals for language processors have been seriously made which embody this assumption (e.g., Schank's conceptual dependency system, 1972). But, appearances to the contrary, cases like (1) are only the most extreme illustration of what may be the typical case; i.e., we process sentence form in the absence of, or perhaps in spite of, lexically based information that is non-syntactic. For example, what we know of talons, speaking and vengeance avails us little and may even interfere with our syntactic processing of (3); but the feeling persists that understanding is there--as it is for prosaic cases like (4).

(3)   Talons speak softly of vegeance

(4)   The foreigner delighted the hostess

Note that even here there is little to be gained, for purposes

of the analysis of the form of the string, from what one knows
of foreigners, delight and hostesses. Only for sentences like
(5) does one begin to feel confident that what one knows of what
the words refer to might usefully constrain processing of the
string. From the point of view that semantically interpretable
sequences like (2) are processed in a fundamentally different
way from strings like (1), something seems to have gone awry.

(5) The canary sang sweetly

What is in fact awry is perhaps the assumption that one should
appeal to the semantic burden of sentences for the purpose of
generating hypotheses about their form. It has been observed,
with some justice, I think, that syntax exists so that we can
say improbable things.[1] Indeed, it is remarkable how infre-
quently the sentences of a spontaneous conversation use lexical
items in a stereotypic relation or exploit stereotypic relations
in sentence construction. This is hardly surprising since the
language would otherwise do remarkably little work for its users.
All this is not to say, of course, that such relations among
words do not ultimately play some role in the comprehension process; it is only to remark on the unreasonableness of making
syntactic analysis contingent on such relations.

These sorts of observations, not at all original, suggest
that we should take seriously the view that most significant
aspects of syntactic processing for sentences are done independently of their ultimate semantic consequence. Evidently there
must be a means of insuring or determining that the forms resulting from such processing have the appropriate (i.e., speaker
intended) semantic consequences. But that constraint in no way
prejudices the possibility that syntactic form is processed
autonomously both for sentence production and sentence comprehension, since semantic selection may be accomplished by means
other than the importation of semantic variables into the domain
of processing rules for establishing sentence form (see, e.g.,
Fodor, Bever and Garrett, Chapter 7).

Clearly, these are matters of potential dispute which have
their parallels in linguistics, artificial intelligence and cognitive psychology. The occasional arguments for a semantic/
syntactic potpourri in the former two fields have inevitably had
their repercussions for models of human cognitive processes. My
remarks are intended to suggest that our common-sense confidence
that _what_ is said is more important than _how_ it is said (both
for comprehension and production) is no grounds for embracing

---

[1] I am not sure whether to attribute this observation to J.A.
Fodor, K.I. Forster, John Limber, myself, some unknown fifth
party, or an ambience generated by our joint contemplation of
such sentences as "John took in washing for his sick pig."

such proposals as being of clearly greater "psychological reality" than systems which represent syntactic processing as independent of semantic consequences of sentence form. The informal observations so far made suggest caution on this point, and there are both formal experimental and observational facts which suggest that the psychological models of both production and comprehension should be represented as having autonomous syntactic processes. In the area of comprehension processes, for example, see Limber's remarks on the Thorn, Bradley and Dewar syntactic analysis routine, and the paper by Forster, both in this volume.

For the case of sentence production, I have argued else-where (Garrett, 1975) that an analysis of speech errors shows a strong indication of specifically syntactic processing systems at two levels. The error corpus[2] used for that analysis (here-after, the "MIT corpus") consisted of some 3,400 errors collec-ted by myself and S.R. Shattuck and has since been augmented by an additional 700 errors. The error "types" in question are, roughly, those in which sounds or words have been added, deleted or moved relative to a speaker's intended utterance. The rele-vant error types can be more fully described as follows: simple additions, deletions and substitutions, e.g., (6)a-e:

(6) a. "...which by itself is the most unimplausible sentence you can imagine." (morpheme addition; intended: "implausible")

   b. "...positive indentication was made." (sound/syllable deletion; intended: "indentification)

   c. "It very could be." (word deletion; intended: "very well could be")

   d. "...to get anythong like a good model of syntactic pro-cessing." (sound substitution; intended: "anything")

   e. "One of them was rejected without any revision at all." (word substitution; intended: "accepted")

There are occurrences of each of these types for sounds, syllables, morphemes and words. These errors, for which there is (apparent-ly) a single "error locus", are somewhat less informative than those errors for which there are two error loci. In such cases elements are mislocated or there appears to be an interaction between two identical elements. These errors include shifts,

---

[2]All errors in the corpus were recorded in written form from spontaneous speech. See Shattuck (1974) and Garrett (1975) for a discussion on the collection, initial analysis and classifi-cation.

exchanges, and <u>complex</u> additions, deletions and substitutions;
e.g., (7)a-i:

(7) a. "...because of band hadwriting" (sound shift; intended:
       "bad handwriting")

    b. "...he get a trips to..." (sound/morpheme shift; inten-
       ded: "gets a trip to...")

    c. "That's what Tomsky was chalking about." (sound exchange;
       intended: "...Chomsky was talking...")

    d. "It waits to pay." (combined-form exchange; intended:
       it pays to wait)

    e. "If I talk it into him." (word exchange; intended:
       "...him into it")

    f. "...but a beach on the bikini is alright." (word ex-
       change; intended: "bikini on the beach")

    g. "Do you know where I can find a clear pliece of..."
       (complex sound addition; intended: "clear piece")

    h. "I think the same may be coming evident..." (complex
       morpheme deletion; intended: "may be becoming")

    i. "...take your foot out of the stirrups and wallop him in
       the chollops." (complex substitution; intended: "...in
       the chops")

In what follows, I will review some of the evidence and arguments raised in my earlier reported analysis of such speech
errors and evaluate it in the context of possible influences
of meaning relations among lexical items.

Sentence Production Processes

     For many linguists and psychologists, the question, "how
do we, as speakers, produce a sentence which corresponds to
whatever particular message we may have in mind?" has seemed to
be naturally answered by the postulation of a series of computational stages corresponding to the several types of linguistic
structures. For example, Fry (1968) characterizes the "encoding
process" in terms of a set of processing levels corresponding
to linguistic types: semantic, lexical, morpheme and phoneme.
These levels are assumed to be successive, but not exhaustively
so. That is, Fry assumes, as have others before and since, that
the elaboration of a complete structure of a given type for a
sentence is <u>not</u> a condition on the initiation of constructions
at subsequent levels. Thus, we may imagine with Fry, the processes as a series of partially overlapping, more or less

independent levels of processing activity corresponding to
major linguistic types.

time →

semantic encod ING
lexical en CODING
morphem E ENCODING
pho NEME ENCODING
m OTOR CONTROL

Figure 1. A characterization of sentence production
as a set of processing levels corresponding to major
linguistic types (after Fry, 1968).

A similar, albeit linguistically more sophisticated, proposal
is made by Fromkin (1971), and MacKay's (1970) interpretation
of some speech errors makes similar assumptions. In fact, this
sort of characterization involves a very powerful claim about
the relation between grammars and the psychological systems
for processing language: namely, (1) that for each linguistic
rule system there is a processing level, (2) that the units of
the computational processes are to be identified with those of
the relevant type of linguistic description, and (3) that the
relation of information flow between the processing levels is
specified by the relation between rule systems of the grammar.
     It will readily be seen that, depending on the character
of the grammar one accepts, these assumptions will or will not
lead to the prediction of an autonomous level of syntactic processing for models of sentence production. This point is important, for it suggests that something very significant turns
on the evaluation of the interactions among informational types
in sentence processing. If we find evidence for the autonomy of
a given linguistic type in the computational procedures for
production or comprehension, it suggests that the grammar from
which the processor is derived should also represent the relevant structural facts in an autonomous component. If, on the
other hand, we fail to find evidence of processing autonomy vis
à vis a given informational type (e.g., semantic vs. syntactic),
the consequences are much weaker. It is virtually inconceivable
that any set of procedures constructed from a grammar which does
not represent, e.g., syntactic relations and semantic relations
by distinct rule systems, would nevertheless process such information by distinct sets of procedures; but the converse is
both conceivable and, in fact, has been a relatively common

suggestion in accounting for effects of semantic and pragmatic
variables in tests of the processing of different sentence types
(see, e.g., the discussion in Forster and Olbrei, 1974, and the
discussion in Walker, this volume). In short, empirical consideration of the interactions among informational types may
tell us not only about procedures of sentence production and
comprehension but also about the form of grammars as well. If
we find strong evidence for processing autonomy for syntax, it
counts heavily against grammars which do not represent such a
distinction among its rule systems.

Let us return briefly to the proposal of Fry before turning
to some of the evidence from speech error analyses, for we must
make an important distinction between "stages" and processing
levels. Note that Fry's characterization comports with a clear
intuition we have about the activity of speaking: we "know" in
detail some of what we want to say before we utter it, and we
know in general most of what we want to say before we utter it.
Even though consciousness or awareness of an activity is a
fickle guide to the nature of mental life, it would be well to
consider the introspective evidence where it makes itself so
naturally felt. Thus, we acknowledge the likelihood that the
levels of sentence planning are simultaneously active, but that
each may be at different temporal stages of progress vis à vis
the final articulatory level target. It does seem greatly unlikely that we must have planned in detail all the syntactic
structure and made all the lexical selections for a sentence
before any activity relating to the phonetic character of the
first emitted element is initiated.

The important point here is to see that to acknowledge this
truism is not to give up the idea that sentence production processes are characterizable by the operation of a series of independent processing systems each yielding a characteristic type
of description for sentences. For, the relevant sense of independence does not require that there be no communication between
levels (an evident absurdity); it requires that there be no
effect on the internal computational processes of a processing
level of the values of its vocabulary or constructions at other
processing levels. (The fact that a verb has two syllables does
not bear on whether it takes complements; more controversially,
neither does the fact that it refers to, e.g., a sensory process.) The complementary observation is commonplace in discussions of language comprehension processes, but there, as here,
no one now takes it as obvious just what levels of processing
there are, or what the "asynchronies" of their relationship
might be.

The final points to consider before examining some results of
speech error analyses are the conditions which we will require
such analyses to meet in order to provide support for the claim
that there are independent levels of processing activity in the

sense just described. There are two such conditions, the first easily met and the second problematic.

(1)   When elements of a sentence interact in an error (e.g., exchange position), they must be elements of the same hypothesized processing vocabulary.

(2)   The structural constraints on a given error type must be of a single processing type.

The strongest outcome is the joint effect of (1) and (2): Are the constraints on an error type stateable in terms of descriptions at the level required if one is to describe the interacting elements in the same vocabulary? For example, there will nearly always be a common description available for the elements of an error interaction even if only as phonetic strings, but the important point is that _if_ one is forced to that level of description, the constraints on the error interaction must be only those applicable to phonological description.

There is, of course, no _a priori_ claim that _error_ mechanisms must be linked to production processes in a systematic way. That is, it is possible to imagine that error distributions would fail to show the sort of regularities that would justify the claim for independent processing levels even though such a characterization of production were correct. Once again, however, the converse is much less likely--if one finds that error distributions _do_ show evidence of such constraints, it would be difficult to maintain that the psychologically correct model of sentence production processes is nonetheless interactive in ways the errors are not.

I will argue that a variety of speech errors can be shown to satisfy conditions 1 and 2, and that the nature of the errors indicates at least four processing levels. These processors correspond in general to distinct rule systems of the grammar, although there are some respects in which that correspondence is limited.

Speech error analyses

In "The Analysis of Sentence Production" (Garrett, 1975; hereafter A.S.P.), I argued, primarily on the basis of several types of exchange and shift errors, that the levels of sentence processing should be (minimally) characterized as in Figure 2. The separation of the levels of processing shown there turns on a number of particular observations which may be summarized as follows:

1. The phenomenon of accomodation. Virtually all investigators of speech errors have remarked on cases like (8) a,b,c.

(8)a "If you give the infant a nipple, then ..." → " ... the nipple an infant..."

   b "...cooked a roast..."   → "...roasted a cook..."
         [kʌkt]   [rowstɪd]   (Fromkin)

   c "...pets rode..."   → "...rodes pet..."
         [pɛts]   [rowdz]

The particular phonetic shape of the article or affix is accomodated to its error induced environment. Though a number of phonological points may be made on the basis of errors like these (see Fromkin, 1971, for a significant discussion), the import of such errors for current purposes lies in showing that there is a level of sound planning separate from the level at which the word or stem exchanges illustrated in (8) a,b,c take place. Two more points might be made which suggest that accomodation is a feature of sound level planning, rather than a general feature of speech errors. One finds departures from "well-formedness", as a consequence of error movements, for syntactic and semantic constraints as a matter of course; but for sound level errors such departures are the rare exception. Further, the following pattern indicates that when an error movement occurs involving irregular representations of affixes, accomodation does not occur. Consider (9) a–d: when the affixes move as in (9) a,b, or when stems move, as in (8) b,c, the affixes accomodate their shape to the new environment; and such things as vowel reduction of word stress are adjusted on the "abandoned" stem. But in (9) c,d the stems do not adjust to their new environment by adopting the appropriate irregular form. Contrast this with the behavior of irregular forms in (10). This example illustrates an error in which the appropriate irregular form appears; but this is an error in which the stems move, an error which by the analysis underlying Figure 2 would be assumed to occur at the functional level of production processes.

(9)a "he goes back" → " he go backs"
         [z]   [s]

   b "...easily enough → easy enoughly .."
         [izəli]   [izi]

   c "I haven't satten down and writ__ that yet."

   d "...was tooken..."

(10)   "...that I would know one if I heard it" →
        "...hear one if I knew it"

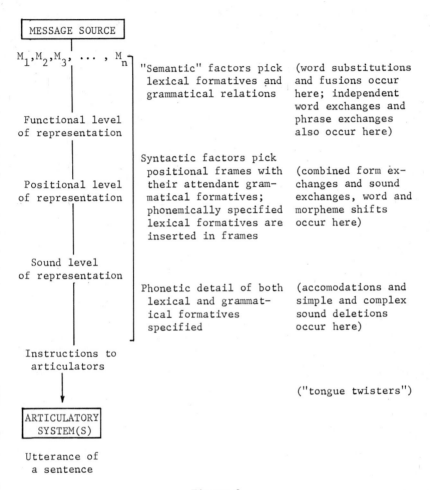

Figure 2

If one assumes that lexical selection takes place at the functional level, and that irregular forms are separately represented in the lexical inventory, (10) should not be viewed as an example of accomodation at all.[3]

    There are a lot of "if" clauses in the preceding paragraph, and the number of relevant examples is small. But barring some

---

[3]I am indebted to Dianne Bradley for examples and discussion of this point.

such argument, the contrast between (9) c,d and (10) must be
assigned (perhaps appropriately) so the simple vagaries of
error data.

2. Exchange errors and syntactic planning. The preceding
argument draws a distinction between the level at which accomo-
dations take place and that at which exchanges like those of
(8), involving stems and words, take place. However, on the
currently available facts, we must also group sound exchange
errors with those of (8) b,c; there is no strong argument for
distinguishing the level at which sound exchange errors take
place from that at which most errors like (8) b,c take place.
The important distinction that does seem to be warranted is between the level at which errors like (8)a take place and that
at which (8) b,c occur. In Figure 2 these levels are called
the "functional" and the "positional" levels. In A.S.P., I
argued that the following differences in the constraints on
"independent word exchanges" (e.g., (8)a and (11) a-d; here-
after simply "word exchanges"), and both "combined-form" exchanges
(e.g., (8) b,c and (12) a-d; also called "stranding errors"), and
"sound exchanges" (e.g. (13) a-d) indicate the need for such a
distinction: (a) the elements of word exchanges are of the
same major grammatical category (or "form class") nearly 90% of
the time (by the current count in the MIT corpus; n = 121 for
word exchanges), while those of combined-form errors (n=57) and
sound exchanges (n = 161) are of differing grammatical category
about 70% of the time; (b) the distance (counted in words) which
separates the elements of sound exchanges and combined-form
errors is significantly less than that for word exchanges; (c)
word exchange errors fairly often involve prepositions and pronouns, but sound exchanges rarely do; (d) sound exchanges and
combined-form errors are usually members of the same phrase, but
word exchanges are usually members of different phrases.

(permuted elements underlined)

(11) a "The whole country will be covered to a _foot_ of one
          depth with dung beetles."

     b "Wait'll you see the one I kept pinned on the _room_
          to my _door_."

     c "Now listen--when I come down in the morning, I don't
          want to find your clothes lyin' _in_ the floor _on_ a heap."

     d "They _left_ it and _forgot_ it behind."

(12) a "They were _Turking_ _talkish_."

     b "You have to _square_ it _facely_."

     c "You _ordered_ up _ending_..."

   d   "There must have been five or six clothing <u>stages</u> on <u>change</u>."

(13) a   "The car sounds like a [kaef] [tʃʌtər]." (intended: chaff cutter)

     b   "They're at Ruvver Frint Stadium." (intended: River Front Stadium)

     c   "...she's a real rack pat--(?)--I said 'rack pat' instead of 'pat rack'." (intended: pack rat)

     d   "...which does not pre-trune shows almost..." (intended: tree-prune)

A summary statement of the properties of these two levels might be as follows:

> a. Exchanged words that are (relatively) widely separated in the intended output or that are members of distinct surface clauses will serve similar roles in the sentence structures underlying the intended utterance and, in particular, will be of the same form class. These exchange errors represent interactions of elements at a level of processing for which functional relations are the determinant of "computational simultaneity"; similarity of the descriptions that govern the selection among elements at this level is asusmed to determine error interactions.
>
> b. Exchanged elements that are (relatively) near to each other and which violate form class represent interactions at a level of processing for which the serial order of the elements of an intended utterance is the determinant of computational simultaneity. Similarity of left and right adjacent elements both phonetically and syntactically, as well as similarity of the elements themselves, is assumed to determine the likelihood of error interactions. (from Garrett, 1975, p. 154).

Note that the difference in the behavior of word exchanges and combined form errors with respect to grammatical category holds where distance is controlled--i.e., combined-form errors and sound errors of one or two words separation are still more likely to change grammatical category than are word exchanges of the same separation. A further point can be made about the difference in the types of constructions these errors occur in: all three error types (and indeed virtually all movement errors) are clausally constrained; both elements of an exchange are members of the same surface clause. However, word exchanges are much more likely to involve elements of distinct surface clauses; and when they do, the constraint of equivalent

grammatical categories is virtually absolute. This constraint
and those discussed in 3 below provide strong grounds for considering the processes at issue to be specifically syntactic.

3. Syntactically active bound morphemes and shifts. The
errors I have been calling "combined-form errors" are of particular interest. Fromkin (1971), Fry (1968) and Nooteboom (1969)
have all commented on one or another aspect of such errors.
These errors provide particularly compelling evidence of the
operation of syntactic processes at the processing level I have
called the positional level. That is the level at which (by
assumption) the integration of the surface order of the lexical
and grammatical formatives is being carried out. The combined-
form errors are, in a very reasonable sense, understood as a
local failure of that process. Note that the morphemes that are
stranded by the permutation of stems in (12) and similar examples given earlier are by and large those introduced by a
syntactic process, not derivational affixes. The set of affixes
which predominates in these errors also shows other unusual behavior in errors which mark them as computationally distinct
from other affixes. They do not themselves undergo exchange,
although they do undergo shift in position (e.g., (9) a,b).
Moreover, these elements are by far the most frequent elements
to undergo shifts at the ends of words; that is, instances of
shifting a word final sound element that is not a syntactically
active bound morpheme are rare (2 of 34 in the MIT corpus, and
5 in Fromkin's published corpus). In general (except for sound
errors), there seem to be a number of reasons to believe that
those elements which shift position (rather than exchange) are
closed class, syntactically active elements, whether they are
bound or free forms (see the discussion of word shift errors in
A.S.P.).

4. The final point to be made concerns an apparent difference in the kinds of elements that word, combined-form, and
sound exchanges span. Word exchanges span content items; combined-form and sound errors rarely do. This could be, but, I
think, is not solely a consequence of the fact that word exchanges span greater distances. When distance is controlled
there are still many more cases of open class items intervening
for word exchanges than for sound or combined-form exchanges.
The numbers of observations are small, however, and this may
prove to be simply a sampling error. If not, however, it would
make sense given the sort of characterization offered of the
positional processing level. If contiguity in the surface
string is a major constraining factor for sound and combined
form exchanges, and if contiguity were defined only in terms of
open class elements (i.e. closed class words not counted), combined-form errors and sound exchanges would be almost entirely
from adjacent elements.

With these remarks as background, let us consider the issue
of condition 1. To what extent are the elements which interact
in errors of the same processing type? It must be obvious that
the answer is: to a very impressive extent. Several investigators (e.g. Fromkin (1971), etc.) have commented on the apparent constraint that only elements of the same grammatical type
interchange. The very success of classificatory efforts in
terms of element types, as well as in terms of error mechanisms,
is testimony to the strength of the constraint. If one were to
encounter errors like (14), one would be given pause if one were
using a classification by element type. But one does not, in
fact, encounter such errors, and hence, is never confronted with
the limitation implicit in the cross-classification of errors
by both element type and mechanism.

(14) "His speech was a disappointment to everyone." →
      "His dis was a speechappointment to everyone."

There is somewhat more to this example of a non-error than
meets the eye, however, for one could describe the error as a
"morpheme exchange". Condition 1 is, by itself, not very constraining given the richness of descriptive resources afforded
by linguistic theory. Thus, the fact that we can successfully
classify both simple and complex errors by element type is a
necessary consequence of condition 1, but it tells us less than
we might expect. More revealing is the fact that certain types
of error interactions do not occur, given that we accept condition 1. Thus, for an error like (14), described as a morpheme
exchange, condition 1 would require that bound and free forms
be computationally equivalent at a level which is, nevertheless,
constrained by their status as morphemes. But, that is just the
sort of conclusion that the error regularities reviewed above
do not seem to indicate; hence, the non-existence of (14).
The major respect in which the observations just reviewed
suggest a departure from a straightforward correspondence of
processing levels and grammatical types is the lack of any
strong distinction between the sound exchange errors and the combined form errors. If, as condition 2 requires, the elements of
a given processing level are of a single descriptive type, this
is an untidy outcome. It may prove possible to disentangle
these error types by a systematic comparison of the sound exchanges with other sound errors. That enterprise will not be
broached here. Barring this issue and those to be taken up in
the next section, however, it appears that the interaction between condition 1 and condition 2 is a reasonable one. The constraints on the various error types do seem to correspond to the
sorts of descriptions that identity of the interacting elements
would commit one to.

"Semantic" effects on movement errors

The properties of error distributions discussed in the preceding section show that there are strong influences of syntactic variables on several types of movement errors. It remains
to be discussed whether these same error types are subject to
nonsyntactic constraints as well. The evidence in favor of condition 1 (interacting elements must be of the same processing
type) is strong, and the syntactic constraints so far discussed
are generally compatible with the structures required by condition 1. However, condition 2 requires that there be no significant influences of processing levels other than those an
error has been assigned to. In particular, those processing
levels I have argued are syntactic (the functional and positional levels) should not show evidence of semantic or phonological
constraints.

Barring the vexatious problem of where to put the various
prosodic effects (see A.S.P.), it is not too difficult to see
what influences of sound structure there are for exchange and
shift errors. It is more than a little difficult to say just
what constitutes a "semantic" influence on such movement errors.
If one sets out to grapple with the detailed proposals (in the
generative semantics literature) about semantic-syntactic alternatives in accounts of sentence structure, the project of showing independence of semantic and syntactic processing in the
error data is virtually insuperable. However, if one initially
confines one's attention to the most obvious sorts of meaning
relations among words, and, moreover, if one uses as a criterion
of contrast those speech errors which do show unmistakable effects of meaning relations (i.e., word substitutions and blends
or fusions), one can get a useful preliminary reading on the
question. Thus, for example, one may note the dominant relations that seem to hold for errors like (15) a-f and (16) a-d,
and compare them with the relations between the members of word,
combined form, or sound exchanges.

(15) a "All I want is something for my shoulders." (intended:
         elbows)

     b "I just like whipped cream and mushrooms." (intended:
         strawberries)

     c "Yeh--they're busy picking up their balloons." (intended:
         batons)

     d "If you can find a garlic around the house..." (intended:
         gargle)

     e "People should take their governor stickers off."
         (intended: bumper; uttered while looking at an old
         bumper sticker which read, "Mike Dukakis for governor")

f   Q. "You sent her a cable?"
    A. "And a <u>letter</u> of myself." (intended: picture)

(16) a   "I'll have to use a whick." (intended: whip/stick)

   b   "...because the price of beef in the U.S. is so
       outreasonable." (intended: outrageous/unreasonable)

   c   "O.K., I'll withract that remark." (intended: with-
       draw/retract)

   d   "Oh, it's dretched." (intended: dreadful/wretched)

This is a somewhat more general approach than it might seem, for
given the intimate relation between the issue of generative
semantics analysis of sentence structure and the issue of lexical decomposition, the failure to find clear consequences of
feature relations between words in those errors presumed to
arise at the level of syntactic processing (the positional and
functional levels) argues against the role of nonsyntactic features in the rules that govern the behavior of elements at those
levels.
       The specific grounds we have for relating the word substi-
tution and blend errors to sentence level processes is the very
strong constraint of grammatical category on such errors.
Nooteboom (1969), Shattuck (1974), and a number of others have
noted this feature of word substitutions.
       Consider the errors of (15) a-f. They are intended to re-
present the three major types of word substitution errors:
those that appear to turn on a similarity of <u>form</u>; those that
are related in <u>meaning</u>; and those with a <u>situational</u> relation.
I emphasize that the decision to so classify the errors is not
transparent; there are, however, some reasonable arguments in
favor of the classification.
       The first point to be made is the complementarity of the
relations between target and intrusion in the word substitutions.
When there is a strong similarity of form, there is simply no
indication of a plausible meaning relation (even taking account
of whatever situational information one might have available).
When there is a plausible meaning relation between the target
and intrusion, there is no very persuasive case to be made for
a similarity of form (although such an observation has been made
from time to time, probably because no distinctions among the
substitution types were made in the analysis). Finally, the
"situational" errors like (15) e,f appear to largely ignore both
meaning and form; I will not consider such errors when evaluating
the relations between members of exchange errors.[4]

----

[4]This is conservative for it is likely that there are unknown
situational determinants for many of the errors that <u>are</u> counted
as semantically related. While this would be unfortunate for

The blends given in (16) a-d are more uniform in their relations; there is little evidence of a similarity of form like
that found for some word substittuions, and they are almost invariably rough synonyms. That synonomy, while not so strong as
the context free cases used to make philosophical points, is
actually somewhat more striking than it appears. When one takes
account of the communicative intent of the speaker (as inferred
from context or gotten directly by questioning), it is clear
that the fused words equally well convey the speaker's intent.
The three lists that follow illustrate some relations in the
error types just discussed.

form related pairs	meaning related pairs	blends
confirmation/ conservation	husbands/wives	draft/breeze (dreeze)
workin'/walkin'	meant/said	lout/lump (lunt)
measured/married	reader/writer	rubbers/overshoes (ruvvershoes)
symphony/sympath	strawberries/ mushrooms	beginning/commencement (begincement)
Auditron/Amphytryon	vouch/account	innovative/inventive (innoventive)
colloquial/colloquium	England/London	umpire/referee (umparee)
Hancock/Hopkins*	lips/kiss	cooking/making (caking)
Baltimore/Buffalo*	ashtrays/ firecrackers	spent/paid (spaid)
discovery/discussion	remember/forget	serenade/melody (melanade)
consisted/considered	reader/writer	flight/plane (flane)
triple/trouble	follow/precede	sewage/pollution (solution)
present/prevent	public/private	evade/avoid (evoid)
surface/circus	believe/doubt	places/people (playple)

any attempt to infer the relevant semantic control parameters
of lexical selection on the basis of such errors, it simply
broadens the type of relations that will be considered "semantic"
in the exchange errors and increases the likelihood of detecting
such influences if they are there at all.

form related pairs	meaning related pairs	blends
advances/advantages	keep/stop	case/question (quase)
hotels/hospitals*	looks/sounds	lawn/yard (yawn)
fire-escape/ fire-place	listen/talk	certainly/greatly (greatenly)
conscience/conscious	asterisk/italics	swoop/scoop (scwoop)

* Possible meaning relation as well

We can summarize the major features of form and meaning relations that we will appeal to as follows:

Form: Related words have the same initial phonetic elements; their stress and syllable length are similar.

Meaning: Related words are: (a) rough synonyms or antonyms (e.g., start/stop; umpire/referee), (b) of the same immediate class (e.g., strawberry/ mushroom; asterisk/italics), (c) associates (e.g., jet/black; desk/chair).

These categories may be used to "prospect" for influences of word form and meaning in exchange errors. Before doing so, an aside on the "reasons" for such relations is in order.

If one assumes that the word substitution errors arise in part because of lexical access processes, the observed semantic effects are not surprising, although the similarities of form are. One cannot help but be struck by the correspondence between the word substitution patterns and those of tip-ot-the-tongue states (Brown and McNeill (1966); see also Rubin (1975)). In TOT states, as in word substitutions, two types of "errors" seem to occur: "semantic", with no apparent form constraint, and form, with little meaning constraint. This is both intriguing and puzzling. That there should be semantic constraints in T.O.T. states or word substitution errors is no surprise; that constraints of form appear so powerful for lexical selection in production is somewhat surprising. Fay and Cutler (1975) have interpreted such errors as those of (15) a-d as evidence for the organization of the mental lexicon. They argue that the word form inventory, which is organized according to the exigencies of comprehension processes, is also used in production. How this is to be spelled out in a way that makes both semantically and phonetically based errors plausible is not yet clear; it is a fascinating problem that bears serious attention. But not here.

If one applies these categories to the elements of exchanges (or the source words in the case of sound exchanges),
there appears to be little basis for claiming a strong semantic
or phonetic influence. Table 1 summarizes the results of my
own classification efforts for the MIT exchanges, and for sound
exchanges in Fromkin's (1973) published corpus (two other naive
"sorters" who also classified the errors yielded even less indication of a relation than did my own ratings). Given the in-
formality of my scaling procedures, the precise numbers in Table
1 are not to be taken seriously, beyond the clear indication
that semantic influences are weak if extant at all. Two points
should be stressed: (1) It is hardly surprising that some evidence of associative relations can be found, given the "loose"
nature of such relations and the fact that the word pairs in
question were, after all, from the same sentence and were
"situationally apposite" comments or remarks. (2) If one contrasts the proportion of meaning related pairs in exchanges
with that for pairs of words from word substitutions and blends,
the "immunity" of the exchanges from semantic influences is made
clearer. Excluding the form related word substitutions, only
15-20% of the remaining substitutions have no apparent connection (other than a "situational" one), and, of course all the
blends are easily interpretible on meaning grounds.

Finally, some notice of relations of form between exchanged
elements (or source words in the case of sound exchanges) must
be made. For sound exchanges there is clearly some similarity
since exchanged sound elements tend to be similar to each other,
as do their immediate environments. However this similarity of
form is to be construed, it seems different from the sort which,
in the case of word substitutions, seems related to lexical
lookup processes. (Further observations relevant to sound exchanges and structure of the mental lexicon are in the next
major section.)

So far as combined-form exchanges and word exchanges are
concerned, the effects of form are, once again not striking.
All exchanges tend to involve words of less than three syllables,
and hence the indication that exchanged elements are of similar
length is hard to evaluate. But, using the criteria of the
word substitution errors, there is no readily apparent relation.
If one were to develop and defend some other metric of similarity than the one I have used, however, one might very well discover some evidence for similarity of form in exchanges. (Such
suggestions have been made by others, but it is difficult to
evaluate how their observational basis would survive the distinctions among error types I have argued for.)

TABLE 1

(entries are proportions of total errors of each type)	Sound Exchanges	Combined Form Exchanges	Word Exchanges
	(n = 118) Fromkin values in parentheses (n = 161 MIT)	(n = 57)	(n = 121)
Types of Relation			
Associative e.g. book/library desk/chair read/write	(.17) .15	.13	.16
Class Membership e.g. car/truck lion/tiger seven/four	(.01) .05	.04	.09
Synonym; Antonym e.g. start/stop come/stay	(.01) .02	.00	.07
No Apparent Relation e.g. idea/guy cigar/briefcase kitchen/coffee	(.62) .58	.64	.52
Names	(.14) .13	.14	.04
Idioms or Formula Phrases	(.08) .08	.06	.12

Lexical Status of Sound Errors

We will consider only sound exchange errors here (although shifts and other complex errors of addition, deletion, or substitution of speech sounds seem to be, if anything, less affected by the lexical status of error "resultants" than are exchanges). Our primary interest will be the evidence we can bring to bear on the question whether the forms which <u>result</u> (such forms are hereafter called "error forms") from an exchange error are affected by their relation to entries in the vocabulary of the speaker. We raise both the question of whether the organization of our lexical or word form inventory affects the

patterns of these sound errors, and whether the form of the
error-produced items themselves is affected by the correspondence to an actual word form. This contrasts with our concern
in the previous section with the evidence for the existence of
nonsyntactic, putatively semantic, relations holding between the
source words for sound errors or between the words or portions
of words involved in combined form or independent word exchanges.

The first point that we can make concerns the effects of
word frequency on sound exchange errors. There is strong evidence that the word form inventory is organized in terms of
frequency of occurrence in the language, with higher frequency
items being placed earlier in the search space than low frequency items. Granting, of course, that this is a fact established
primarily for word recognition processes, we must nonetheless
concede that some access to an inventory of representations for
word forms must be assumed by any theory which claims that error
forms which correspond to words are more likely to be emitted
than error forms which do not correspond to words. For those
cases (virtually all) in which the semantics of those error
forms which do correspond to words do not relate to the communicative intent of the speaker at the time of the production of
the error, there seems no alternative but to suppose that the
error form must be "evaluated" for its correspondence to an
entry in the actual vocabulary of the speaker by accessing the
stored representation of word forms--hence one would expect the
organization of that word inventory, as it is indicated by comprehension processes, to be reflected in the distribution of the
error forms. In particular, one should expect that high frequency word forms should be found more often as error forms than low
frequency word forms. This follows from the view that the error
forms which correspond to high frequency words would be more
likely to have their lexical status confirmed prior to the operation of whatever error checking routines we have for monitoring
our speech (e.g., those which allow us to note the impending
occurrence of an error and to inhibit its output).

Such a finding of a frequency effect would be a powerful
confirmation of the view that there exists an editorial process
which normally applies at the level(s) where sound errors take
place, and which has access to the specific lexical identify
of the forms being processed, including perhaps facts about
their interpretation. Such a circumstance runs counter to both
the argument about irregular forms (e.g. "know/knew") I presented in discussing the phenomena of accomodation, and to the
requirements of constraint 2 (depending, of course, upon how
intimately one construes the relation of editorial and planning
functions).

If we look for frequency effects among the 35 to 40 percent
of the error forms that do correspond to word forms, we find no
indication of a preference for high frequency forms in either
the M.I.T. corpus or in the corpus of errors recently published

by Fromkin. Table 2 gives a classification of the error forms
that are also word forms (Kučera and Francis (1967) values for
the exact forms are used).

TABLE 2

Frequency Classification for Error Forms that are also Word Forms
(Entries are proportions of total error forms corresponding to words)

	Low (less than 20)	Intermediate (20-50)	High (more than 50)
M.I.T. corpus n=161 errors (322 potential word forms; 123 actual)	.63	.22	.15
FROMKIN corpus n=118 errors (236 potential word forms; 97 actual)	.62	.20	.18

The proportion of error forms that are not words is:
(MIT corpus) .62; (FROMKIN published corpus) .59.

One might suppose that the incidence of error forms in
Table 2 which correspond to high frequency words is greater than
would be expected by chance. Deciding on "chance" is a non-
trivial problem for speech errors (see below), but given that
length and frequency are correlated, and that sound exchanges
tend to involve short words, one might have expected a more
striking outcome than the observed one if occurrence frequency
of word forms is related to error form frequency.
One might, reasonably enough, argue that failing to find
an effect of occurrence frequency on the distribution of error
forms is not strong evidence against "wordhood" being a relevant factor; there may be several explanations for the lack of
frequency effects even though wordhood were a significant deter-
minant of the likelihood of a sound error. What about a number
of somewhat weaker tests of the hypothesis?
The most obvious initial hypothesis, of course, is simply
the frequency with which error forms do or do not have word
status. On the face of it, the facts provide no comfort whatever for the view that word status is relevant: in the MIT
corpus 62% of the error forms resulting from sound exchanges are

non-words; in Fromkin's published corpus 59% of the error forms
are non-words. Thus, if there is a bias in favor of word forms,
it is not a powerful one; it is a statistical bias at best. The
evaluation of such a statistical bias is difficult. One is somewhat at a loss to determine precisely with what frequency one
would expect random exchanges of sound elements to yield words,
given the structural constraints on sound exchange errors. This
latter point is very important. There are a variety of strong
constraints on sound errors which are not specifically related
to the identity of particular lexical items, but which might be
expected to strongly affect the probability of exchanges yielding phonetic sequences corresponding to words. For example,
sound exchanges take place between elements occupying corresponding syllable or word positions, they generally take place
between elements that are relatively close together, the words
involved in sound exchange errors are likely to be monosyllabic
or bisyllabic, the source words for an exchange are likely to
be within the same noun phrase, and finally, the elements involved in an exchange are likely to be of corresponding levels
of stress. If one attempts to observe these (and other) sorts
of constraints in one's evaluation of the possible value of a
word factor in the random exchange of sounds, the problem becomes difficult to manage. I have attempted to sample from a
number of transcripts of spontaneous speech while observing some
of these constraints, and to determine the rate of word forms
which result from sound exchanges in those transcripts. The
following constraints were observed: the proportion of proper
names sampled was matched to the proportion of proper names involved in the MIT corpus of sound exchanges, the exchanges were
sampled only for open class sources in the same noun phrase with
no more than one closed class element intervening, and only word
initial sounds were exchanged. The spontaneous texts were entered at a random point, and the first 100 successive pairs of
words, subject to the constraints just enumerated, were selected. Table 3 gives the frequency of words and non-words which
resulted for the first and second serially occurring items in
each of the six transcripts sampled. For whatever this sort
of enterprise is worth, it does not indicate any very striking
difference between the incidence of words in the error corpus
and the incidence of words in the randomly selected samples
chosen.

　　　　Another aspect of this question that we might consider is
the possible asymmetry in the frequency with which the first of
the two serially occurring error forms is in fact a word.
Clearly the editorial/planning function has "more time" to pick
up the consequences of the error exchange in the case of form
2, the serially second error form. Thus one might predict the
frequency of both complete and incomplete error exchanges with
respect to the lexical status of first and second occurring

error forms. One would predict that for <u>completed</u> exchanges the
frequency of possible outcomes would be: (1) word, word; (2)
word, non-word; (3) non-word, word; (4) non-word, non-word. For
<u>incomplete</u> exchanges the predicted ordering of complete exchanges
also indicates that the errors in which a word form occurs
should greatly exceed those in which the error element is a nonword. That is, where the first element of the error exchange is
a non-word, it is detected and output inhibited much more often
than when the first error element is a real word. There is no
evidence for such an effect in either the MIT corpus for either
complete exchanges or incomplete exchanges. In fact, the ordering is reversed: for the completed errors the <u>least</u> common case
is the "word, word" combination, the <u>most</u> common is the "nonword, non-word", the other two cases are about equal to each
other. This is true for Fromkin's published corpus as well.

TABLE 3

Lexical Status and Serial Order
of Pseudo "Error" Forms
(n=100; entries are proportions of error forms)

Passage*	Form 1		Form 2	
	Word	Nonword	Word	Nonword
1	.25	.75	.26	.74
2	.30	.70	.35	.65
3	.33	.67	.31	.69
4	.39	.61	.37	.63
5	.36	.64	.38	.62
6	.29	.71	.33	.67

*Passages are from Playboy interviews, 1974 issues.

These findings contrast sharply with those recently reported for an experimental task which produced involuntary sound
exchanges. Baars, Motley and MacKay (1975) report a significant
influence of lexical status on the likelihood of (word initial)
sound exchanges in a short-term memory task. From this they
argue for an editorial function which inhibits nonsense forms in
real word contexts. That conclusion is just the one which
naturally occurring speech error distributions seem to provide
no support for.
The apparent rationalizations of this divergence are simply
to (a) deny the relevance of the experimental task to normal

processing, or (b) to deny the representativeness of the natural error corpus. Neither solution is appealing. There are aspects of the experimental task used by Baars, et al. which might
yield an "unusual" influence of word form, but the case is
sufficiently similar to normal speech to warrant serious consideration. The error corpora are likewise to be interpreted with
care, but the major features of the error distributions do seem
pretty stable across various investigators. The likely explanation seems to be in terms of "sensitivity". Though the effects
of wordhood are not strong enough to show up in natural error
data, the controlled circumstances of the experiment show their
presence; i.e., the effect is relatively weak, but statistically
significant. How we evaluate the theoretical significance of
such an effect is very difficult to determine at this point. In
broad terms, it is hard to see how the editorial function being
tapped in the experiment could be <u>directly</u> relevant to the level
at which the normal exchange errors are occurring, given the
simple fact that, more often than not, the error forms are nonwords. It may be that the editorial function which we normally
exercise (roughly, running the "last level" of production
through the comprehension system to see if it matches our communicative intent) is what accounts for the experimental results. At all events these findings present something of a
paradox that will require further attention to resolve satisfactorily.

Conclusion

What I have tried to do with the speech error data is, in
some measure, what Marslen-Wilson (this volume) is arguing for.
That is, to take natural language processing performance on its
own merits, so to speak, and see what it suggests about the
underlying computational systems. Surprisingly enough, we find
that the outcome is near to what a straightforward interpretation of linguistic rule systems as processing systems would lead
one to expect.

For the sense of independence I discussed in the beginning
of this paper, speech error distributions seem to indicate syntactic processing systems which are unaffected by at least the
sort of semantic relations that produce word substitutions and
blends. The effect of sound structure on the putatively syntactic levels of processing is less easy to evaluate, particularly if one assumes that the sound exchange errors are the results of processes at the same level as the combined form errors.
That error type and its relation to other sound errors needs to
be more carefully examined. Similarly, the conclusions about
semantic effects on syntactic processing levels are restricted
to the type of semantic relation discussed here. The search for

effects of subtler semantic constraints <u>might</u> yield a different
outcome; my bet at the present is that it will not.

Acknowledgment

This research was supported in part by NIMH grant HD 05168.
Helpful comments by K.I. Forster, J.A. Fodor, S.R. Shattuck and
E.C.T. Walker are gratefully acknowledged.

References

Baars, B., Motley, M. and MacKay, D.G. (1975) Output editing
    for lexical status in artificially elicited slips of the
    tongue. J. of Verbal Learning and Verbal Behavior, 14,
    382-391.
Brown, R. and McNeill, D. (1966) The "tip-of-the-tongue" pheno-
    menon. J. of Verbal Learning and Verbal Behavior, 5, 325-
    337.
Fay, D. and Cutler, A. (1975) You have a dictionary in your
    head, not a thesaurus. Texas Linguistic Forum, 1, 27-40.
Fromkin, V.A. (1971) The non-anomalous nature of anomalous
    utterances. Language, 47, 27-52.
Fromkin, V. (Ed.) (1973) Speech Errors as Linguistic Evidence.
    Janua Linguarum, Series Maior, 77. The Hague: Mouton.
Fry, D. (1969) The linguistic evidence of speech errors.
    BRNO Studies of English, 8, 69-74.
Garrett, M.F. (1975) The analysis of sentence production. In
    Psychology of Learning and Motivation, Volume 9, G. Bower
    (Ed.). New York: Academic Press.
Kučera, H. and Francis, W.N. (1967) Computational Analysis of
    Present Day American English. Providence, R.I.: Brown
    University Press.
MacKay, D.G. (1969) Forward and backward masking in motor
    systems. Kybernetik, 2, 57-64.
MacKay, D.G. (1970) Spoonerisms: the structure of errors in the
    serial order of speech. Neuropsychologia, 8, 323-350.
Nooteboom, S.G. (1967) Some regularities in phonemic speech
    errors. Instituut voor Perceptic Onderzoek, Annual pro-
    gress report.
Rubin, D. (1975) Within word structure in the tip-of-the-tongue
    phenomenon. J. of Verbal Learning and Verbal Behavior,
    14, 392-397.
Shattuck, S.R. (1974) Speech errors and sentence production.
    Unpublished doctoral dissertation, Massachusetts Institute
    of Technology.

ACCESSING THE MENTAL LEXICON

Kenneth I. Forster

Monash University

Introduction

It is impressive that a mature speaker of a language is able to recognize words of that language so rapidly and so effortlessly. Even more impressive is his ability to immediately recognize that an item is not a word of his language, even though it is a possible word.

This ability involves a highly structured information retrieval system, which apparently has at its disposal an extremely rapid search procedure. Understanding how this system operates is obviously important in a theory of sentence comprehension and production, since understanding the meaning of a sentence requires that information about each of the words in the sentence be recovered. On the production side, we obviously cannot speak until we have located words which will serve our communicative purpose.

The study of information retrieval systems is also important in the larger context of the study of mental processes, since perception, memory, learning and thought itself all depend critically on efficient information retrieval. In fact, understanding how we locate and recover the information we have stored about a particular word can be regarded as a paradigm case of pattern recognition.

In what follows, I will attempt to sketch the emerging outlines of a theory of word recognition. I have taken the advice of the editors of this volume at face value, and have given a "progress" report of the activities of a small group of researchers working with me at Monash University. Much of the work I will report is unpublished (perhaps unpublishable), but it would be senseless to try to restrict this paper to just the published material, since the structure of the overall argument would be lost. I will also be highly selective in my treatment of the existing literature, and will draw only on those experiments which bear directly on the issues we are investigating.

Our general approach owes much to the work of R.C. Oldfield (1966) who first developed the notion of a mental dictionary and who first raised the question of how information about the meaning of a word is recovered. We have also been heavily

influenced by the work of H. Rubenstein, and the model I describe is in fact based on the system described by Rubenstein,
Lewis and Rubenstein (1971).

Theories of Lexical Access; Direct-Access Versus Search

The essential feature of associationism in psychology was
the claim that familiar stimuli somehow contacted their appropriate memory traces directly. Thus, if a word is presented,
then we automatically produce the meaning of that word, or the
ideas connected to it, or the mediating responses associated
with it (whatever terminology we use, the concept is the same).
Thus, words and the mental events that they give rise to are
directly wired together.

The implications of this theory are best understood by means
of an analogy. Suppose we had an actual dictionary in which it
was always possible to predict in advance from the spelling of
the word exactly where it would be listed. The actual computational machinery for making this prediction would use something
like the decision tree shown in Fig. 1.

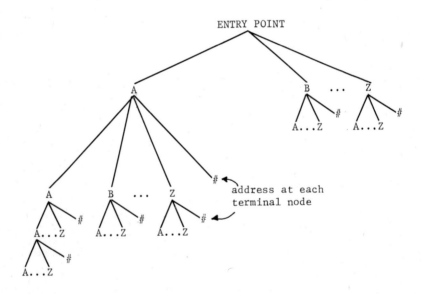

Figure 1.   Decision-tree for a direct-access lexicon

The tree is used by beginning at the topmost mode and descending
via the path labelled with the first letter of the letter sequence that we wish to investigate. At the next node, we des-
cend via the path appropriate to the next letter in the sequence.
The final "letter" (the blank letter, or #, which indicates the
end of the sequence) leads to a terminal node with no further
branching. At this terminal node is an "address", which is simply a number telling us which page and which column, etc., in
the dictionary we should consult. The tree is constructed so
that the constraints of English orthography are preserved. That
is, not _every_ combination of letters is represented; thus, there
would be no branch for a sequence beginning _ptl-_, since there
can be no English word beginning with these letters. This is
actually a vital assumption, since if all combinations of letters were included, we would need a tree with 27^{10} branches just
to cope with words up to ten letters long.

If the presented letter sequence is a word, then the meaning can be found at the address specified at the terminal node.
If it is _not_ a word, then there will be nothing entered in that
location at all. Thus, if we are given the test item _atishnet_,
we would trace the path for A, T, I, S, H, N, E, T and # in sequence, take the address specified at the terminal node, and
then discover no information in the lexicon at this address.
From this we would conclude that _atishnet_ is not a word.

Such a dictionary would be enormously expensive, since
there would be millions of empty slots (one for each _possible_
word of English). It would have to impose an arbitrary limit on
the length of a possible English word, since otherwise the tree
would be infinite. A further interesting property is that there
would be no real need to have words of similar spelling stored
in similar regions (although this could be arranged if necessary),
since any arbitrary assignment of numbers to terminal nodes
would suffice.

However, the dictionary would at least have the property of
being _content-addressable_. This means that one can compute the
exact address of information from a knowledge of the description
under which it is filed (i.e., the spelling). Recovering information from this memory would thus be _direct access_ recovery.
The decision-tree described in Fig. 1 would constitute the mechanism of _association_ and is a complex form of direct wiring.

At the opposite extreme of a continuum from fully content-
addressable models to non-content-addressable models, we have
the possibility that the spellings of words and the addresses of
their dictionary entries are simply listed in random order.
Finding the entry involves a look-up procedure in which the
spelling of the target item is successively compared with each
member of this list until a match is obtained. The essence of
this model is that a serial search is involved. If the target
item is a word, then the search terminates when a match is
found. If the target item is not a word, then the search must

be exhaustive. That is, we cannot recognize that <u>atishnet</u> is not a word until we have examined every member of the list.

Between these extremes, there are a number of intermediate, or mixed models. Our ultimate conclusion will be that the best working hypothesis for a model of lexical access is to adopt a mixed system.

Returning to the model depicted in Fig. 1, it might be suggested that it is pointless to have terminal nodes which correspond only to possible but not actual words, since this must increase the necessary wiring by a very substantial amount. This is quite easy to arrange; all one need do is to prune the tree in Fig. 1, so that the only branches remaining are those that lead to actual words. A fragment of such a tree is shown in Fig. 2.

The principle of construction in this tree can be seen by examining the node at the end of the path A–B–A. Since there is no word beginning <u>abaa-</u>, there is no need to have a further branch for the letter <u>a</u>, and similarly there is no need for a branch for <u>b</u>. However, since there <u>is</u> a word beginning <u>abac-</u> we need a branch for the letter <u>c</u>. Since for most people, there is only <u>one</u> such word (<u>abacus</u>), there is no need to have branches for each of the remaining letters, and all that remains is to check that the remaining letters are in fact correct (allowing for the fact that <u>abacan</u> would be recognized as a nonword).

Although we have now simplified the associative machinery considerably, it is not without cost. In a sense, we have made the system <u>too</u> efficient. Consider what would happen with a nonword such as <u>atishnet</u>. Descent would be via the path A–T–I (necessary for words such as <u>atilt</u> and <u>atingle</u>), but there would be no branch corresponding to <u>s</u>, since there is no word beginning <u>atis-</u>. Hence nonwords will be recognized as such with great efficiency, and will in fact be recognized as nonwords more rapidly on average than words will be recognized as words.

But this does not square with the facts. By means of the so-called <u>lexical decision</u> experiment, we can estimate the time required for lexical access to occur. In such an experiment, a letter sequence is presented visually for as long as the subject requires to classify the item as a word (in his vocabulary) or as a nonword as rapidly as possible. Since there is no way to perform this task without accessing the internal lexicon (with one exception, see footnote 1), we can estimate the time for this operation by measuring the subject's reaction time to make the decision.

In such experiments, it is typically found that familiar words are classified in around 500 msec., but that nonwords require about 650 msec. Thus, rather than taking <u>less</u> time to classify, nonwords take substantially <u>more</u> time to classify

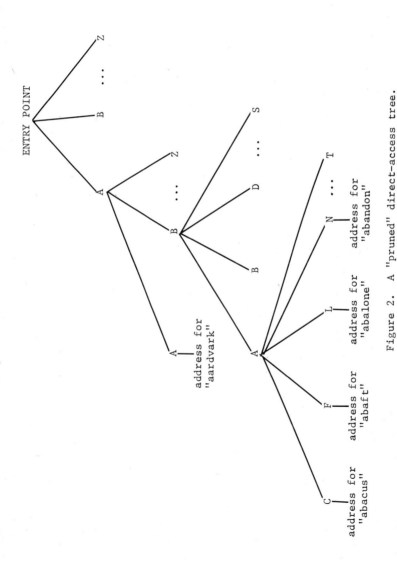

Figure 2. A "pruned" direct-access tree.

than words.[1] This is an extremely robust finding, and has been
reported by a number of different investigators (e.g.,
Rubenstein, Garfield and Millikan, 1970; Stanners and Forbach,
1973; Forster and Chambers, 1973; Forster and Bednall, 1976).

It is not easy to explain this discrepancy between theory
and experiment. Since there is no natural way to explain the
result using the decision-tree, extra assumptions must be made,
and these will always involve processes occurring _after_ the non-
existence of a branch has been detected. One such argument is
that the subject is not consciously aware of the current status
of the processing within the decision tree until an address is
discovered. That is, he is never aware that no address could
be found for a given item, and hence must set a deadline, such
that a "no" decision will be made if an address has not been encountered before the deadline expires. For error-free performance, this deadline would need to be set so that the addresses
of all words would normally be found before the time limit was
up.

With such a model, one can explain why nonwords will, on
the average, take longer than words. Although ad hoc in this
case, the notions of limited awareness of the status of processing and deadlines are not implausible, and have been invoked
in a number of reaction-time models.

Fortunately, it is not difficult to eliminate this line of
argument (and a number of similar lines of argument), since it
can be shown that nonwords do not _always_ take longer to process
than words. For example, Forster and Bednall (1976) have shown
that if subjects are asked to classify items according to
whether they have more than one meaning or not, then orthographically legal nonwords such as _flink_ are classified faster than
unambiguous words, such as _year_ (the correct response being
"No" in both cases), and also faster than ambiguous words, such
as _chest_ (where the answer is "yes"). Similarly, it takes _less_
time to recognize that _to flink_ is not a possible phrase in
English than it takes to make the same decision about _to year_.

Given the previous assumptions about limitations on conscious awareness, nonwords should always take longer than words,
since the retrieval system is incapable of indicating that there
is no information at all about these items. Hence it seems that
this particular direct-access model should be discarded.

The same conclusion seems appropriate for the 'unpruned'
model in Fig. 1. The implication of this model is that words
and nonwords should take the _same_ amount of time to classify.
This model could be patched up in the same way as the pruned

_____

[1]The only exception to the rule (first noted by H. Rubenstein)
is that _impossible_ and not actual words, such as _thptxt_, are
classified in about the same time as words. Presumably, such
items can be rejected without the lexicon being consulted at all.

model, but would run afoul of exactly the same facts.

There is another critical fact that these theories are quite incapable of explaining in a natural way. The fact is that words which have a relatively high frequency of occurrence are classified faster than words with a low occurrence frequency e.g., mildew, perspire, radiate, although the latter are still perfectly familiar to the subjects of the experiment (e.g., Rubenstein, Garfield and Millikan, 1970; Forster and Chambers, 1973; Forster and Bednall, 1976). There is simply no way of arranging the decision-trees so that frequency of occurrence of the word itself controls access time. It is of course possible to arrange matters so that letter frequency is a relevant parameter (e.g., by changing the order in which the paths are listed), but this typically has no detectable impact on processing time (e.g., Chambers and Forster, 1975). About the only variable that these models clearly implicate is the number of letters in the word, but even this is inappropriate, since in at least two experimental situations, length appears to play almost no role in word recognition (Frederiksen and Kroll, 1974; Forster and Chambers, 1973; Chambers and Forster, 1975).

Our conclusion then, is that if we do have direct-access to entries in the internal lexicon, then it certainly cannot be via letter-based decision-trees of the sort we have described. If this is the case, then it may well be asked what possible alternative remains? To my knowledge, there is only one remaining direct-access alternative that is different in kind from the decision-tree approach, and that is to use some kind of word-detector model (for a fuller discussion of such models, see Selfridge and Neisser, 1960; Morton, 1970; Meyer and Schvaneveldt, 1976).

The essence of such a theory is that for each word there is a separate detector which is selectively tuned to perceptual features characteristic of that word. Thus, the detectors for the word dog would be activated to some degree by any letter sequence having either an initial d, a medial o or a final g. It would also be activated, although to a lesser degree, by sequences having letters similar to these. It might also be activated by any sequence having exactly three letters, and to a lesser degree by two and four letter strings. Thus each detector has its own tuning curve, and is responsive to a variety of inputs.

Obviously, presentation of any word will activate a large number of word detectors to varying degrees, as will the presentation of a nonword. The problem now is to make a decision as to which detector is the one being activated most strongly. One method would be to scan all detectors and make comparisons between them. This alternative has to be discarded since this is the exact antithesis of a direct-access system. Another method would be to set thresholds on each detector, such that when the

level of activation reaches a certain level, it automatically
fires. If no detector reaches its threshold level, then the
item is declared to be a nonword.

There are two problems with this account. The first is
that it is technically difficult to ensure that the correct detector will always be the one to fire first. This stems from
the fact that it is usually assumed that the thresholds of high
frequency words are lower than the thresholds of low frequency
words, thus allowing the model to explain frequency effects.[2]
In this case, there will obviously be a problem when the stimulus is a low frequency word that is very similar to a high frequency word. For example, consider the case depicted in Fig.
3, where the test item is the low frequency word blight, and we
examine the levels of activation in the detectors for blight
and bright. The rate at which the blight detector is activated
is fastest, since the test stimulus has more features in common
with the word blight. But since bright has a higher frequency
of occurrence, its threshold is lower. Given the situation depicted in Fig. 3, the bright detector will be the first to fire,
since its threshold is reached first. Doubtless there are other
ways of drawing Fig. 3 so that this does not happen (e.g., by
making the overall rate at which activation levels increase much
slower), but it is nevertheless clear that the theory would have
to be extended to guarantee that the correct detector will be
activated first.

Of course, sometimes the word blight will in fact be mis-
read as bright, and on such occasions, the correct account will
be given. But in a typical reaction time task where the stimulus is not impoverished in any way, e.g., a word naming task,
such errors are quite infrequent.

But there is a far more serious problem, and this concerns
the procedure for deciding that a test item is a nonword. The
best method would be to set a suitable time limit so that if no
detector reaches threshold before the time limit expires, a "No"
response is executed. However, the problem with this procedure
is that there is now abundant evidence that nonwords can activate word detectors before the time limit is reached. This is
demonstrated by the fact that nonwords which are similar to
words take longer to reject than other comparable nonwords
(Amey, 1973; Chambers, 1974; Coltheart, Davelaar, Jonasson
and Besner, 1975). For example, nonwords formed

---

[2]There are several ways of explaining the faster access of high
frequency words. For example, we could instead assume constant
thresholds, but postulate higher "resting" levels of activation
for high frequency words. Or we could assume that the rise in
activation level takes place more rapidly for high frequency
words. As far as I can determine, there are no important differences between these competing accounts.

by transposing adjacent letters of a word take longer to reject
than suitable controls, even though they contain orthographically
illegal sequences, e.g., vaiation, obttle, huamn, etc. It is
also the case that interference effects (lengthening of the reaction time) are produced when the item is one letter different
from a word, e.g., destair. Other types of interference involve
similarity to parts of words, e.g., bezzle (Taft and Forster,
1975), and cases where the nonword contains a word, e.g.,
footmilge (Taft and Forster, in press). Given the variety of
interference effects uncovered so far, it seems likely that
there are still more to be discovered. For example, would
changing two letters (e.g., diblussion) still produce interference? Leaving out a letter (e.g., manifst)? Adding a letter
(e.g., offbice)? Moving a letter to a new position (dawerr)?

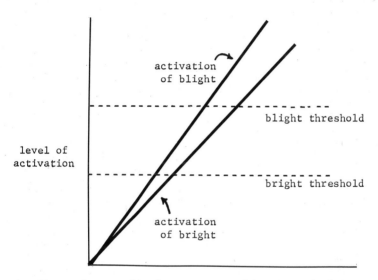

Figure 3. Levels of activation of bright and blight
           detectors when blight is presented.

It seems inconceivable that anyone should attempt to explain these effects without assuming that the nonwords activate
detectors to threshold levels. Hence it will be necessary to
postulate a further stage of processing which takes the set of
detectors activated by a given item and evaluates each in turn
to see whether the correct detector has been activated (presumably by checking the spelling in the lexical entry against
the target item).

Of course, it is difficult to see how this post-activation checking procedure differs from a search process. In fact, we can regard the detector system as being designed merely to generate a set of plausible hypotheses about the correct interpretation of the stimulus item, hypotheses which then must be checked for veracity as they become available (i.e., as the detectors reach threshold). In the case of the nonwords which are similar to words, this subsequent check fails, and the item is correctly assigned to the category of nonword.

Although this modification of the theory is quite reasonable,[3] it should be recognized that we have also given up the assumption of direct access. If the term direct-access means anything, it means that the correct lexical entry is specified automatically without any other entries being specified as possible candidates.

Thus, we have arrived at the conclusion that lexical access will inevitably involve some kind of search process. That is, there are preliminary processors which operate on the target item itself and specify a subset of the total lexicon such that there will be a very high probability that the correct entry will be found within that subset.

This is equivalent to giving up the claim that lexical memory is fully content-addressable, and instead assuming that it is only approximately content-addressable. The final precise locating of the correct entry will require a serial examination of a range of entries, each entry being examined to see whether its orthographic properties match the target item.

This is very like the procedure we would use with an actual dictionary when asked whether an item such as atishnet is a word. Initially, we would use only one property of the item to guide the search, namely the fact that the first letter is a. This property would fix the probable search area as, say the first twenty pages of the dictionary. Using the guide words listed at the top of every page, we would then search until we found the actual page that must contain atishnet. Up to this point, we have merely narrowed down the actual search area (although a search procedure was still involved, namely a search of the guide words). Now the real search begins, since we have to examine actual words on the page until we find that position where atishnet would have to be if it was a word. If an entry is found, a "Yes" decision is made. If some other word is listed in that position, then a "No" decision is made.

In order to make this a satisfactory account of the results, we would need to modify only one thing. The words on each page should not be ordered alphabetically, since if they were, then

---

[3]For an interesting alternative treatment of this problem see Coltheart et al. (1975).

words and nonwords would take the same (or very nearly the same) amount of time in a lexical decision experiment. This is because in an alphabetical sequence, there is only one place where atishnet could be, and the correct decision is made by finding that place and then checking to see whether atishnet is listed there. If instead we assume that the entries on any given page are organized by frequency of occurrence, with high frequency words at the top of the page and low frequency words at the bottom, then we will be able to explain the effects of frequency (the detailed search starts from the top of the page) and the increased time for nonword decisions (all entries on a page will have to be searched before a "No" decision can be made).

A Search Model of Lexical Access

We will now attempt to provide a more detailed model of lexical access, incorporating the assumptions we have just made, that is, assuming that accessing the mental lexicon is not too dissimilar from looking up a word in a printed dictionary.

The first point to notice is that the lexicon has to be accessed under three rather different conditions: namely, when we are reading, listening and talking (writing is perhaps a fourth, but we will defer that issue). When we are reading, it would seem sensible to have lexical items organized into pages so that the words on each page have similar orthographic properties. But for listening, it would seem more sensible to organize entries by phonological properties. Finally, since we seldom care what words will either look or sound like when we construct sentences, but we do need to find words with the right semantic and syntactic properties, it would seem desirable to organize entries by semantic and syntactic properties for the purpose of sentence production.[4]

Of course, it is impossible to organize the same set of entries in three different ways, unless we list each entry in three different locations. Since this is somewhat uneconomical, we assume that there is only one lexicon proper, and we will refer to this as the master file. In addition, there are three peripheral access files, one organizing words by orthographic properties, one by phonological properties, and one by semantic

---

[4]I am assuming without argument that the contents of memory are structured and organized in some way, since any search model which denies this would have to assume, for instance, that before we could classify an item as a nonword, we would have to search through all the familiar faces we have stored. This seems an absurd proposal, although it is hard to disprove. For a recent discussion of such a memory system, see Landauer (1975).

and syntactic properties. The entry for a word in the master
file contains all the information that we have about that word,
while the entry for the same word in each of the peripheral access files simply contains a description of the stimulus features of word (the <u>access code</u>) and a pointer to the corresponding entry in the master file. This situation is depicted in
Fig. 4.

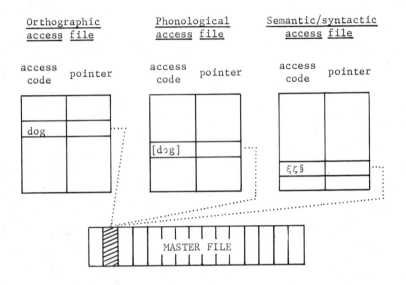

Figure 4.   Organization of peripheral access files
            and master file.

     Thus, accessing the entry for a word in the master file is
accomplished by finding the entry for that word in the appropriate peripheral access file. This involves preparing a coded
description of the target item (the stimulus word) and then
searching through the access file, comparing the description of
the target item with the <u>access codes</u> in each actual entry.
When a sufficiently accurate match between these is obtained
(there being a variable criterion of sufficiency), the search
terminates, the pointer specified in that entry is used to
access the master file, and then a detailed comparison between
the properties of the stimulus item and the properties of the
word specified in the master file must be made. We will later
refer to this as a <u>post-access check</u>.
     As a concrete illustration, let us trace through the steps
involved in the access of the visually presented word <u>henchman</u>.

The initial perceptual operations performed will convert the
input stimulus into a format that is compatible with the access
codes (e.g., there is no point taking the shape of the word into
account if the word is not listed under a shape access code).
Let us assume that the access code is defined in terms of letters. But we need not assume that all letters are involved,
since it would be computationally expensive to make a large number of comparisons involving all eight letters. So, we might be
able to take just the first four letters, or perhaps the first
syllable, hench. We now proceed through the orthographic access
file, comparing h-e-n-c-h with the access code in each entry.
When the similarity between them exceeds some previously defined
criterion, the search stops, and the pointer is used to direct
the system to the entry in the master file. At that point, the
full orthographic specification of henchman needs to be extracted and compared with the properties of the input stimulus (the
format in which this comparison is made need not be the same as
the one used for access; indeed, if the system is really effective as an error-check, it ought to use a quite different format).

As we have already seen, the criterion for a match must be
well below the maximum possible, since nonwords which are similar to words take longer to reject. This is presumably due to
the fact that the search stops at an incorrect entry, and time
is lost during the entry to the master file and the performance
of the post-access check, the search in the original access file
then recommencing.

As we assumed earlier, the entries in the access files are
grouped together, and we shall refer to each such grouping as a
bin. Thus the first stage of lexical access involves calcula-
ting which bin, or group, the test word is likely to belong to.
Entries belonging to the same bin will obviously have similar
descriptions. This internal structure of an access file is
depicted in Fig. 5.

Within each bin, the entries are listed according to the
frequency of occurrence of the word. Actually, this frequency
may vary from one file to another. For example, the frequency
of the printed form of a given word may differ widely from the
frequency of the spoken form. Further, the relevant frequency
in the case of the third file, the one used for talking, is
likely to be the frequency of occurrence in the speech of the
person possessing the lexicon.[5]

---

[5]It has been recently argued that it is not frequency of occurrence that controls access time, but rather order of acquisition
(Carroll and White, 1973). For purposes of the argument, this
is immaterial, since all we need assume is that entries are listed in some order, and that word frequencies can be used to predict that order. Of course, there are a number of problems with

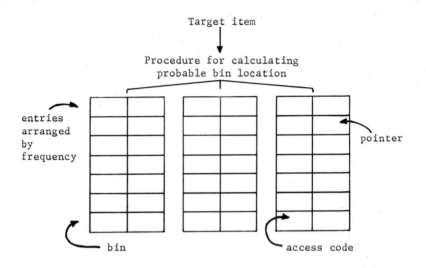

Figure 5.   Approximate content-addressing.

Before going on to consider further properties, we should ask whether there is any evidence that supports this particular analysis. At the moment, there is very little that can be said. One might point to the fact that some people can access words from their orthographic representations without being able to spell them correctly (assuming this is a fact), which implies that orthographic properties must be represented twice--once in the access file (correctly represented) and once in the marker lexicon (incorrectly represented). This would explain how children can check their oral spelling of a word by writing it down; if their written version leads back to the same entry as they started with, then it is very likely correct. These pheno- mena would be very difficult to explain if there were only one listing of words, with a single representation of orthographic information.

But perhaps the strongest evidence comes from the fact that it is counterproductive to arrange the system any other way. For example, it is now generally agreed that the orthographic file cannot be discarded, as was once assumed in the so-called phonological recoding hypothesis (for a discussion, see Marshall's paper in this volume). This hypothesis suggested that orthographic representations were first converted to

---

the acquisition view, but these go beyond the scope of the pre- sent paper.

phonological representations by rule, taking advantage of the
fact that everyone who learns to read already has a phonological
access file (i.e., can understand the spoken word). Thus print
is converted to sound, and access is via the sound. There are
many objections to this theory (for a review, see Bradshaw,
1975), but there is one experimental observation that is crucial.
If the recoding hypothesis is correct, then it should take no
longer to decide that <u>trane</u> is pronounced the same way as an
English word than it takes to decide that <u>train</u> is an English
word. A moment's reflection reveals that this cannot possibly
be correct. In actual fact, the former task takes nearly twice
as long as the latter (Taft, 1973; Bower, 1970). Thus, one cannot collapse the first two access files.

One might wish to collapse either the first and third, or
the second and third files. For example, one could imagine a
decision tree in which the initial categorization was by semantic category, with a sub-classification by orthography or phonology, as in Fig. 6. The problem in this case is to make sure
that frequency can be represented in some way. If we preserve
the bin arrangement originally suggested, with frequency controlling order of search within a bin, then we have constructed
a sub-classification tree, rather than the cross-classification
scheme suggested earlier.

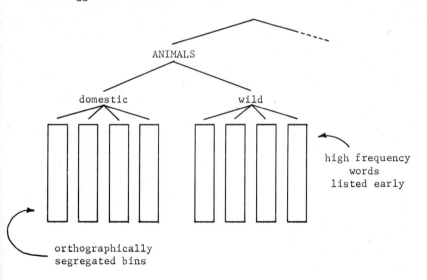

ANIMALS

domestic   wild

high frequency
words
listed early

orthographically
segregated bins

Figure 6. A semantic/orthographic/frequency search tree.

But this system makes exactly the wrong predictions about
frequency. When the semantic category in which a word belongs

is known (e.g., the word is in a sentence context) then a high
frequency word will be found before a low frequency word and
hence normal frequency effects will be observed. But when the
semantic category is not known, as in a normal lexical decision
experiment when the words are presented in isolation, then
there should be no frequency effect at all, since the tree would
have to be searched at random, and many low frequency words will
be searched before many high frequency words. But of course,
the strongest effects of frequency are found when the semantic
category is not known, so we must abandon either our interpretation of frequency effects, or the notion that entries are
organized into semantic categories with an orthographic sub-
classification.

We now return to a discussion of further properties of the
search model. It should be clear from the previous discussion
of decision times for nonwords that the current model postulates
an exhaustive search for nonwords and a terminating search for
words. The main source of evidence for the exhaustive nonword
search stems from experiments in which the task calls for information that is not contained within any single entry. For
example, if we ask whether a word such as year is ambiguous or
not, then the information in the entry for year will not answer
the question (unless words are specifically marked as unambiguous), and hence the search must be continued on beyond the initial entry to find whether a second entry for year exists. Similarly, if we ask whether year can be used as a verb, then an exhaustive search will be required to establish that it cannot.
The consequence of such a decision procedure would be that frequency effects would no longer occur, since no matter how quickly the first entry was located, an exhaustive search is still required. This is in fact what happens (Forster and Bednall, 1976).

However, these experiments do not indicate whether the
search continues only to the end of whatever bin the entry
should have been in, or whether more than one bin is searched.
What evidence we have suggests that the search might extend
beyond the initial bin. For example, consider the following
nonwords: xecause, bxcause, bexause, becxuse, becauxe, and
becausx. In each case, it is easily seen that the nonword is
very similar to the word because, and in each case, this similarity is perceived quickly enough to interfere with the "No"
response (Amey, 1973). This implies that the set of entries
searched in each case included the entry for because. Since
it seems unlikely that the same bin was searched in every case
(e.g., a word beginning xe- would surely be allocated to a different bin than a word beginning bx-), it seems there are only
two alternatives. Either we assume that because is listed in
many different bins (which defeats the purpose of having bins),
or we assume that the search continues beyond the first bin if
no entry is found. In this case, we would have to postulate

that a sufficiently large number of bins were searched to guarantee a high probability of encountering the distracting entry.
This latter proposal essentially argues that all, or nearly
all of the entries in the master file must be searched before a
"No" decision can be made. Although this seems very inefficient,
it should be kept in mind that the overall system was designed
for accessing familiar forms, not classifying unfamiliar forms.
If normal day-to-day language processing regularly required us
to identify nonwords as such, then no doubt we would have
evolved more efficient procedures (as perhaps we may have for
faces, where classification as known/unknown has more utility).

The next property that needs to be outlined has to do with
cross-references between entries in the master file. Meyer and
Schvaneveldt (1971) have shown that lexical decision time for a
given word is decreased if it is preceded by an associatively
related word. That is, the decision time for the word doctor
will be faster if it is preceded by the word nurse. This effect
has been explained in terms of word detectors by postulating
that detectors are interconnected, so that activation of the detector for doctor will also tend to activate the detector for
nurse (Meyer and Schvaneveldt, 1976). However, for the purposes
of the search model, this explanation is equivalent to postulating a system of cross-references between entries in the master file, such that once the entry for doctor is located, it is
possible to transfer immediately to the entry for nurse without
going through any access file.

If this is the case, then the speed with which the first
word of such a pair (i.e., doctor) is accessed should be controlled by frequency, since access is via the normal peripheral
access file. However, the frequency of the second word (nurse)
should be irrelevant, since it is not accessed via a frequency-
organized access file. This hypothesis has been tested in an
unpublished experiment carried out by Elizabeth Bednall. The
procedure involved presenting two words simultaneously (one
above the other), and requiring either a lexical decision about
both items (respond "Yes" only if they are both words) in one
situation, or a semantic relatedness judgment in another (respond "Yes" if the two words are related in meaning). The word
pairs were constructed so that the frequencies of Word 1 (the
topmost word) and Word 2 were jointly varied, but independently
of whether the words were related in meaning (calibrated by
ratings of semantic relatedness) or not. There were 56 related
word pairs, and 56 unrelated pairs. The results for the related
pairs are summarized in Table 1. For both tasks, there was a
strong effect of frequency for Word 1 (64 msec for lexical decision, 68 msec for semantic relatedness), but in neither task
was there a significant effect[6] of frequency for Word 2,

---

[6]Throughout this paper "significant" means "significant at the

although the lexical decision task comes closer (44 msec) than does the semantic relatedness task (15 msec). This seems a reasonable result, since in the lexical decision task, it might sometimes be faster to locate Word 2 through the normal access file, hence we might expect a reduced effect of frequency. But in the semantic relatedness task, there is very little point in accessing Word 2 through a peripheral access file, since it is only by searching through the network of semantic cross-references that we can determine whether the words are related in meaning. Hence we assume that the semantic relatedness task is the better task to use if one is interested in exploring the cross-referencing system.

TABLE 1

Lexical decision times and semantic relatedness decision times for semantically related word pairs.

Frequency of Word 1 and 2		Lexical task	Semantic task
High–high	(finger–leg)	645	792
High–low	(fun–mirth)	715	848
Low–high	(monsoon–wet)	734	900
Low–low	(bug–grub)	754	875

N.B. Average rated semantic similarity equated in all conditions.

For both tasks, related words were processed faster than unrelated words (66 msec for the lexical decision task, 98 msec for the relatedness task), as would be required if the conditions of the Meyer and Schvaneveldt experiment were to be duplicated. However, it is worth noting that in Bednall's experiments, the semantic relation was never specified as an associative relation. That is, Word 2 was chosen so that although it clearly belonged to the same semantic field as Word 1, it never appeared as an associate of Word 1 (e.g., fun–mirth: although related in meaning, nobody gives mirth as an associate of fun). This means that the cross-references responsible for the semantic facilitation effect are not associative in nature.

The semantic relatedness task represents an interesting addition to our test battery. Our assumption is that decisions

5% level or better using the min F' procedure".

can be made only by searching the cross-references, and if an entry is found that matches the spelling of Word 2, a "Yes" decision is made, otherwise a "No" decision results. One interesting consequence of this view is that Word 2 would not be accessed via a peripheral access file even when the items were unrelated, since this is quite unnecessary for the semantic relatedness task. That this is the case is strongly suggested by the fact that there is no frequency effect for Word 2 for unrelated items. The effect here (11 msec) contrasts sharply with a normal frequency effect for Word 2 (81 msec) when a lexical decision must be made about a pair of unrelated words. This latter effect is to be expected, since failing to find Word 2 in the system of cross-references hardly determines whether Word 2 is a word or not; hence it must be accessed through an access file in the normal way, and hence frequency effects should be observed.

The implication of this view is that a semantic relatedness judgment on a pair of unrelated words is made without knowing whether the second item is a word or not. This is highly counter-intuitive, but apparently true, since a "No" decision for a word pair such as sum-crate takes the same time as a "No" decision for a word-nonword pair such as sum-trate (Bednall, unpublished experiment). This is restricted, of course, to semantic relatedness judgments. For lexical decisions, the normal result is obtained, and a pair containing a nonword in the second position takes longer to classify.

It would be most instructive to ask whether any semi-direct access model would be able to make any sense of these results. As far as I can determine, one would have to argue that the activation process would be identical for both kinds of tasks; any differences between the tasks would reflect post-activation processes. Thus, one would have to expect normal frequency effects for Word 2 in all situations. One might construct a special theory of activation-summation which argues that the frequency effect will be reduced when the activation level has been boosted by semantic "cross-talk", but one could not explain the total absence of any Word 2 frequency effect for the relatedness task, whether the items are related or unrelated.

The cross-reference network obviously extends the power of the system considerably, and effectively defines yet another kind of search. However, given phenomena such as the semantic facilitation effect, semantic confusion errors in paralexia (Marshall and Newcombe, 1966), and various effects reported in the semantic memory literature (e.g., Collins and Loftus, 1975), there seems very little point in resisting this addition. The only serious possibility is to collapse the network system and the production access file, so that one semantic search process will do the work of both. The problem with this proposal is that the descriptions under which words must be filed for purposes of planning sentences may not always coincide with the descriptions used in a semantic network.

This completes the preliminary description of the overall structure of the search model. In the end, it turns out to be much more like a library than a dictionary. The essential problem in both a library and a mental lexicon is how to arrange information so that it can be accessed efficiently in a number of different ways. In the case of a library, the solution is either to buy several copies of each book and store one copy at each of the locations predicted by the various access functions, or to have just one copy of each book, but several different catalogues (e.g., one organized by author, one by title, another by content). Thus, the books of the library are analogous to the lexical entries in the master file, the catalogues are analogous to access files, and the reference numbers correspond to pointers.

Lexical Access in Sentences

It is often remarked that there is little point in studying the recognition of isolated words, since the entire system might be quite different when a sentence context is supplied. Of course, this remark quite misses the point, since we would have no notion of the distinctive role played by context unless we could contrast the characteristics of performance with and without a context. But in any event, we certainly ought to ask how the system might take advantage of the context provided by a sentence.

For example, it has been almost universally assumed that the semantic context of a sentence somehow reduces the number of possible words that can occur at a given point in a sentence, and hence facilitates the process of word recognition. In terms of the search model, we would have to say that the size of the search set has been reduced prior to access.

But notice that this immediately creates a number of problems. Remember that the size of the search set has already been reduced by the procedure which computes the approximate location (the bin number) on the basis of orthographic or phonological features of the target word (see Fig. 5). How are we to organize the access files so that we can reduce the search set still further by taking into account the semantic properties of the context? The most obvious way it to construct a search tree such as the one depicted in Fig. 6, where semantic categories have been subclassified by orthographic categories (we will restrict our attention to reading, but it should be remembered throughout that the same arguments will apply to listening). However, we have already seen that such a system predicts no frequency effect when the words are presented in isolation, so we would have to give up the notion that frequency effects reflect

the order of search. The same conclusion applies if we alter
the structure of the search tree so that orthographic categories
are subclassified into semantic categories.

Evidently, there is no way out. We cannot assume that context acts to restrict a search set already restricted by the
stimulus itself, simply because we would be unable to explain
how access took place when there was no context.

As far as I can determine, the most sensible alternative is
to propose that there are two quite independent access functions:
one that computes an approximate address on the basis of the sensory features of the target word, and one that computes an
approximate address based on presumed semantic properties. Thus
two search sets are defined, with neither set being a proper subset of the other. To explain how context can facilitate access,
we would need to assume that both sets are searched simultaneously, and that the semantic search is often the fastest.

Within the model, there are two ways of carrying out a
semantically governed search. One is to use the network of
cross-references, and the other is to use the production access
file. The disadvantage of the former method is that there must
always be a particular word in the context that establishes the
link to the target word. This seems to be a most implausible
assumption. For example, in the sentence The little boy fell
off the ----, the last word is often guessed to be dock or pier,
but it seems unlikely that there is a specific link between any
one of the words in the context and either of these words (if
there is, then nearly every word will be connected to nearly
every other word). The second method, namely using the production file, suffers from no obvious disadvantages, except that
we are committed to the view that perceiving a sentence requires
the use of the sentence production apparatus (a strong claim).
It also seems improbable that this system would ever be fast
enough to beat out the search guided by sensory properties.

This last point suggests an interesting line of argument.
Most of the existing demonstrations of the effects of semantic
context on word recognition (e.g., Miller and Isard, 1963;
Rubenstein and Pollack, 1963; Tulving and Gold, 1963) have used
impoverished stimuli, and, as Meyer, Schvaneveldt and Ruddy
(1975) point out, have allowed the subject plenty of time before
a response has to be made. Both factors would tend to favor a
production-based search over a sensory-based search. This leads
to the obvious question. Can context effects be demonstrated
when the stimulus is not degraded and the response must be
executed rapidly?

There are two sets of results which suggest that the correct answer to this question is "No". First, consider what
ought to happen to frequency effects when the semantic context
is effective. If the search set is reduced in size, then the
impact of frequency ought to be reduced substantially. However,

the following experiment shows that this is not the case
(Forster, 1974). Subjects were asked to classify visually presented sentences as meaningful, grammatical sentences or as
non-sentences (for details of procedure, see Forster and Olbrei,
1974). If frequency controls access time, then clearly it will
control sentence processing time, since the sentence cannot be
processed until the words have been accessed. Hence it is not
surprising that when the frequency of the major substantives in
the sentence is varied, as in The girl surprised the teacher
(high frequency substantives) compared with The bishop preached
the sermon (low frequency substantives), then there is a substantial effect of frequency on decision times (137 msec). This
is the effect obtained when the sentences are semantically
plausible (i.e., the individual words are all relatively predictable from the remainder of the sentence). But if the sentences are made implausible, then the frequency effect should be
magnified considerably. For example, compare The women measured
the road (high frequency) with The board organized the kitchen
(low frequency). However, if anything, the frequency effect
was slightly reduced (104 msec) when the individual words become relatively unpredictable, although this reduction was not
significant. Thus, there was no change in the frequency effect,
even though the implausible sentences took far more time to
process (1621 vs 1258 msec). The implication of this constant
frequency effect is that the size of the search set was constant
for both plausible and implausible sentences--a conclusion which
is very difficult to reconcile with the assumption that the context of the sentence acts to restrict the search set.

   Of course, if it turns out that the frequency effect has
nothing to do with the size of the search set, then there is no
problem; the results are simply irrelevant. For this reason, we
need supplementary evidence which looks at access times in a
more direct fashion. The word-naming task is particularly suitable here. We know that lexical access is involved in rapid
pronunciation, since vocalization is initiated faster for words
than for pronounceable nonwords, and high frequency words can be
named faster than low frequency words (Forster and Chambers,
1973). We also know that word-naming time shows semantic facilitation effects of the doctor-nurse variety (Meyer, Schvaneveldt
and Ruddy, 1975). Given these facts, then it ought to be the
case that words which are predictable from a sentence context
should be named much faster than words which are not.

   Several experiments have been completed in our laboratory,
and the conclusion has been negative, with only one exception.
The sentences were of the following type, where the word to be
pronounced is underlined.

   The family enjoyed the picnic among the trees.
   The family enjoyed the picnic among the teeth.

Tony hated wrapping _parcels_.
Tony hated wrapping _pickles_.

The campers were scared when they heard strange _noises_.
The campers were scared when they heard strange _nurses_.

The sentences were presented visually, one word at a time, at
speeds of three words a second in some experiments, one word a
second in others. The target word was in italics. The only
response the subject had to make was to pronounce the target
word as rapidly as possible. In one experiment, predictable
target words were pronounced only 5 msec faster than unpredictable target words, this difference being well within chance
expectations. In a subsequent experiment, this effect was increased to 36 msec, but it was still insignificant. Because
we were worried that the subjects might not be attending to the
context, we ran a further study in which _every_ word had to be
pronounced (the presentation rate here was one word every
second). In this case, the predictable words were read 17 msec
faster than unpredictable words. Once again, the effect was
insignificant.

However, there was _one_ experiment that produced a clear and
significant effect of context (64 msec). In this case, however,
the target word duration was reduced considerably (from 333 msec
down to 83 msec), and the target word itself was followed by a
masking stimulus. This was not sufficient to make the recognition task exceptionally difficult (as it is in a tachistoscopic task), since 88% of responses were still correct. It
was, however, enough to increase the naming times on correct
trials by about 50 msec.

The combined effect of these experiments lends weight to
the hypothesis that the semantic context provided by a sentence
only exerts an appreciable effect on access time when the stimulus has been degraded. Why should this be so? One possible
answer is that stimulus degradation makes access by the normal
stimulus-based methods either impossible, inaccurate or very
slow. With normal stimulus conditions, the stimulus-based
method is always the fastest and most reliable method, but when
the stimulus becomes degraded, the context-assisted methods
become more important. In this respect, it would be expected
that the _doctor-nurse_ facilitation effect would be enhanced if
the second word were degraded, since this increases the probability that information about the second item will be accessed
via the semantic network, and just such an effect has been
reported by Meyer et al. (1975).[7]

---

[7] Given this argument, it is particularly interesting to observe
that stimulus degradation does _not_ enhance the frequency effect
(Stanners, Jastrzembski and Westbrook, 1975), which would argue

It is even possible that sentence context has no effect at all _prior_ to access. It may be simply that in uncertain stimulus conditions, the plausibility of the sentence as a whole is used merely to check on the accuracy of the lexical analysis.

But whatever conclusion is reached, it seems clear that the semantic context provided by a sentence fragment does not provide anything like the same facilitation as a semantically related word. I would argue that this stems from the fact that the semantic network can be used effectively in the latter case, but not in the former. It seems quite clear that in the case of sentences, the appropriate cross-reference would have to come from an internal representation of a _situation_, not a word or any other kind of linguistic entity. Thus, the way in which a sentence fragment constrains the possible words that could plausibly appear has more to do with our knowledge of likely situations, and this cannot be adequately captured in a set of cross-references between lexical entries.

Extensions of the Model

I would now like to outline very briefly what I consider to be the interesting questions that should be explored with the aid of this model. Since these are not inter-related issues, a listing seems the most appropriate format.

1. How should "malapropisms" be explained? In a most interesting paper, Fay and Cutler (1974) point out that speech errors such as substituting magician for musician suggest that the master file is organized according to phonological similarity. In the current model, this finding is difficult to handle, since once the appropriate entry has been found in the master file, the details of the pronunciation should be available, and the only types of error that should occur would be misarticulation errors (which would produce words only by chance). The conclusion has to be that the actual articulatory commands necessary for speech are not represented in the master file, but are instead listed elsewhere, and are accessed from the master file by pointers. This file must be organized according to phonological (or articulatory) similarity.

2. Are the semantic confusion errors observed in paralexia mediated by the cross-reference system? As Marshall and Newcombe (1966) observe, patients make semantic errors in reading aloud, e.g., reading canary as parrot. We could describe this as a kind of "spill-over" effect, in which the search continues on past the correct entry in the master file and onto the set of

---

against a slowing down of the search process.

entries specified by the semantic cross-references. But in this case, then we should expect such patients to make the same kinds of errors in a task which used a different access file, but the same master file entries, e.g., a dictation test. If it turns out that the effects are restricted to a particular access mechanisms, then the errors will have to be explained in terms of defective pointers. To explain how a semantically similar word could be selected by a defective pointer, we would be forced to assume that the master file itself is organized in a systematic fashion according to some set of semantic principles, rather than being very loosely structured by a set of cross-references.

3. <u>On what basis are bin numbers computed?</u> Functions which compute probable locations are referred to as hash coding functions (Knuth, 1973). It has been suggested that the input to the hash coder consists of the initial and final letters of the word (Stanners, Forbach and Headley, 1971; Stanners and Forbach, 1973). This proposal is based on the fact that the initial and final segments of a word are the most effective cues for prompted recall of previously presented words (Horowitz, White and Atwood, 1968), and the fact that transpositions of letters in the initial and final positions are more disruptive for word identification (Bruner and O'Dowd, 1958). Stanners et al. (1971) reasoned that the size of the search set would be a function of the frequency of occurrence of the initial and final letters; that is, words beginning and ending with unusual letter combinations would be more likely to be located in sparsely populated bins than words beginning and ending with common letter combinations. From this assumption it follows that lexical decision times for nonwords beginning and ending with low frequency consonant clusters should be faster than for nonwords with high frequency initial and final clusters, since in the former case, the bin specified by the hash code contains relatively few members and hence can be searched more rapidly. Although this prediction was confirmed experimentally, there are problems in interpreting the results, since the same finding should also be observed for <u>words</u>. However, the reverse finding was obtained, with faster decision times for words with high frequency initial and final clusters. This finding was also obtained by Stanners and Forbach (1973). Further, there are problems with the assumption that there is substantial variation between bins in the number of entries that they contain, since the most <u>ef-</u><u>ficient</u> way to design a hash code is to divide the lexicon up into equal-sized subsets.

The problem with the results for words might be handled by arguing that <u>word</u> frequency was confounded with cluster frequency, which would tend to produce quite the opposite effect. Also, it might be suggested that the "density" effect would only be obtained for low frequency words, since a high frequency word

would be positioned so that the density of the bin would be irrelevant.

A somewhat different approach to this problem uses the so-
called "priming" effect. If the extremities of a word are used
to compute an approximate location, then providing advance information about the extremities should facilitate lexical access,
compared with a condition in which no such advance information
is given. This situation can be arranged by presenting the first
two and the last two letters of a word slightly in advance of
the entire word (an adaptation of a procedure used by Ericksen
and Eriksen, 1974, and also Manelis and Atkinson, 1974). From
the subject's point of view, the fact that the extremities of
the word are presented briefly (62.5 msec) prior to the entire
word is barely noticeable. However, if the first stage of processing involves identifying the letters at the beginning and
end of the word and the determination of an approximate address,
then this phase of processing can at least begin even though the
total word is not yet displayed. It may even be the case that
the search process itself can also be initiated, since lexical
entries that do not have the right beginnings or ends can be
eliminated.

The results obtained with this technique (Forster and
Gartlan, 1975) are encouraging, but not easily explained.
Briefly, it turns out that priming with the extremities of a
word produces faster lexical decision times than priming with
the interior. However, most surprisingly, priming with the
first half of a word produces no advantage over priming with the
second half. In fact for words, the only priming condition that
produced a priming effect (faster than no prior information at
all) was the exterior condition. For nonwords, where one might
expect exactly the same set of results (since the faster a bin
is located, the sooner the search of the bin will be completed),
a quite different picture emerges. There is no difference between priming with the exterior and the interior portions, and
no difference between first and second halves. However, all
conditions showed a priming effect. That is, any prior information about a nonword appears to facilitate lexical decision.
Needless to say, a coherent interpretation of these results is
currently unavailable.

4. How many searches? It might be imagined that in reading,
for example, there would be just one process assigned the task
of locating the lexical entry for a given word. However, the
deeper one probes, the more search processes we seem to encounter. For example, in Taft and Forster (1975), it is argued that
a morphological analysis of an item is attempted prior to access. Thus, a prefixed word such as rejuvenate would be analyzed into something like (re(juven(ate))). But this means that
items that appear to be prefixed, e.g., repertoire, would have
to undergo the same analysis. Since there is no item

(re(pertoire)), and since such pseudo-prefixed words do not seem
to present any special difficulties, we can only conclude that
we look for both a morphologically analyzed and an unanalyzed
form simultaneously.

However, there is quite independent evidence (Taft and
Forster, in press) to suggest that polysyllabic words are recognized by a system that takes letters from left to right, execu-
ting a new search with each new letter that is added. Thus a
word such as neighbour would be accessed by a system which took
as successive targets n, ne, nei, neig, neigh, neighb, etc.
The evidence for this is as follows. Nonwords containing a word
in initial position (e.g., footmilge) take longer than nonwords
which contain no word (e.g., mowdflisk) and also nonwords with
a word in final position (e.g., trowbreak), the latter two conditions being equivalent. Clearly, if a lexical entry is actually encountered, the "No" decision will be substantially longer,
and the system we described would encounter an entry only in the
case of footmilge. However, the same result would be obtained
if the first syllable were chosen as a target, so the left to
right letter model seems redundant, until it is demonstrated
that the interference produced by a word in initial position is
just as strong when the syllable boundary position is ambiguous
(e.g., trucerin, pagelont).

Such a strategy may seem quite pointless. However, it does
permit postcard to be accessed through the entry for post, along
with post-office, postal, postman etc. In fact, the evidence
shows that compound words such as headstand are accessed with a
speed predictable from the frequency of head rather than the frequency of the word as a whole. Presumably this access system is
designed purely for such compound words.

The conclusion then, is that each word is likely to be
filed under multiple descriptions, and that lexical access consists of selecting a whole range of techniques for recovering
the entry.

5. How should frequency effects be interpreted? Since so many
arguments turn on the correct interpretation of the frequency
effect, we really need strong evidence that the order of search
interpretation is correct. The alternative is some post-access
mechanism, such as decreased read-out time for high frequency
words. The best evidence against these alternative interpretations is that they imply constant frequency effects for all
tasks. However, as shown in Forster and Bednall (1976), the
search model successfully predicts the circumstances under which
frequency effects will be absent. It should not be inferred, of
course, that there are no problems with the order of search explanation. For example, in the same paper, it is shown that
although frequency correctly predicts the speed of access of the
most commonly used meaning of an ambiguous word, it completely

fails to predict the speed with which the less commonly used
meaning is accessed.

Fortunately, the list of interesting questions we can ask
is very long indeed, and I have done no more than sample at
random from it. If many of the topics seem too narrow, or to be
overly concerned with the mechanisms of retrieval, rather than
with the information itself that is being retrieved, then I can
only say that this is my bias, and that I believe that none of
the really interesting questions can be approached until we
know far more about these mechanisms.

References

Amey, T.J. (1973) Perceptual factors in word recognition. Unpublished thesis, Department of Psychology, Monash University.

Bower, T.G.R. (1970) Reading by eye. In H. Levin and J.P. Williams (Eds.), Basic Studies on Reading. New York: Basic Books.

Bradshaw, J.L. (1975) Three interrelated problems in reading: A review. Memory and Cognition, 3, 123-134.

Bruner, J.S. and O'Dowd, D. (1958) A note on the informativeness of parts of words. Language and Speech, 1, 98-101.

Carroll, J.B. and White, M.N. (1973) Word frequency and age of acquisition as determiners of picture-naming latency. Quarterly Journal of Experimental Psychology, 25, 85-95.

Chambers, S.M. (1974) Word similarity and interference in lexical decision tasks. Paper read at the First Experimental Psychology Conference, Monash University.

Chambers, S.M. and Forster, K.I. (1975) Evidence for lexical access in a simultaneous matching task. Memory and Cognition, 3, 549-559.

Collins, A.M. and Loftus, E.F. (1975) A spreading-activation theory of semantic processing. Psychological Review, 82, 407-428.

Coltheart, M., Davelaar, E., Jonasson, J.T. and Besner, D. Access to the internal lexicon. Paper presented at Attention and Performance VI, Stockholm.

Fay, D. and Cutler, A. (1974) You have a dictionary in your head, not a thesaurus. Paper presented at the 46th annual meeting of the Midwestern Psychological Association, Chicago, May 2-4.

Forster, K.I. (1974) Separation of the effects of meaning on word recognition and sentence processing. Paper read at First Experimental Psychology Conference, Monash University.

Forster, K.I. and Bednall, E.S. (1976) Terminating and exhaustive search in lexical access. Memory and Cognition, 4, 53-61.

Forster, K.I., and Chambers, S.M. (1973) Lexical access and naming time. Journal of Verbal Learning and Verbal Behavior, 12, 627-635.

Forster, K.I. and Gartlan, G. (1975) Hash coding and search processes in lexical access. Paper read at the Second Experimental Psychology Conference, University of Sydney.

Forster, K.I. and Olbrei, I. (1974) Semantic heuristics and syntactic analysis. Cognition, 2, 319-347.

Frederiksen, J.R. and Kroll, J.F. (1974) Phonemic recoding and lexical search in the perception of letter arrays. Paper presented at Psychonomic Society, Boston.

Horowitz, L.M., White, M.A., and Atwood, D.W. (1968) Word frag-
    ments as aids to recall: The organization of a word.
    Journal of Experimental Psychology, 76, 219-226.
Knuth, D.E. (1973) The Art of Computer Programming. Volume 3:
    Sorting and Searching. Reading, Mass.: Addison-Wesley.
Landauer, T.K. (1975) Memory without organization: Properties
    of a model with random storage and undirected retrieval.
    Cognitive Psychology, 7, 495-531.
Manelis, L., and Atkinson, R.C. (1974) Tachistoscopic recogni-
    tion of syllabicated words. Quarterly Journal of Experi-
    mental Psychology, 26, 158-166.
Marshall, J.C. and Newcombe, F. (1966) Syntactic and semantic
    errors in paralexia. Neuropsychologia, 4, 169-176.
Meyer, D.E., and Schvaneveldt, R.W. (1971) Facilitation in
    recognizing pairs of words: Evidence of a dependence be-
    tween retrieval operations. Journal of Experimental
    Psychology, 90, 227-234.
Meyer, D.E. and Schvaneveldt, R.W. (1976) Meaning, memory struc-
    ture and mental processes. Science, 192, 27-33.
Meyer, D.E., Schvaneveldt, R.W. and Ruddy, M.G. (1975) Loci of
    contextual effects on visual word recognition. In P.M.A.
    Rabbit and S. Dornic (Eds.), Attention and Performance V,
    London: Academic Press.
Miller, G.A. and Isard, S. (1963) Some perceptual consequences
    of linguistic rules. Journal of Verbal Learning and Verbal
    Behavior, 2, 217-228.
Morton, J. (1970) A functional model of human memory. In D.A.
    Norman (Ed.), Models of Human Memory, New York: Academic
    Press.
Oldfield, R.C. (1966) Things, words and the brain. Quarterly
    Journal of Experimental Psychology, 18, 340-353.
Rubenstein, H., Garfield, L., and Millikan, J.A. (1970) Homo-
    graphic entries in the internal lexicon. Journal of Verbal
    Learning and Verbal Behavior, 9, 487-492.
Rubenstein, H., Lewis, S.S., and Rubenstein, M.A. (1971) Evi-
    dence for phonemic recoding in visual word recognition.
    Journal of Verbal Learning and Verbal Behavior, 10, 645-657.
Rubenstein, H. and Pollack, I. (1963) Word predictability and
    intelligibility. Journal of Verbal Learning and Verbal
    Behavior, 2, 147-158.
Selfridge, O.G., and Neisser, U. (1960) Pattern recognition by
    machine. Scientific American, 203, 60-68.
Stanners, R.F., and Forbach, G.B. (1973) Analysis of letter
    strings in word recognition. Journal of Experimental
    Psychology, 98, 31-35.
Stanners, R.F., Forbach, G.B., and Headley, D.B. (1971) Deci-
    sion and search processes in word-nonword classification.
    Journal of Experimental Psychology, 90, 45-50.
Stanners, R.F., Jastrzembski, J.E. and Westbrook, A. (1975)
    Frequency and visual quality in a word-nonword

classification task. Journal of Verbal Learning and Verbal Behavior, 14, 259-264.

Taft, M. (1973) Detecting homophony of misspelled words. Unpublished paper, Monash University.

Taft, M. and Forster, K.I. (1975) Lexical storage and retrieval of prefixed words. Journal of Verbal Learning and Verbal Behavior, 14, 638-647.

Taft, M., and Forster, K.I. (in press) Lexical storage and retrieval of polymorphic and polysyllabic words. Journal of Verbal Learning and Verbal Behavior.

Tulving, E. and Gold, C. (1963) Stimulus information and contextual information as determinants of tachistoscopic recognition of words. Journal of Experimental Psychology, 66, 319-327.

AUTHOR INDEX

SUBJECT INDEX